D1544234

03/22
STRAND PRICE
$ 5.00
EACH

SAINT UNSHAMED

A GAY MORMON'S LIFE

Healing From the Shame of Religion,
Rape, Conversion Therapy & Cancer
To Find My True Self

While this is a true story, certain names, events, and identities have been changed to protect both the innocent and the guilty.

Copyright © 2018 by Kerry Ashton.
All rights reserved.

ISBN/SKU Number: 9780692170519

Printed in the United States of America.
First Edition, Hardcover: November 20, 2018

Jacket Cover Art & Design by Kerry Ashton
Author's Photograph on Cover by Victor Ramirez

No part of this book may be used or reproduced
in any manner whatsoever without written permission.

For more information, write to
Lynn Wolf Enterprises at
LynnWolfEnterprises@gmail.com

PREVIOUSLY PUBLISHED BY KERRY ASHTON

THE WILDE SPIRIT (Printed Book)
A One-Man Play Based on the Life of Oscar Wilde

THE WILDE SPIRIT Performance DVD
Including DVDs if Ashton's restaging of the 1996 Off-Broadway show

THE WILDE SPIRIT
Original Off-Broadway Cast Recording on CD

THE WILDE SPIRIT (Audio Book)
Written & Performed by Kerry Ashton

THE WILDE SPIRIT (The Musical) DVD and CD
Kerry Ashton Sings Wilde
As Performed Live in Provincetown, MA in 1992

THE WILDE SPIRIT Performance DVD
Live From Provincetown
As Performed Live in Provincetown, MA in 1990

THE WILDE SPIRIT VOCAL SELECTIONS
Musical Selections from the Play

MY LIFE AS OSCAR WILDE
A Multi-Character Two-Act Play

RED HOT MAMA: The New Sophie Tucker Musical
A Two-Character Two-Act Musical

BUFFALO HEAD NICKELS
A One-Act Play (Published by Pioneer Drama Service)

For more information about the author's work, visit
www.KerryAshton.com

The author at age six.

SAINT
UNSHAMED

A GAY MORMON'S LIFE

Healing From the Shame of Religion,
Rape, Conversion Therapy & Cancer
To Find My True Self

A MEMOIR

KERRY
ASHTON

LYNN WOLF ENTERPRISES * FORT LAUDERDALE

*First and foremost, for my loving life partner
Victor Ramirez. Without his love and support
I could not have completed this book.*

*Also for my therapist of twelve years,
Jim Enders, CSW, who introduced me
to my inner child.*

*And for all of the members of my family
and for all of my friends. This is sent as a valentine
from my heart to each one of you.*

*Lastly, in loving memory of my Mormon parents,
Allan William Ashton and Millie Jane Ashton.*

PART ONE

I told this story once as fiction in the 1980s, but this time I tell the truth. I even tell the truth, in #MeToo fashion, about being violently raped by another man when I was 18, with a knife held to my throat—a secret I kept from everyone, including myself, for over 40 years. The rape, like other experiences I endured while a student at Brigham Young University, where I came out in the early 1970s, had a profound impact on my later life. But this story is not so much about my rape or my coming of age at BYU, as it is about the lifelong effects of shame itself, not only about how I internalized and inherited a wounding shame from my Mormon upbringing, but also how I eventually *unshamed* myself. It is about a lifetime journey of spiritual growth, self-discovery and healing, including many miraculous events along the way that pushed me forward through the darkness toward the light.

Growing up in Pocatello, Idaho in the 50s, in the heart of Mormon Zion, was like growing up in Oz, where Mormons kept me on a religious path the way the Munchkins told Dorothy to follow the yellow brick road. Most American families felt pressure in those years to appear like the perfect U.S. family seen in TV shows like *Father Knows Best* and *Ozzie and Harriet*. But in our insulated Mormon community in southeastern Idaho, the expectations of appearing like a perfect family increased dramatically.

With a population of 35,000, Pocatello was Idaho's second largest city in the 1950s. It is now twice that size if you count the suburbs. Home to Idaho State University, Pocatello was and still is very LDS—as members of The Church of Jesus Christ of Latter-Day-Saints call themselves.

In Pocatello, like all LDS communities, church membership divided into wards. My family and I were members of the Pocatello 15th Ward, one of several wards within Alameda Stake, and among the more than 40 LDS wards in Pocatello. As LDS Brothers and Sisters, we proselytized Gentiles—as we preferred to call non-Mormons—but we never socialized with them, since the Prophet had warned us "to avoid the mere appearance of evil."

To survive in my LDS family and Mormon community, I had to pretend to be a perfect Saint the way my parents did.

Both of my parents were raised dirt poor during the Great Depression. Mom was barely 17 and Dad only 20 when they married during his military furlough, prior to Dad shipping out with the Navy to serve in the South Pacific during World War II.

After Dad returned from the war, my parents had four babies in six years. The firstborn, my oldest brother Dennis, was expected to be the responsible one. When he couldn't live up to all that was expected of him, he became the family scapegoat. My sister Denise was assigned the role of Daddy's little girl, his perfect Mormon princess, and the sweetest of all of us. Craig would later make Dad proud as a popular athlete in school and in his later and highly successful career in public education.

Without knowing it, Dad had claimed the first of his three children as his own. So when I came along, being the youngest and Mother's last chance, she claimed me entirely for herself. As my New York therapist noted decades later, "Whether you were a boy or a girl, she knew she would name you Kerry, since she expected you to carry and meet her emotional needs from then on."

Both of my parents had dormant and repressed shame boiling within each of them. Sometimes, as my siblings and I made our way down the LDS yellow brick road, my parents' shame came sailing at us like the fireballs thrown by the Wicked Witch.

I don't know how old I was when Mom lay me out naked on a changing mat, as I waited for a new diaper. I only remember that when she wiped down my genitals, my "little pee-pee," as Mom called it, sprang to attention. "Oh, dear!" Mother exclaimed, removing her hand from my penis as though she had just touched a hot poker. What Mommy had been doing to my pee-pee had felt pleasurable. I wanted the feeling to continue, but when I reached down with my right hand, to rub the spot that had felt so good, Mom smacked my hand away. "No, Kerry Lynn!" she said. "You mustn't do that. That's naughty!"

My little hand stung and I cried, but the real pain was in the shame I had just internalized. It was sinful to give myself pleasure!

The next time I remember being shamed happened when I was five. My father Allan Ashton, an insurance salesman, was 35 at the time. My mother Millie Jane Ashton was a 32-year-old homemaker. At 11, my oldest brother Dennis was already a bully. At ten, my sister Denise was the saintliest among us. At seven, my brother Craig already fit in the way he was expected to. And I was Mom's "baby."

Getting in our car after spending hours in church, I announced my true feelings from the backseat: "I hate church. It's so boring!"

Enraged, Dad turned to face me in the backseat. Looking directly into my eyes, he gave me a dire warning: "Kerry, I don't ever want to hear you speak that way again about our Church!"

"I'm sorry, Daddy," I whimpered, already repentant for my outspoken honesty, behaving like the best little Mormon boy in the entire world. Yet, it was not my father's rage but the look of disapproval on my mother's face that had me cowering.

My mother was the only source of love I knew or had ever known. I could no more live without her approval than the earth can live without the sun. Clearly, I was trained from an early age not merely to be her baby boy, but to behave like her exclusive property. Not that Mom or anyone in my family would have seen it that way; her complete commandeering of my psyche and all that I was, of my very soul, was not something that she was aware of consciously, any more than any member of my family was consciously aware of their assigned roles in our dysfunctional family system. But the fact that I was my mother's personal slave is true nonetheless.

Mom had trained me well: A lifted eyebrow meant she was displeased with me, that my only source of love and companionship might abandon me. At five, I had already learned the truth: To survive, I had to lie; I had to become inauthentic and false.

When I was six, I performed in a church play with my family on the stage of our LDS ward's reception hall. It was my first appearance on stage and I was nervous. Some little girls giggled backstage as Mom stripped me out of my clothes for a quick costume change. Naked and mortified, I was Mother's property to do with as she pleased. Once dressed, I stifled my tears and made my entrance holding my owner's hand.

That same year, our family visited my Aunt Ruth and her family at their home in Ogden, Utah. Aunt Ruth had a little girl named Carrie who was just my age and, like me, loved to sing and dance. After Carrie got up on the kitchen table and sang, "On the Good Ship Lollipop," we all applauded.

Wanting me to have my turn in the spotlight, Mom encouraged me to sing "If I Were King of the Forest" from *The Wizard of Oz*, since I did a good impression of Bert Lahr's performance, complete with dialogue and dance steps, and I always got rousing applause. "Go on, Kerry Lynn!" she said, nudging me onto the kitchen table. "Sing the Cowardly Lion's song!"

I got up on the table, but when I sang, *"It's hard believe me Missy, when you're born to be a sissy,"* Dad yelled, "Stop singing that song!"

"What?" I asked, surprised as everyone else.

"Get off that table, young man!" he hollered. "No son of mine is going to perform on a table like a ... like a ..."

"Like a what?" Mom interjected, getting up in Dad's face.

Dad shouted back at her, "Millie Jane, pack up! We're leaving!"

Before I knew it, we were in the car driving home. Sitting in the backseat, I knew Dad was ashamed of me, but I didn't understand why. "Why didn't you let me finish my song, Daddy?" I asked.

As I began to cry, Dad warned, "That'll be enough, Kerry Lynn! I don't want to hear any more about it!" Dad gave my mother a warning glance. "This is your fault, Millie Jane!"

"My fault?" Mom retorted. "Why? Because I stand up for him against you and all your bullying?" Clearly, I was the reason for their fight, but I still didn't understand why.

As my parents fought over me, I cried even more.

"Stop crying, young man," Dad shouted, "or I'll give you

something to really cry about!" But the more I tried to repress my tears, the more I sobbed.

"That's it!" Dad shouted, pulling the car to the side of the road. "You're getting a beating, Kerry Lynn!"

Wild with shame, Dad jumped out of the car. Deciding that his belt was not harsh enough, he went along the road and tore a two-by-four from a nearby fence. Bringing the board back with him, he dragged me out of the car.

"Allan Ashton!" Mom exclaimed. "You are not going to beat our child with that two-by-four! I will not allow it!" But Dad already had my pants down and was paddling me when Mom got between us. "Allan, that's enough! What is wrong with you?"

Undeterred, Dad continued my beating as the drivers passing by looked on in horror.

That incident was so emotionally painful for me that I blocked out any memory of it. It was only after years spent in therapy decades later, and only after my sister Denise shared with me her memory of the entire event, that I finally faced the truth.

Regardless of what had made my father so angry that day, he made it clear to me then that I was a source of shame for him, one he either had to ignore or obliterate.

******

The *Holy War*, as I have come to think of it, began on a hot day in early September 1971, the day I left Pocatello to drive four hours south to Provo, Utah, to attend Brigham Young University. As in all wars, whether holy or unholy, it would not be without its casualties.

I spent the morning packing things in my '56 Chevrolet, parked in the spot on the lawn where our driveway would have been had my parents ever had the money to pave it. A yellow-and-bronze, two-door coupe with cream interior, a huge cream steering wheel, and black dashboard, the car had class, which is why I named it Oscar— after the Academy Awards I hoped to win one day.

As I packed Oscar full of boxes, Dad worked under the hood of

6

the car. Once Oscar was filled with boxes, I sank down on our front lawn. Knowing this would be my last day at home, I tried to capture everything I saw and felt around me: The red of Mom's roses framing our side porch, the hazy blue of the late morning sky, the large pine tree at the front of our corner lot, and the blue-grey crag of Scout Mountain in the distance, where I had always imagined Santa's sleigh flew over on Christmas Eve.

Hearing Mom humming in the kitchen as she prepared lunch, everything seemed right in my Latter-Day-Saint world.

Getting up from the grass, I walked over to where Dad was still working under Oscar's hood. "Everything look okay, Dad?" I asked.

"Oh, sure," Dad replied in his folksy way. "I just wanted to make sure everything's good with your car. I don't want you stranded on the highway."

Though I had fulfilled every church obligation, I was not the mechanic that Dad had hoped each of his three sons would become. I left mechanical jobs to Dad or to my two older brothers, both married by then.

"I love you, Dad," I said suddenly. He stopped tinkering with the spark plugs and looked up at me. "I love you, too, son," he replied, embracing me with a greasy hug.

Mom came out on the side porch just then. Wiping her hands on her apron, she called out to us, "Okay, you two! Lunch is ready!"

I washed my hands at the kitchen sink and let Dad wash his hands in the bathroom. Then I joined Mom at the kitchen table while we waited for Dad.

"Kerry Lynn," she whispered, stroking my dark brown hair as she often did, "I don't know what I'm going to do without you."

Now a grown-up, or so I thought, I bristled at her calling me by both my given names as it sounded so girlish. But since it was my last day at home, I chose to ignore it.

"With all the kids married," Mom continued, "and you going off to college, this house is going to feel awfully empty without you."

"Maybe you and Dad will finally get some peace and quiet," I kidded. "Maybe now you two can finally go on that second

7

honeymoon you've talked about."

"Maybe," she said, laughing as she reached out to hold me. "I love you, Kerry." As she held me tight, I never wanted to let go.

Once Dad joined us at the table, he said a blessing on the food, as we always did in our home.

After the blessing, we tore through the food. Mom had made some of my favorites: Her wonderful potato and egg salad, savory burgers with all the trimmings, and delicious corn-on-the-cob bought fresh from the farmer's market.

After lunch, we went into the living room where Dad anointed my head with oil, laid his hands upon my head, and gave me a sacred Father's Blessing—the blessing of a Melchizedek Priesthood Elder—warning me to be "mindful of the Adversary."

Before I left that day, Dad took a photograph of me standing in front of Oscar. Barely 18 and dressed neatly, at 6'3" and 190 pounds, I was the very image of a conservative, clean-cut, LDS young man who loved his Mormon family, the LDS Church, and his Heavenly Father.

I arrived at Salt Lake City three hours later. From there, it took me another hour driving south on Interstate 15 before I arrived in the city of Provo.

Taking my first glimpse that day of Provo through Oscar's wide windshield, I could see the white LDS Temple huddled against the Wasatch Mountains, its golden steeple gleaming in the late afternoon sun. Further north, Mount Timpanogos reached heavenward, while a sign at the main entrance to the BYU campus read: "The World Is Our Campus." In reality, the campus became my world.

Driving north past the immense Cougar Stadium, and then into the foothills just beyond the BYU campus, then turning east and heading toward the mountains, I came to the huge Marriott Sports Arena under construction on my right, and stopped at the light. Once the light turned green, I made a left turn onto Sumac Avenue, climbing dramatically into the foothills, before pulling into the driveway in front of my new off-campus apartment.

Getting out of the car, I could see Utah Lake shimmering at the south end of the valley. The white Provo Temple stood just up the road and across a field, with a huge whitewashed Y on the Wasatch Mountains looming in the background above me, to the east.

Walking up through the home's carport and using my key to enter my new apartment—the one Mom and I had chosen earlier in the summer when we had first visited Provo together—I was glad to see that my roommate Mickey, a friend from high school, had not shown up yet. It would give me time to unpack all of my belongings.

The living room was covered in blood-red shag carpet, just as I remembered it, and the view of Mount Timpanogos and my landlord's yard through the back window were just as stunning as I had remembered them, when Mom and I had first looked at the place earlier that summer.

With my single bed set up in the living room, as I had asked, and another single bed set up in the adjoining alcove, awaiting my roommate Mickey, and set up that way at his request, the apartment already felt like home.

My landlady Mrs. Dixon had even put out some flowers in a vase on the top of the living room dresser to welcome us. It was the same spot where I would place my portable color TV that I had brought with me.

I was now at 'the Y'—what BYU's 26,000 students called the university—and a new resident of Utah Valley, or Happy Valley as it was termed, since most living in the valley seemed stuck somewhere in the 50s. In truth, while American students across the country were rioting, burning their draft cards, and calling for an end to the Vietnam War and an end to the establishment, the residents of Happy Valley were blissfully removed from the social revolution of the 70s.

Since BYU was the showplace for clean-cut and clean-living LDS youth, 'the Lord's University' required all of its students to obey the laws of God. This meant obeying *The Word of Wisdom*, abstaining from alcohol, cigarettes, tobacco, coffee, tea, and recreational drugs. And students were expected to observe chastity and to abide by a dress code. Since a young man's hair length indicated his politics at that time in a way it hasn't done since, males were required to keep their hair cut above the ear and the collar, while sideburns, long moustaches, and beards were forbidden.

Unfortunately, I had my first run-in with the BYU Standards Office at registration the next afternoon, when a man in a black suit walked up to me and said, "Young man, please step out of the line."

"What's the matter?" I asked.

"You are in violation of standards," he replied.

It was only then that I noticed the badge on his lapel, identifying him as a Standards Monitor. "I'm sorry," I said, "I don't understand."

"Your hair is touching the tip of your upper ears," he replied. He pulled out a book of regulations from his suit pocket. "The rules are explicit," he said, and then he read aloud from the pamphlet: "Hair must not extend below the upper tip of the ear."

"I know," I responded, perhaps a bit defensively. "I got my hair cut yesterday; my folks said it looked fine."

He took out a notepad. "Young man, may I have your full name?"

"It's Kerry. Kerry Lynn Ashton," I replied, taken aback.

"May I see your activity card application?" he asked, as though he were with the Gestapo. I handed him my papers. He glanced at my registration papers only for a moment, before he suddenly grabbed my hair, stretching it below the tip of my upper ear.

"Hey! What're you doing?" I asked.

"Proving that your hair length does not comply with our dress code," he explained. "Unless you cut your hair, you can't finalize your registration."

"I don't believe this! I want to talk to someone in charge."

"Brother Ashton," he replied, "I think that's a good idea. If you'll come with me, I believe we clear up this matter."

I followed him out of the huge Smith Fieldhouse and up the steps to upper campus, aware of students looking at me as though I were a criminal.

As we walked across the wide sidewalks of upper campus, I saw trimmed lawns lined with perfectly shaped shrubs and trees. Everything was immaculate. Climbing the steps to the white, x-shaped Administration Building, we passed Brigham Young's statue in front of the main fountain. The statue sported a full beard, and the stony hair of the statue fell a good five inches below Brigham's back collar. Neither Brigham Young nor Jesus Christ would have met the university's standards, unless they cut their hair and shaved their beards. Nonetheless, I felt apprehensive as we approached the Administration Building with its largely glass façade.

Bounding up the wide glass steps to the second floor, Ferguson guided me to the end of the building's southeastern wing, where we entered the Office of University Standards.

"Take a seat," Ferguson said.

I sat down on a wooden bench, not daring to move, as Ferguson whispered to the secretary, a thin middle-aged woman with glasses, who reached for the desk intercom, buzzing the adjacent office. "Sir, Brother Ferguson is here with a problem student," she announced. A male voice replied through the intercom, "Please send Brother Ferguson in."

After Ferguson disappeared into the inner office, I heard him talking in low tones to an unseen male figure, while the secretary eyed me suspiciously over the rims of her glasses, until the intercom buzzed again. "Yes, Sir?" the secretary asked. I heard an intimidating deep male voice reply in a most somber and ominous tone, saying, "Sister Smith, please get me the file on a Kerry Lynn Ashton."

"Yes, Brother Clarke," she responded, as she found my file and took it into the inner office.

She returned in a moment with Ferguson behind her. "Please come in, Brother Ashton," Ferguson said, motioning me inside.

The inner office had plush carpeting, a large wooden desk, and handsome bookshelves neatly stacked with religious books. Through a large window behind the desk, I could see the Harris Fine Arts Center parking lot where I had parked my car that morning, and the whitewashed Y on the Wasatch Mountains rising dramatically just beyond campus. Behind the desk sat a large man with grey, balding hair—cut above his ears, of course—with an unwavering smile.

"Brother Ashton," Ferguson said, "This is Brother Gilbert Clarke, Head of the Office of University Standards."

"How do you do, Sir," I replied, trying to sound polite.

"Please sit down, Brother Ashton," Clarke said softly. As I sat down in a chair facing him, Brother Clarke added, "Brother Ferguson tells me that you two had a disagreement at registration."

"Yes, Brother Clarke," I said. "He thinks my hair's too long!"

"I see," Clarke replied. He walked around his desk and took my hair in his fingers, gauging its length with the ruler in his other hand. "The length is borderline, but that isn't good enough."

"But Brigham Young had hair way longer than this," I said, deciding to stand up for myself, "and so did Jesus Christ."

Brother Clarke grimaced. "Brother Ashton, our standards are our standards. The question is, can you live by the standards and dress code that you have agreed to?" I started to protest, but Clarke's face flashed impatience. "Young man, you signed a contract when you applied for admission to abide by our rules. If you won't get a haircut that meets with our approval, you can find yourself another school."

After my hair was cut at the barbershop in the Wilkinson Student Center, Brother Ferguson walked me back to registration, where papers were finalized and I received my activity card.

Walking back across campus to where I had parked my car, I again came upon the statue of Brigham Young. It made me recall my visit at age 11 to the Beehive House in downtown Salt Lake City, when I had stood in the same long hallway in which Brigham Young had once stood, deciding which of his 27 wives he should sleep with next. Not unlike a gay bathhouse—as I would later discover—the hallway had 27 adjacent rooms, and behind each door was a bed where Brigham had sexual relations with each wife. "How," I wondered, "had Mormons evolved from 19th century pioneers to the 20th century establishment?" But Brigham's stony lips didn't offer me any answers.

Later I drove Oscar back to my apartment on Sumac Avenue, rebelliously singing the hit song from *Hair*, "Give me a head of hair, long beautiful hair!"

Bursting into my apartment, I threw my new schoolbooks on my bed in the main room. My roommate Mickey—who had settled into his sleeping alcove the night before—emerged from behind the partition that divided our studio apartment into two bedrooms, eyeing me carefully where I sat on the sofa next to my single bed. "What's wrong, Kerry?" he asked.

"Nothing!" I retorted, still fuming inside.

"Something's wrong. I can tell." His eyes got round with discovery as he noticed my new haircut. "What happened?" he squeaked. "It looks like you got scalped!"

Jumping up, I caught a glimpse of myself with my new crew cut in the mirror above my dresser. "I had a run-in with Standards! They said my hair was too long! Now I look more conservative than Charles Nixon!" Slumping back on my bed, I tried to calm myself down as quickly as I could.

"I think you look fine," Mickey said, sitting down on the bed beside me. "Hey! You wanna see if we can catch a movie at the Varsity Movie Theater? Since we've now got our new student activity cards, we can get in free. Then maybe we can do dinner in the Wilkinson Center cafeteria."

"Let's do it!" I said, putting my clash with Standards behind me. Or so I thought.

******

Everything my siblings and I knew about my father we learned from Mom. She was his spokesperson; she clarified what Dad was feeling and thinking at any moment as he moved about the house.

When we were little, Dad carried each of us on his back and played horsey, or got us on the floor and tickled us into senseless giggles. Dad played checkers with us, or pulled out the ice cream and offered it up to us, as if to say, "I'm not good at sharing emotionally, but look what I bought for you!" So none of us, to our detriment, ever learned how to say no to a big scoop of ice cream from Dad.

Dad played a great game with us that we called *Werewolf*, which caused shivers of both delight and fright. It was hide-and-seek, but Dad would howl as we stood breathlessly in our hiding places throughout the house, knowing for certain that sooner or later the werewolf would come and find each of us.

I felt genuinely scare me as I waited in the dark, usually hiding behind the oil furnace in the washroom in our basement, knowing that the werewolf would soon find me. And when he did, he would tickle me, and growl and howl and I would squeal with both horror and laughter. It wasn't that Dad looked like *The Wolf Man*—one of the horror movies played on TV's Chiller Theatre on Friday nights—that scared me, but that I had experienced the monstrous part of my otherwise gentle and loving father, who could, if provoked, become a violent and seething monster.

In my family, you could lie like a doormat and eat humble pie, as Dad usually did, until the rage and shame burst out of him, or you could hurt people's feelings, as Mom often did, like a knife cutting into flesh. Dad called this backbiting. Yet, Mom could— and did—love all of us. Despite everything else, I knew that Mom loved me. I knew that Dad loved us, too, but it was harder for me to trust in his love, since I knew he might beat me with a two-by-four if ever I made him angry. As hurtful as Mom could be when telling her truth, Dad was the one who hurt Mom worse than any person should ever be hurt.

I had just turned seven when Bishop Ronald Anderson announced from the pulpit that it was our LDS duty to vote for Nixon in the presidential election of 1960. A Democrat in a sea of Republicans, Mom stood up in our pew and confronted him. "Bishop," she said, "our ward chapel is no place for politics!"

Bishop Anderson's face turned bright red.

As spiritual head of our family, Dad was embarrassed. His wife had shamed him in front of our entire ward congregation. Besides, being Republican, Dad agreed with the Bishop: Nixon was the righteous choice. Being entirely Mom's property, I totally agreed with her.

"Sit down, Millie Jane!" Dad ordered, trying to pull her back into our pew, but Mom shook him off, as our ward congregation watched.

The Bishop took control of the situation, when he spoke from the pulpit saying, "Sister Ashton, your point is well taken. From now on, I will avoid sermons about politics."

"Fine," Mom replied and sat down.

Mom seemed satisfied. But Dad was still fuming, managing only to hold himself in check until we got home.

Grandpa Hamp used saltier language than most LDS folks would, when he frequently said, "Mormons won't say shit even when they have a mouthful!" My grandfather could have been talking about my father, since Dad always held his true feelings inside until he burst, cussing a blue streak and taking the Lord's name in vain—something he felt terrible about afterward and always apologized for later. But it happened again and again, whenever he became upset with us or with himself.

As soon as we were behind closed doors at home, Dad brutally berated my mother. "Jesus H. Christ, Millie Jane!" he screamed. "How could you do that to me in front of our entire ward?"

"Someone needed to take a stand against the Bishop," Mom retorted, "turning our church meeting into a political rally!"

"Millie Jane, you disgraced the family and you disgraced me!" Dad's face was red and puffy, and he began shouting far more loudly than before. "You will call the Bishop and apologize!"

"I won't!" Mom began to cry. "I only spoke the truth."

"No one wants or needs that kind of truth!" Dad spurted back at her. "You will call the Bishop and apologize right this minute!"

Dad's verbal pummeling went on until Mom was on her knees, sobbing. "I'm sorry if I embarrassed you and the family," she stammered, as Dad physically forced her to the telephone.

Humiliated, Mom called the Bishop and apologized.

It was also that year I suggested to Little Mack, a kid younger than myself who lived next door, that we play a game called *Master and Slave*. "How do ya' play it?" Little Mack asked.

"I am your master and you're my slave. You have to do whatever I say, no matter what."

15

"Okay," he replied innocently.

"Lie down on the grass and don't move," I ordered, already in my role. "You can't move no matter what I do."

"Okay," he agreed.

I ran my hands down his body until I came to the zipper of his pants. He giggled as I slowly unzipped his fly, and then he began fidgeting. "Don't move!" I said. "You're my slave. As your master, I get to do whatever I want to you."

"Okay, master," he replied, still giggling. But this tantalizing game ended when his mother called him home for lunch.

"Gotta go!" he said, quickly zipping himself up.

"Okay," I said shamefully, knowing even at my young age that I had behaved in a perverted way. "See ya'."

"See ya'," he replied, running into his house.

I have often thought about that first S&M scene. Why did I want to play that particular game at such a young age? Did I want to feel, if only for a moment, the total control over another, like the control Mom exerted over me constantly? Or was I, as I suspect, reenacting what a shameful older male had already done to me?

When Christmas morning arrived in 1960—the year that I turned seven—Santa brought me a life-size Shirley Temple paper doll, which I had wanted badly, since my favorite TV show at that time was *The Shirley Temple Hour*. I also received the china closet that I had asked for, albeit a far more masculine version of the glass china closet that Grandma Hamp had in her living room, since mine looked like a child's desk with wooden shelves above and below. And I got the set of dishes that I had begged for. As if to balance all of these items with a gift that my Dad found more appropriate for a young boy, I also received a Tonka trunk. I loved it, too.

I was so proud of all of these items that after the holidays, I invited my friend Howie from my second grade class to return with me to my home after school so I could show him my Christmas presents. When I proudly showed Howie my new china closet and my new set of dishes that fit so neatly inside the charmingly carved wooden shelves, he didn't react with delight, the way I thought he would. "Those are little girl's things!" he scoffed. "You're just a big sissy!" Not only did Howie refuse to play with me after that, he ran out of my house as though I had molested him. The shame that crept over me then seemed to color me in scarlet from toe to head.

I should have shown him my Tonka trunk and left it at that.

******

Just as Mormonism required all of its members at that time to attend all church meetings—including as many as eight meetings on a Sunday alone—BYU required its students to do the same. In addition, all students were required to take a religion course every semester. As students, we didn't attend church at wards but at student *branches*, and instead of Bishops we had *Branch Presidents*. My branch, like all church branches at BYU, met for church meetings in a campus classroom turned into a makeshift chapel. It was at my first Priesthood meeting on Sunday morning when I met Harlan.

While Branch President Cyrus W. Wilkinson addressed the priesthood holders of our branch, I listened intently. A man in his mid-50s, he was of medium-height, pudgy, with a gray crew cut. And, like most Branch Presidents on campus, he was also a Professor of Religion at the Lord's University.

As I looked around the classroom, I saw a handsome stranger in a Navy-blue suit sitting a few rows away, staring at me. I looked at him quickly, did a double take, and then I returned his stare with equal intensity.

He appeared to be a few years older than me.

I knew I had never met him before, yet I felt as though I had always known him. In many ways, he represented a conglomerate of my favorite male movie stars of the 50s and 60s: He had the sandy-brown hair of Paul Newman, the deep brown eyes and masculine appearance of Rock Hudson, and the sensuous lips of Tony Curtis, but overall he most resembled James Dean. Then suddenly and without warning, the James Dean lookalike flashed me a smile!

17

I averted my eyes, as feelings stirred within me like the rumblings of a dormant volcano.

Later, when all of the Brethren waited in the hall to separate into Priesthood Quorum Meetings, I focused on the handsome stranger standing at the end of the hall, when suddenly Mickey ran up and touched my arm. "Hey, Shakespeare! What's the matter?" he queried.

"Oh, nothing," I replied. "I guess I was just daydreaming."

As I followed Mickey toward the Aaronic Priesthood Meeting, I felt a strong hand grab my arm from behind.

I turned to see the handsome stranger facing me. We both stood 6'3", but we had opposite builds: I was 20 pounds overweight and I was soft, where he was athletic with a tight body; his shoulders were broader than mine but his physique narrowed at his waist; where he went in, I went out. Tanned everywhere that I could see, his bronze skin contrasted with the blond highlights in his sandy-brown hair. His deep brown eyes seemed filled with heaven. "This must be what God looks like," I thought.

He smiled again, revealing perfect white teeth. "Excuse me," he said. "I wanted to apologize for staring at you." His voice was as sensitive as his eyes and every bit as deep. "You reminded me so much of a friend of mine," he explained.

My insides felt as though they were melting. "Oh?" I managed breathlessly. "Someone nice I hope?"

"Very nice," he responded slowly. His deep resonant voice sent shivers cascading up and down my back. "I guess I should introduce myself," he added, shaking my hand. "I'm Harlan. Harlan LeClair."

Not only did he look like a movie star, he had a name like one!

As we shook hands, the mere touch of him—with its magnetism and strength—made me tremble.

"I'm Kerry Ashton," I managed to reply.

"Nice to meet you, Brother Ashton," he replied.

"Nice to meet you, too, Brother LeClair," I gushed, pulling my hand away, hoping he hadn't felt me tremble. "That's quite a name you have," I stammered. "Is it French?"

"It is," Harlan replied. "I mean I am. I mean my family is."

18

As Harlan stammered out his response, we both laughed.

"Is that Kerry with a C or a K?" Harlan added, still chuckling.

"It's Kerry," I said, spelling it out for him.

"Oh," he said. "Like Kerry County, not like Cary Grant."

"I wish I were like Cary Grant. He's a true movie star."

"I agree. He's so at ease," he replied. "That's what I hope to achieve as an actor someday."

"You want to be an actor?" I asked, hardly believing what I had just heard.

"That's why I'm here at the Y," he replied, "to get my degree in professional acting."

"Oh, my gosh! Me, too!" I said, before adding. "You certainly have the looks for it!" As soon as I added that sentence, I wished I hadn't, though I wasn't quite sure why.

"Thanks," he replied humbly, "but I never thought of myself as anything special."

He had to be lying; I felt unworthy to be in his presence. "As you can see," I replied, rubbing my soft and hefty waistline, "I'm more of a character actor."

"Kerry Ashton sounds theatrical. Is that your real name?"

I nodded. "But Kerry is not as bad as Lynn. That's my middle name. Having one bisexual name is bad enough, but having two is ridiculous!"

"You could have worse middle names," he said, "like mine."

"What could be worse than Lynn?"

"Alphonse," he replied, smiling broadly and chuckling.

"Alphonse!" I gasped. "You're right: It is worse!" We both laughed in unison, decreasing the tension between us. "How did you end up with a moniker like that?" I asked.

"It's an old French family name, going way back."

"Harlan Alphonse LeClair," I pronounced. "Now that has a theatrical sound to it!" I paused, noticing the ringed collar of the holy Temple undergarments beneath his shirt. "Hey! You're an RM, aren't you?" RM was LDS slang for Returned Missionary.

"How could you tell?" He smiled. "Do I have a halo?"

19

His comment made me laugh. "No! You've got the missionary ring," I explained, pointing to the neck ring of the holy Temple undergarments visible underneath his shirt.

He chortled. "Stuck with it now, aren't I?"

"Yea, verily!" It was an expression used in *The Book of Mormon*, one I had incorporated into everyday slang. "You must be an upperclassman," I added.

"No, I'm a freshman. But I was here for a semester before my mission back in the fall of '68."

Just then Mickey poked me. "Hey, Kerry, our meeting's starting."

"Okay, Mick. I'll be right there." Then turning to Harlan, I said, "Sorry, but I gotta go."

There aren't many of my BYU courses that I care to remember, other than my Creative Writing class that first semester. Taught by Miss Lowell—a spinster in her late 60s—she arrived at our first class looking prim and elegant with her silver hair impeccably coiffed. We had each arrived with essays already written about our personal goals in life, as Miss Lowell had required in advance, and each of us stood one at a time before the class, and read each of our essays aloud.

I wrote about wanting to become an actor and playwright. Bridget Peters wrote about her desire to become a journalist. "I want more than anything to be a writer of merit," Bridget read nervously from her paper, while her bright hazel eyes sparkled with intelligence. "That's why I'm taking this course."

I decided that Bridget Peters must be insecure about her height of 5'11", since she wore flat penny-loafers and styled her auburn hair so that it lay flat on top, falling gracefully down her back. Both slender and statuesque, Bridget was wearing a light blue skirt with a navy blue sweater. I thought she looked lovely.

After gathering up my belongings at the end of class, I approached Bridget, still seated at her desk. "Miss Lowell liked your essay," I said. "Congratulations!"

Bridget looked up from her desk, a look of astonishment on her face. "Thank you," she replied, a smile forming on her lips. "She liked yours even more, and so did I."

"Thanks," I said happily. "Do you have another class right now?"

"No," she replied.

"Would you like to have some lunch with me at the Wilkinson Center cafeteria?"

She smiled broadly. "I'd love to."

As we walked on the wide sidewalk from the English building to the Wilkinson Student Center across the quad, I learned that Bridget was a freshman from Salt Lake; that her father was a stockbroker; that she was majoring in Journalism and working at the student paper, and that she was a terrible cook.

"I hate housework and I hate cooking," Bridget confided. "I'd rather work at *The Daily Universe*. I want a family but I want to write, too. I hope you can understand."

"Are you kidding? Of course, I understand," I said.

Bridget breathed a sigh of relief.

"I wouldn't give up my writing for anything," I added.

"But the church asks women to give up their careers for their husbands." She stopped herself from talking further, checking my reactions with inquisitive eyes. "You must think I'm an apostate talking like this," she rushed to explain. "I know the Gospel is true. I just want to have a career, too."

She took a meaningful pause before changing the subject. "I have a confession to make. When you read your essay in class today, I thought you had written it just so you could get in good with Miss Lowell." She paused, making her point clear. "But you really are serious about becoming a professional actor and writer, aren't you?"

"Deadly serious," I replied. "Someday I'm not only going to write plays for the New York stage, I'm going to act in them, too!"

"Most of the people I've met who act in plays don't seem that serious about it," she said. "About doing it professionally, I mean."

"I know. Most of them dabble in it for fun and hope someday they'll get a chance to act in a church play. As for me, I'm headed to Broadway!"

"Broadway! Wow!" she exclaimed, full of admiration.

"Someday, I'll be produced in New York or die trying."

"I don't know why, but I believe you, Kerry," Bridget replied.

"It's just a matter of time and lots and lots of hard work and determination," I said, picturing my speech at the Tony Awards.

"I wish I was as confident as you are," she responded quietly.

"You should be. You're a good writer, Bridget."

She smiled happily as her face flushed with embarrassment. "Thanks," she replied.

Bridget's long Maybelline eyelashes fluttered. I felt a sense of relief. I was normal after all, since I could see and appreciate how pretty she was. Not realizing how long I was staring at her beautiful face, Bridget suddenly asked, "Is there something wrong?"

I felt embarrassed to have been caught eyeing her so closely, and I did my best to hide it. "You know what's wrong with you, Bridget?" I asked, smiling.

She shook her head no, surprised by my question.

"Absolutely nothing!" I exclaimed. I had stolen the line from the film *Charade*. Her hazel eyes lit up. What girl doesn't love being told something like that? "In fact," I added, "I was just noticing what beautiful eyes you have."

Soon Bridget and I could be found playing canasta on the lawn beneath the campus bell tower, or watching my portable color TV from Oscar's front seat in my driveway. And we became closer far sooner than I thought we would.

******

Mormon children are expected to be baptized at the age of eight—what Mormons call *The Age of Accountability*—when the LDS Church believes that an LDS child should know enough about church history and doctrine to freely choose to be baptized.

Rest assured, all LDS children always choose baptism over the threat of being abandoned, and prepare for their interview with the Bishop by memorizing *The Thirteen Articles of Faith*, which they must recite from memory. In my case, I had memorized the

Articles of Faith by repeating every word over and over again that Mom had read aloud to me.

During my interview, I sat on a couch facing our newly appointed Bishop behind his desk.

"Now, Kerry," Bishop Fannin asked, "Can you recite *The Thirteen Articles of Faith?*"

"Yes, Bishop." I had it memorized. *"The First Article of Faith,"* I began. *"We believe in God, the Eternal Father, and in His Son, Jesus Christ, and in the Holy Ghost."*

"Very good, Kerry!" Bishop Fannin replied, as though patting my head like a puppy and rewarding me with a bone. I went on to recite all of the *Articles of Faith*, until Bishop Fannin exclaimed, "And last but not least, *The Thirteenth Article of Faith?*"

"Yes, Bishop," I replied. *"We believe in being honest, true, chased by an elephant, virtuous, and in doing good to all men..."*

The Bishop cackled uproariously, interrupting me. "We believe in being chased by elephants?" Bishop Fannin asked, still trying to contain his laughter. "No, Kerry, we believe in being *'chaste, benevolent,'* not *'chased by an elephant.'"*

I had wondered about that myself, but I had repeated each and every word the way I had heard them coming out of my mother's mouth, deciding that the angry mobs must have used elephants to chase the Mormon Saints out of Illinois.

"Begin the Thirteenth Article again," Bishop Fannin said, "but this time, leave out the elephants."

"Yes, Bishop," I replied, as shame heated my face. *"The Thirteenth Article of Faith: We believe in being honest, true, chaste, benevolent, virtuous, and in doing good to all men; indeed, we may say that we follow the admonition of Paul—We believe all things, we hope all things, we have endured many things, and hope to be able to endure all things. If there is anything virtuous, lovely, or of good report or praiseworthy, we seek after these things."*

"Very good!" the Bishop proclaimed. "With the exception of the elephants, that was perfect! I am very proud of you!"

"Thank you, Bishop," I replied.

"Kerry, a young man your age should already have learned a great deal about the church in Mormon Primary classes and in Sunday School. Can you tell me what you've learned about Joseph Smith?"

Having been told everything there was to know about Joseph Smith from the cradle up, I unreeled my memorized answer like a computer emitting data. "Joseph Smith grew up in the farming community of Palmyra, in upstate New York."

"That's right, Kerry," the Bishop said, smiled pleasantly. "When Joseph was only 14, just a few years older than you are now, he went out to pray in a secluded grove of trees that we now call the Sacred Grove, asking God which church he should join, as they all claimed to be true. In answer to his prayer, both God the Father and His Son Jesus Christ appeared to young Joseph. And do you know what the two Holy Personages told him?"

The story had already been hammered into me a thousand times. "That none of the churches were true, that the true Gospel of Jesus Christ needed to be restored to the earth."

"Good!" he exclaimed, giving me a big smile. Suddenly I felt very proud of myself. "I can see you've been paying attention in Sunday school!" Bishop Fannin added. "In fact, Jesus said: 'They draw near to me with their lips, but their hearts are from me.'"

I listened to the Bishop's words with faith and respectful obedience. "Joseph Smith was also visited many times by the Angel Moroni," Bishop Fannin explained. "Moroni was the last great Prophet of an ancient people known as the Nephites who lived and died on the North American continent many centuries earlier. Moroni told Joseph about the Golden Plates that contained the ancient history of the people of this continent that he had buried nearby. Do you remember where Moroni buried the Golden Plates?"

I thought of the Mormon Primary song I had always loved:

"The Golden Plates lay hidden
Deep in the mountainside,
Until God found one faithful
In whom He could confide."

"They were buried in the Hill Cumorah," I replied.

"That's right, Kerry!" Bishop Fannin said, as he walked around the desk and took a seat by my side on the small sofa. "After Joseph dug up the Golden Plates, he translated this ancient record through divine power, and published it as *The Book of Mormon*, naming it after Moroni's earthly father Mormon, the famed Nephite prophet."

Bishop Fannin must have noticed that I was growing restless, as he added gently, "I know this is a lot to digest, Brother Kerry, but you can't be baptized otherwise." Even at eight, I understood. I had to know the basics of LDS doctrine before I could be baptized.

"When the church was organized in 1830," he continued, "Joseph Smith received a revelation from God designating him our Prophet, Seer and Revelator. In addition to *The Book of Mormon* and the *Holy Bible*, we have two other sacred texts based on the Prophet Joseph's divine revelations from God, *The Doctrine and Covenants* and *The Pearl of Great Price*. From these four sacred works, we know God expects us to obey *The Ten Commandments,* and to obey *The Word of Wisdom*, which makes it a sin to smoke cigarettes or any type of tobacco or to drink any alcohol or beer or any coffee or tea. And we must obey *The Law of Chastity* and *The Law of Tithing*."

I already obeyed *The Law of Tithing*, giving 10% of all that I earned from my paper route to the Bishop at Tithing Settlement, held at the end of each year in the Bishop's office at our ward building.

The Bishop continued to talk, telling me how the Prophet Joseph Smith established the first Mormon Zion in the town of Nauvoo, Illinois, how the Latter-Day-Saints built their first LDS Temple there, and how many of the Saints were attacked or murdered by mobs, and how even the Prophet Joseph and his brother Hyrum were attacked and murdered while being held in an Illinois prison on trumped up charges. Whenever I heard the story of how our Prophet Joseph Smith was killed and how the Saints were persecuted, I always cried.

"You mustn't feel sad, Kerry," Bishop Fannin explained kindly. "Jesus Christ preserved His church, and gave the Saints a new Prophet, Brigham Young, who led us out of bondage to our

Promised Land in Salt Lake City."

"Yes, Bishop," I replied, feeling grateful for the sacrifices of my Mormon ancestors.

Bishop Fannin got up from the sofa and took a seat behind the desk. "Brother Ashton, you're a fine young man. Someday, you'll make a wonderful missionary."

"Thank you, Bishop Fannin."

"The Gospel is true, Brother Kerry. I know that with all my heart. Once you are baptized on Saturday, and confirmed with the Spirit of the Holy Ghost on Sunday at Sacrament Meeting, you too will have a similar burning conviction within you."

When Saturday came, Dad walked me into the water of the baptismal font at the Alameda Stake House while all the members of my family, dressed in their Sunday best, looked on.

I knew that baptism in the Mormon faith required complete immersion in the water, but I was terribly frightened of the water at that age and I feared that I might drown. Dad had reassured me many times during the previous week by saying, "You'll feel so great when I bring you up out of the water, and you are born again!" But when I emerged from the water, I felt only relief.

At Sunday's Sacrament Meeting, Bishop Fannin and his First and Second Counselors joined with Dad to lay their hands upon my head, confirming upon me the Spirit of the Holy Ghost.

I thought I would feel very different after my confirmation and that somehow I would be spiritually transformed once I became an official member of The Church of Jesus Christ of Latter-Day-Saints, but I only felt gratitude that the entire ordeal was over.

At the time of my baptism, I already knew the straight and narrow path that I was expected to follow throughout my life. When I turned 12, I must be ordained a Deacon in the Aaronic Priesthood—the lesser of the two orders of the Holy Priesthood. At 14, I must be ordained an Aaronic Priesthood Teacher. At 16, I must be ordained a Priest. At 19, I must be ordained an Elder in the Melchizedek Priesthood, accepting even more responsibilities. Then, after receiving my Temple Recommend entitling me to go to the LDS

Temple for the first time, I must make secret covenants with God, known as Temple Endowments. Then I should serve a two-year mission for the church, marry in the Temple, have children, and raise them to follow the same LDS path.

This was the Mormon yellow brick road that I was expected to tread with unswerving diligence. More importantly, it was the path that I wanted to follow. The Mormon Gospel was the only truth I had ever known; it had answered all of life's questions and explained all of life's mysteries; it was the truth I embraced with devotion.

When I was eight, my ten-year-old brother Craig and I were both sick with a cold and kept home from school. By the afternoon we were both feeling well enough that Mom left us alone briefly to run an errand. Once we were alone, Craig and I got naked and pranced about the house. Craig led me to Mother's makeup chest, where he had me put on rouge and lipstick and eye shadow and then we each dressed in our parents' holy undergarments.

As a child I already knew that the garments symbolized a Mormon adult's faith and commitment to our Heavenly Father, but this was precisely what my brother Craig and I chose to desecrate.

With Craig pretending to be Dad and me pretending to be Mom, we stood in the hallway, looking in the mirror as we rubbed our garment-covered bodies against each other. When my brother took me in his arms, as though he were about to kiss me, I suddenly felt overcome with shame. Breaking free from Craig's embrace, I said, "We shouldn't do this. It's not right."

"You're right," he agreed abruptly.

We both removed the Temple undergarments quickly and got dressed. Craig ran to his bedroom and closed the door. I ran to the sofa in the living room, where I was resting earlier when Mom had left the house.

My face felt hot with shame, much hotter than I felt earlier when I was running a slight fever. I wanted to cry, but couldn't. Somehow I knew that I had shamed my older brother without meaning to. Craig and I never played that way again together, nor did we ever acknowledge that we had once shared a sexual exploration together that was both innocent and healthy. Up to that time, my brother Craig and I were inseparable. After that, nothing was ever the same between us. Such is the power of shame.

******

As Harlan and I got to know each other that first week at BYU, he told me more about himself. "I'm from Layton," he explained, as we ate lunch in the student center cafeteria on campus. "It's a suburb north of Salt Lake."

I knew exactly where Layton was, since we had always passed the signs for Layton, Utah every time our family had made a trip to Salt Lake City, usually to attend the LDS General Conference held in the Tabernacle at Temple Square once a year.

"I don't have much family left who live there," Harlan continued. "Only my brother Warren and my sister Katharine. Warren was 22 and Katharine was 18 when I was born, so I basically grew up as an only child." He paused briefly. "Mom died when I was 14," he added, his voice growing quiet. "Then my dad died last March."

Having never experienced such loss, I tried to imagine how I would feel if both my parents had died. "Wow!" I murmured softly, "You must feel like an orphan."

On the next Sunday after attending our church meetings, Harlan came to see my apartment, and later that afternoon he invited me back to see his place in downtown Provo. It was hot outside, but I decided not to change, going in my Sunday best.

With Harlan backing out of my driveway in his red Volkswagen bug, I followed close behind in Oscar.

Driving past the block-wide Marriott Center, our new basketball arena nearing completion, Harlan suddenly pulled into the Cougar Stadium parking lot and I followed suit.

"Why the stop?" I asked, as we both got out of our cars.

"I want to show you something," he explained, looking at the stadium. "See Cougar Stadium?" I nodded. BYU's football stadium was huge, seating over 25,000 people, and difficult to miss. "I played

28

football in the stadium back in '65 when I was a freshman my first semester, before going on my mission in March 1966, just after my 18th birthday."

We walked across the street to the bleachers surrounding a baseball field. "What position did you play?" I asked, sitting in the center on the front row of bleachers.

"I played tight end," he said, as he sat down beside me.

"I wouldn't know a tight end from a loose one!" I said.

"Just keep it that way!" Harlan replied, making a joke.

I didn't understand his joke, so I ignored it. "What does a tight end do, anyway?" I asked.

"I was an offensive lineman but I also run downfield and tried to catch passes from the quarterback. I was good at running and catching, but I usually dropped the ball," he explained, smiling broadly. "That's why they used to call me Slippery Hands LeClair!"

"If you say so," I said, laughing. "As for me, I hate sports!"

"What about baseball?" he asked, looking at the ball field.

"I hate baseball the most!" I replied.

Looking out across the baseball diamond, I remembered the catcalls and the taunting jeers. "In Pocatello, a boy wasn't a real boy if he didn't play baseball. My brothers played sports, but I spent my time alone, reading, writing, acting, and doing puppet shows. I didn't have friends, only puppets. I couldn't wait to grow up! But it's a funny thing; now that I'm here in Happy Valley, I wish I could be Peter Pan and never grow up!"

He nodded. "When did you decide you wanted to be an actor?"

"Always. But more than that, I've always wanted to be a star!" I paused. "I think my dad found my dreams silly, but Mom took them very seriously. When I told her that I wanted to write, she bought me a typewriter for my birthday."

"She sounds like a great lady," Harlan said.

"She is." I paused. Suddenly realizing that for the first time in my life I felt like someone was not only deeply listening to me, but also understanding the words that I was saying, I reveled in the moment. "How about you?" I asked. "When did you decide you wanted to be

29

a professional actor?"

"I still haven't. It's just that people keep telling me that I have the looks for it."

"They're right, you know!" I reiterated. "You have movie star written all over you. In fact, you look so much like James Dean that it's uncanny." I blushed when I said the words, and he blushed, too.

"But I don't have the confidence or the experience that you have," he replied. "I just hope to make some quick money at it."

"Which you will," I enthused. "You're so handsome."

"Thanks, Kerry," he said shyly. "But you're embarrassing me."

Then Harlan grabbed my knee suddenly, saying, "Come on, Kerry. I want to show you my place before it gets too late."

I trailed Harlan's red Volkswagen to University Avenue, where he made a right turn onto a side street and then another right into the alley behind his house. After we parked, Harlan guided me to his apartment entrance in back. "Welcome to my little slice of heaven!" he exclaimed as he held the door open for me.

"It's cute!" I said, eyeing the stuffed sofa and matching chair in his living room, and the small TV on a dresser. Adjacent to the living room was a small but charming kitchen area with a tiny table and four chairs.

"Come on, and see the rest," he said, guiding me down a narrow hall to his bathroom and then on to his bedroom with two twin beds.

"You must have a roomie," I noted.

"Nope. That's how the place came. I didn't want a roommate, until now, that is, since I met you. But I guess it's too late for that now, at least for this semester. But you're welcome to sleep over anytime you want."

I blushed, not knowing quite what to say. "Thanks," I muttered.

"You're welcome!" Then he paused. "Mind if I change, Kerry?" he asked, as he began pulling off his tie. "I've been in these hot Sunday clothes all day!"

"Go right ahead!" I replied. But as Harlan stripped out of his clothes, I panicked. "Hey!" I added, "I'm thirsty! Can I get some water in the kitchen?"

"Help yourself! There are glasses above the sink."

I ran down the hall. From the kitchen, I could see Harlan standing in the hallway, wearing only his Temple undergarments. Though the garments covered his body as long johns would from neck to mid-thigh, they barely covered his nakedness, since they were made of a see-through nylon fabric. Worn only by LDS adults, these holy garments served as a constant reminder of the covenants made with God in a secret Temple ceremony. I would not wear the garments myself until I entered the Temple when I turned 19, to make similar secret and holy covenants with my Heavenly Father, prior to serving my mission.

I took the glass of water with me into the living room, taking a seat on the sofa. Harlan returned to the living room a moment later wearing jeans and a plaid shirt, sitting in the overstuffed chair next to me. Now that he was dressed, I could breathe again. But the intensity of the eye contact between us forced me to look away—at the TV, then at the built-in bookshelf where I saw Harlan's leather-bound copies of LDS scripture that he had, no doubt, used on his mission.

"You know, Kerry," he said softly, "you seem as innocent now as I was when I was a freshman here, back in the fall of '65."

"I hope you mean that as a compliment," I said, sitting the glass on a coaster on the adjacent table, as I began to blush.

"Oh, I do." He smiled gently, making me tremble all over. "In some ways," he continued, "I wish I could trade in the last five years of my life and go back to being the freshman I was then, instead of the freshman I am now. Except this time, I'd skip the football."

"Were the last five years that rough?" I asked, half-kidding.

"Actually, they were." Harlan paused, breathing heavily. "I guess the hardest part is adjusting to life back here in Happy Valley."

"Where did you serve your mission?" I asked, deciding it might be best to change the subject.

"In France," he replied. "Mostly in Paris."

"Paris must be wonderful." I looked through his window at the mountains of LDS Zion that had blocked my view of the world for the first 18 years of my life.

"What I saw of it was nice," Harlan answered. "When you're in the mission field, almost all of your time is spent proselytizing and tracking converts. You're not allowed much time for sightseeing."

"Even on your one day off a week?"

"On your day off you do laundry, shopping, and chores." Harlan grinned. "But the hardest part of being a missionary," he continued, "is learning a language at the Language Training Mission."

"Did you learn to speak French fluently?"

"With the Lord's help."

"Can you say something in French?"

"Oui, Monsieur." He took a moment to think of what to say, before adding, "Vous-etes tres aimable."

"I love it." Hearing the French words had conjured up images of romance in Paris. "What does it mean?"

"It can either mean 'you're very nice,' or 'you're very lovable,' depending on how you say it and who you say it to," he explained.

"Well, thank you." I laughed. "Either way, it's a compliment."

"Oui."

Harlan stared at me again, his soulful deep brown eyes penetrating me to the core. "I've always had a problem learning other languages," I said. "I hope they send me someplace where people speak English."

"If you pray hard enough, the Lord might arrange it that way."

"I doubt it," I replied, remembering the song we sang in church:

> *"I'll go where you want me to go, dear Lord,*
> *Over mountain or meadow or sea.*
> *I'll say what you want me to say, dear Lord.*
> *I'll be what you want me to be!"*

"But wherever it is," I continued, "I'll go wherever the Lord sends me. I just hope it isn't to some African village, where I have to go to the bathroom in the jungle!"

Harlan laughed. "Missionary life isn't quite as bad as all that. Even if it were, the spiritual rewards more than make up for it. I may not have seen Paris like a tourist, but I got to know the people. I lived among them, and visited them door-to-door. I experienced more of the real Paris than tourists ever do. And I baptized many new converts to the gospel." He paused. "Nothing in this world can compare with the thrill of saving even one soul. It's the greatest joy a man can ever know."

I was filled with genuine admiration. Harlan was obviously in-tune with the Holy Spirit.

"I was lucky, Kerry," he added quietly. "The Lord in His mercy prepared me on my mission for other tests."

"Other tests?" I asked, not knowing whether I should pry.

"Let's just say that I had a lot of growing up to do." Harlan smiled again. "You're so young. The world out there is not as beautiful as it is here in Happy Valley." He paused. "Take my advice, Kerry, and stay Peter Pan in Happy Valley for as long as you can!"

******

Since we weren't a well-to-do family, my siblings and I were each expected to do chores at home, and deliver the Idaho State Journal. Working on our family paper route was first the job of my eldest brother Dennis, then handed down to Denise, then to Craig, and lastly to me. Each of us, in turn, learned how to gather the bundle on our front step, fold and prepare the newspapers, stuffing all inserts into one, putting a rubber band around each, then cramming all into a canvas bag, before riding on our bikes, delivering a paper to each customer. We did this every afternoon, summer or winter, after school or after play, in blizzard, rain or intense heat, just as we did it every Sunday morning prior to the crack-of-dawn, so that the papers were delivered long before we were expected to attend church. I worked the paper route for nine years, starting at eight until I was a junior in high school.

We all were taught how to manage the money we made, and that ten percent of all that we earned was to be given to God at Tithing Settlement, handing it over to the Mormon Bishop at the end of each year. Even so, I saved enough money from the paper route to buy myself a portable color TV on my 13th birthday, when color TV was still in its infancy. And I managed to save enough money to pay for my mission, which I was expected to serve when I turned 19.

I was nine when I asked my parents if I could miss our ward's Sacrament Meeting to watch *The Wizard of Oz*.

"Please," I pleaded. "Can I please stay home from church just this once, to watch *The Wizard of Oz* on TV? It's my favorite, and it only comes on TV once a year. Please!"

Mom relented, intoning Glenda the Good, "Yes, you can stay home but just this once. You can't make a habit of missing church meetings."

"You're making a sinful decision, Kerry Lynn," Dad retorted, sounding like the Wicked Witch, as he threw a fireball of shame directly into my face. "I'm ashamed of you!" he added loudly, as he locked the back door behind him, even as Mom and my siblings were already making their way out to the car.

Watching from the living room window as my parents and siblings pulled away from the curb in our family Volkswagen on their way to Sacrament Meeting, shame began eating away at me from the inside out.

Sometime during that particular televised trip down the yellow brick road, I burst into tears. I felt lost like Dorothy, imprisoned by the Wicked Witch, hoping to find my way home.

I went down on my knees, putting my hands together on the couch in a reverent sign of prayer. "Heavenly Father, please forgive my sins. Help me become a better boy. And help me to make the choices that would please my parents. I ask for these favors and blessings in the name of Jesus Christ. Amen."

That year I did something that took me decades to understand. Dressed in my Sunday best and sitting on the wooden bench between Mom and Dad at Sacrament Meeting, I listened as our Bishop ranted from the pulpit, preaching that even our thoughts, if sexual, could damn us forever. Suddenly I tugged on Mom's arm, whispering that I had to go to the bathroom. Having been excused, I walked quietly up the aisle and out of the main chapel. But I didn't go to the men's room. Instead, I went up the stairs to the Junior Sunday School chapel on the second floor.

Alone in the smaller upstairs chapel, I stripped off my clothes, lay out naked like a sacrificial lamb on the same altar where the sacrament was sanctified, and jerked myself off to a dry climax.

Afterward, I got off the altar, dressed, put everything back in order, and returned to the congregation in the lower chapel, as though nothing out of the ordinary had just happened, giving both Mom and Dad an innocent smile when I returned.

When I described this incident to my therapist years later, he explained: "Your inner child knew you had to bury him to survive your childhood, so he did something outrageous so you wouldn't forget him."

"My inner child?" I asked. I had never heard the term before.

Jim gave me a gentle smile. "When I talk about your inner child, I'm talking about your true self—your authentic self, if you will—the person you were before you began pretending you were someone else, someone that they found more acceptable than who you really were."

Then I finally understood: My true self, my inner child, was saying goodbye and with a plea in his heart: "Don't abandon me forever. Find me again someday, please!"

That year my family had two terrible car accidents nearly back-to-back in a period of three months. In the first case, Dennis and Craig had opted out of attending a family reunion, so it was just my parents and my sister and I that went to the family reunion at Downata Hot Springs near Downey, Idaho on Saturday.

After a fun day of picnicking and swimming, we left the reunion to head home. Almost immediately, we began having car trouble, so Dad drove our cream-colored Volkswagen bug at not more than 20 miles an hour, on the shoulder of the road.

The drive home had become so slow and monotonous that my sister had fallen asleep in the back seat. I tried to nap as well, but couldn't get my eyes to stay closed.

Then, hell itself seemed to explode within our little VW.

I didn't know until later that a drunken truck driver, going upwards of 75 mph, had come up behind us in his semi-truck, and had plowed into the backend of our little Volkswagen bug.

All I knew at the time was that there had been the sound of something crashing into us from behind. And then our car had tipped over on its side, and spun round and round, rolling over and over again, like a nightmarish carnival ride, completely out of control. When our car finally came to a halt on its side, with the driver's side down, all was silent.

Still in the backseat and with the car on its side, it was difficult for me to stand up inside the car without standing on my sister Denise, who lay silently beneath me. Thinking she had slept through the accident, I tried to wake Denise again and again, but to no avail. Eventually I faced the reality that she must be dead, even as I realized with sudden dread—as though in a waking nightmare—that Mom and Dad were not inside the car.

After struggling to push the car door open above me on the passenger's side, I was finally able to look around at the crash site. What I saw when I finally managed to push the car door open, horrified me. Dad and Mom were lying near each other on the ground surrounded by bits of the car and sagebrush. Neither of them moved, and Mom—who was bleeding profusely from a rip in her leg—lay in a pool of her own blood.

Believing that both of my parents had died, a feeling of terror, unlike anything I had known before, gripped me as I froze in shock. Everything, including my convoluted thoughts, seemed to slow to a crawl, as though I were trapped in a surreal dimension, in another time and space. Slowly I processed the numbing reality: They were all dead. Only I had survived the terrible accident. In one brief instant, my parents and my sister had been taken from me. A loneliness that only orphans know flooded my senses. What would I do now? To whom could I turn? Praying as hard as I could, I whispered, "Please, Heavenly Father, help me. Don't let them all be dead. Please!" Then, to my utter astonishment, I heard a calm male voice comforting me, as though an invisible presence was inside the car with me.

"Be at peace, Kerry," the loving voice said. "All will be well."

Was it the voice of a ghost? At first, I wondered if I had died, too, and I just hadn't realized it yet. Then I decided it must be the voice of an angel sent from Heaven, much like the Angel Moroni who had appeared to Joseph Smith when the Prophet Joseph was just a boy, except that my Angel was invisible.

It was the first time that I had heard such a voice, but it would not be the last. Indeed, this was only the first of many deeply spiritual experiences in my life that would follow. Though I didn't understand it then, these experiences would eventually call me to a deeper spiritual path, separate and apart from the religious path that I was required to follow. Today, I think of the voice as that of an inner spiritual guide—one I believe that we all have, particularly in the dark times when we need inner guidance most.

Regardless, breaking into the sacred revelry of my thoughts, I suddenly heard Mom screaming, "My kids! Where are my kids?" And then I heard my father's response to Mom, "They both must still be inside the car!" Just hearing their voices was an answer to my prayer. My parents were alive! And Denise might be, too!

The next thing I knew Mom and Dad were lifting me out of the car, while the gash in Mom's leg spurted blood like a geyser.

"Millie Jane," Dad shouted, "I've got to take care of that cut on your leg or you'll bleed to death!" Tearing a sleeve from his shirt and wrap-ping it around her wounded leg, he tied it tight.

Suddenly we became aware of the smell of gasoline, as a fire started in the engine at the back of our VW. Realizing that the car might explode any second, fear overcame our shock. "The engine in back is going to blow!" Dad exclaimed, who knew everything about cars. "We have to get Denise out the back window!"

I was pushed to safety, as Dad ripped the other sleeve off of his shirt, wrapping it around his fist before smashing it through the back window, as glass flew everywhere.

Mom and Dad frantically reached with their bare hands to pull all of the broken glass from the frame in a race against time. I ran forward to help, grabbing the cut glass from the sides of the window, cutting my fingers. As it was, we barely managed to pull my sister's body through the back window to safety, before our car exploded in flames. With my sister Denise still lifeless, lying just beyond the edge of the fire, I heard Mom ask, "Is she dead?"

Dad put his hand on my sister's wrist to check her pulse. "She's still alive," Dad replied. "But we have to get you and her to a hospital, and soon!"

As it happened, Good Samaritans—who had seen the accident happen—had stopped to help, and quickly raced the three of us to the nearest hospital in Pocatello. It wasn't until we arrived at the hospital that Denise finally awoke, and blissfully unaware of anything that had happened.

Denise was later diagnosed with a concussion, while Mom's severed artery required surgery.

When we were finally allowed to go home in a taxi hours later, Mom came home with painkillers.

Mom was in so much pain that she had to take the prescribed opioids frequently, and within two weeks she was utterly addicted to them.

******

Each church branch at the Y was divided into BYU families, so students could attend Family Home Evening on Monday nights, as LDS families do throughout the world. BYU families were both our student fraternities and our sororities. Harlan, Mickey, and I were all assigned to the same BYU family, and Harlan was chosen as our family father.

When we gathered in Harlan's living room for our first Family Home Evening on the following Monday night, while Harlan gave a lesson on *The Word of Wisdom*, I noticed that some of my BYU brothers were showing interest in their BYU sisters and vice-versa.

I have never been more aware of the beauty in the world than as a new freshman at BYU. I was young, and for me the world was young, too. Flowers were in bloom along the clean wide sidewalks, and the mountains were colored with wildflowers, pine trees, and sage. It was September in Happy Valley—a time and place where youth and innocence seemed as natural to the earth as springtime—a perfect time to fall in love.

Harlan and I went for a picnic on Saturday. With Carole King singing "You've Got A Friend" on the car radio, we took the Alpine Loop through mountain canyons covered with pine trees, until we found a picnic spot beneath majestic Mount Timpanogos. I thought it such a perfect spot for a picnic that I promised myself to bring Bridget there on a date the following Saturday afternoon.

While we were sharing a blanket and eating our picnic, Harlan admitted, "I have something to confess, Kerry." He paused, and gave me a sheepish look. "I lied to you last week when I told you how I felt about my mission. To tell you the truth, it wasn't the greatest experience I've ever had."

"You told me last week that it was," I said.

"Last week I told you what I thought you wanted to hear. But just in this last week, I've learned that you want to hear how things really are, and that you deserve to hear the truth." He paused dramatically before continuing to speak. "Serving a mission isn't as wonderful an experience as most RMs say, at least I didn't think so." He paused, as though he were trying to read my reaction. "Don't get me wrong, Kerry. I loved living in another culture, learning a new language, seeing more of the world, but being a missionary was one of the worst experiences I've ever had."

Undoubtedly my eyes were as wide as the paper plate I held in my hand. I had never heard an RM express such blasphemous feelings. Holding my half-chewed drumstick in midair, I replied, "I don't know how you can say that, Harlan!"

Sounding exasperated, Harlan retorted, "Once they lock you up inside the Language Training Mission, while marching you through hundreds of missionary discussions and cramming a new foreign language into you, then you'll know what I mean."

"I can't believe you're saying this!" I protested loudly.

"You'd better believe it, Kerry!" he replied. "Once you're in the mission field, you'll go door-to-door, proselytizing and mouthing canned sentences like a programmed robot."

I stared at the peaks of Mount Timpanogos high above us. Harlan's reversal on the subject of his mission had shocked me. I thought I knew Harlan, but now I was seeing him for the man he actually was. Having never met a Mormon as honest as Harlan, I finally spoke up. "I don't know what to say. It makes me think twice about going on a mission," I admitted.

Harlan seemed suddenly overcome with guilt, particularly when the potato salad fell off my plate. "I'm sorry, Kerry," he offered suddenly, "if what I said turned you off to the idea of a mission. I shouldn't have said those things. It wasn't my place. I apologize."

"Don't apologize, Harlan," I replied. "You're the first and only person who has ever talked to me honestly about anything related to the church." My throat choked with emotion. "I've only known you a couple of weeks, but it's already been the best time of my life!"

"It's been a good time for me, too, Babe," he said quietly.

I looked away from his handsome face to take in the view of Mount Timpanogos. Sometimes I found it painful to look at Harlan for too long. He was too handsome by far, at least in my estimation, and taking in his physical maleness and masculine beauty caused an ache inside me that I didn't want to understand and certainly didn't want to acknowledge.

"Timp is beautiful, isn't it?" I asked, hoping to change the subject.

"Beauteous," he said, using Dad's word in describing nature.

"You told me about your mission, but what did you do when you returned home after your mission?"

"I went to live with Dad," Harlan explained, "and worked at various jobs for over a year. Then—since I didn't want to go back to school just yet—I decided to join the Marines."

"The Marines?" I choked on my fried chicken. "You were a Marine?" Harlan slowly nodded his head yes. "Did you … did you serve in … in …" I stammered awkwardly.

"In Vietnam?" he asked, completing my question. I nodded yes. "Of course!" he replied. "My Dad served as a Marine in World War II," he explained. "I wanted to serve with the Marines, like Dad."

"Geez! I didn't know anybody still joined the Marines!"

"Well, they do," he said quietly. I took a bite of the potato salad that I had put on a fresh paper plate, and waited for him to continue. "It seemed like the right thing to do at the time," he added.

"I still don't understand," I replied, hoping to find out more.

"I believed in what we were fighting for," Harlan explained, "to stop communism and all that. I spent years out of country, first in France on my mission, then fighting in Nam." A shadow crossed his face. "But going to Vietnam was an even dumber decision than going on my mission."

Harlan walked over to a nearby log and sat down.

"What I saw and did in Nam are unspeakable," he added haltingly. "It was horrible. The thing that saved me was meeting Danny. He was so much like you." He paused and looked at me for a long time. "He died over there, Kerry." He paused again. "When I saw you in church that first day, you reminded me so much of him, I knew that I had to meet you."

"Whew!" I exclaimed. "You sure have been through a lot."

Harlan stared at me long and hard, before he spoke again.

"As hard as Nam was, coming home was harder," he explained. "I still can't adjust. It's all sweetness and light here at the Y, but young men like you are still dying every day over there in that shithole!" He exhaled deeply, already feeling guilt for swearing. "I shouldn't have sworn like that, Kerry. I'm sorry."

I realized then how much Harlan was like my father. "I've never been through anything like Vietnam," I replied quietly. "I can't even begin to comprehend it." In truth, I knew nothing about the Vietnam War except what I had seen on *The Huntley-Brinkley News Hour*.

Harlan had experienced too much of life, and I too little. Like

41

drowning survivors in a vast expanse of ocean, we clung to each other in a need to forget and a desire to know, never letting go until the sea swallows one or the other or both.

******

Three months after the first car accident when I was nine, Mom and Dad went on a second honeymoon to Los Angeles, leaving the four of us with my grandparents.

After attending Sacrament Meeting at our ward chapel on Sunday without my grandparents, Dennis and Denise each invited a teenage friend to join us for a ride in our family car, a '57 Chevy, entering the Fort Hall Indian Reservation on a narrow gravel road curving dangerously through sagebrush-covered mountains.

Unwisely, Dennis chose to go even further off-road, driving onto isolated farmland high in the mountain canyon and directly into deep mud, where we promptly got stuck.

While Dennis and his teenage buddy Gary went to borrow a tractor from a local farmer, Denise and her teenage girlfriend Sharon decided to hitchhike back to town, leaving Craig and me in the car.

Once Dennis and Gary got the car out of the mud, Gary took the tractor back, while Dennis tore up the gravel road at 80 mph, searching frantically for Denise and Sharon.

When we ran over a cattle guard installed in the gravel, our car flew off the road, hurtling end over end, all the way down the mountain. My brothers and I were not wearing seatbelts; they weren't yet required in vehicles back then. So the three of us were bounced around inside the car as though we were pinballs bouncing from one object to the next inside an out-of-control pinball machine. When the front end of our Chevy slammed into a huge boulder three times the size of our car—and with full force—not only did it throw the three of us into the backseat, it flattened the engine and the front seat of the car like a pancake. Had we been wearing seatbelts and remained in the front seat, my brothers

42

and I would have been flattened like pancakes, too, since the front seat now only had an inch or two of breathing room. Miraculously, smashing into the boulder had saved our lives, since it had stopped our car from dropping into the deep river canyon below. Clearly, my brothers and I had also, quite magically, escaped drowning.

What I experienced from inside the car felt similar to what I had experienced during the first accident a few months earlier, as though we were turning inside a washing machine, going end over end. But the experience felt radically different in the final impact, when we plowed suddenly and with ferocious force into the boulder that had saved us from dropping into the river below, even as all three of us were thrown into the backseat.

Then there was only the eerie sound of spinning wheels, gradually giving way to deafening silence.

Finally I heard Craig ask, "What happened?"

"We crashed," I explained, having been the only one in the family to experience both car accidents. "Come on," I added, pulling myself out of the side rear window of our smashed car, utterly flattened in the front and turned upside down. Then I helped Craig and Dennis get out of the car through the same, narrow window.

In shock, my older brothers and I tried to keep our balance as we surveyed the wreckage, and began hiking back up the mountain. Once we reached the road, we spent several minutes on the isolated gravel road, waiting for someone, anyone, to come along. The three of us were alone, lost and abandoned in the Indian Reservation with only sagebrush and mountains in sight.

When an old, red and rickety pickup finally came into sight up the road from us 15 minutes later, it felt like a Godsend.

"What happened to you boys?" the driver asked, sticking his head out of his pickup window as he pulled up to the three of us standing in the middle of the road. "What are the three of you doing way out here all alone on a Sunday afternoon?"

Both Craig and Dennis were still deep in shock, so I was the one who spoke up. It was surprising since I was the youngest. "We wrecked our car," I explained, pointing down the side of the mountain where our flattened Chevy was still smoking from the violent accident that had occurred only a few minutes earlier.

He gasped when he saw our car, or what little was left of it, smashed into the one huge boulder by the edge of the deep river canyon. "Holy Jesus! You boys are lucky to be alive!"

Introducing himself as a member of the Bannock-Shoshone Tribe, the kind stranger invited the three of us to hop into the back of his pickup truck, offering to take us to the nearest police station in the city of Fort Hall.

Later that afternoon, after the police dropped us off at our grandparents' home in Pocatello, where we were united with my sister, Grandma Hamp confronted Dennis. "What were you doing up there on the Indian Reservation anyway?" she shouted. "You were supposed to be taking care of your little brothers! Instead, you nearly killed them!"

"I just thought it would be fun to go for a drive," Dennis explained lamely.

"Fun!" Grandmother shrieked in anger. "I'll show you fun, young man!" Grandma Hamp took her shoe off and struck him in the head with it, as she sometimes did to Grandpa Hamp, and Grandpa on occasion had the bruises to prove it.

For the first and only time that I can ever remember, I detected some measure of guilt and regret in my oldest brother. It was something that I would never see in him again, as though such feelings within my brother Dennis died that day.

When my parents were told about the accident, they cut their trip short in California and raced back home.

Upon their return, they decided not to punish Dennis for the accident, feeling that he had already suffered enough guilt about it.

After that, my oldest brother's rebellion took over our family completely, as though he were acting out more and more, simply as a way of earning the punishment he felt he rightfully deserved. And the worse that Dennis behaved, the more attention he received.

******

Standing on the patio of BYU's Fine Arts Center overlooking campus, I could see thousands of students walking on sidewalks between classes. The sidewalks were crammed with RMs seeking an LDS wife, and young LDS women searching for an RM husband.

Every student clung to the sidewalks; no one dared walk on the grass. They all moved in lockstep.

In truth, I marched in lockstep with them, though I was just beginning to explore, apart from the dictates of parents and church, what I might want to become.

In September, Dr. Preston Gledhill cast me as the lead in my first major production at BYU, his Reader's Theatre presentation of an original play, *Starlight*. I felt like a star when the play opened in early October to a good review in the campus paper.

I had also received joyous news from home that week. My sister Denise had given birth to her first child—my niece Tara Lee—on October 2. In addition to my nephew Doye, I now had a precious little niece! Denise and Lee would later have two more children, my niece Joy and my nephew Adam. Naturally, I cherished my new role as uncle, and performed my duties as an uncle quite joyously.

Harlan and I went to Cougar Stadium sometime in October to watch our first BYU football game together. When the Cougars ran onto the field, we leapt to our feet to sing BYU's fight song:

> *"Rise and shout! The Cougars are out!*
> *They're on their way to fame and glory!"*

As the crowd sang, the bleachers rumbled beneath our feet, and I sang louder than anyone. "For someone who hates football," Harlan observed, "You're having a good time!"

"Oh, I love watching football," I said. "I just hate playing it!"

After the game, Harlan walked me up the hill to my apartment where he had parked his red VW bug. As we walked, the moon rose above the mountains. The moonlight gave Harlan's sandy-brown hair silver highlights. "The moon's pretty, isn't it?" I asked softly.

"It's an October moon," Harlan replied. "October moons are always magical."

I shivered under my red windbreaker. "It's getting cold. I should have worn a heavier jacket."

"Here, Babe," he said, calling me by the new nickname he had given me (and one that I loved), taking off his letterman's jacket and offering it to me. "Put this on."

"What about you? You'll freeze."

"No way! I'm hot-blooded like all Marines," he said, laughing.

I put the jacket on. It was quite tight on me, but I didn't care.

"Warmer now?" he asked tenderly.

"Much," I replied, as my spirit soared to the moon.

It was my first glimpse beyond Utah's mountains.

Harlan met his girlfriend, Jennifer Wells—a petite and pretty blonde—in Freshman English near the same time that I met Bridget. Since Harlan and I both wanted to meet each other's new girlfriends, we all met together as a group at Heaps of Pizza—a popular hangout on the south edge of campus—sometime in October. We all had a good time together that night, and we quickly coalesced as friends. In fact, Jennifer invited us all to her apartment for dinner the next night.

Like Bridget's apartment, Jennifer's place was in a three-story building approved for female students, a few blocks from the south edge of campus, in between Bridget's place and Harlan's. Jennifer's whole apartment was decorated in true Molly Mormon fashion with Holly Hobby paraphernalia everywhere. Aside from the decorating, as well as being both pretty and petite, Jennifer Wells was also a great cook. After dinner, Harlan complimented Jennifer. "Sister Wells, that was a great dinner, from first to last!"

"Thank you kindly, Elder LeClair," she replied demurely.

I could tell that Harlan and Jennifer were attracted to each other by the way they kept eyeing each other across the dinner table, and soon the four of us began double dating.

On our first double date, we went to Hawkins Drive-In, a red-and-white burger stand across town that Bridget and I had discovered earlier that fall. After going inside, Jennifer exclaimed, "This place is so neat! It's right out of the 50s!"

With the four of us sitting at one of the few tables in the small red-and-white dining room, I announced enthusiastically, "Bridget and I love this place. They make the best burgers and fries I've ever eaten! And their milkshakes are out of this world yummy!"

When our burgers and fries arrived at the table, Bridget made a suggestion: "Kerry, you should show them the way to eat fries, the way you showed me at the Wilkinson Center the other day!"

"Okay," I replied. "First you need great fry sauce, which they have. Then you take a fry, dunk it in the sauce, and stuff it in your mouth and chow down. But the most important part is that you have to mmm once you start eating the fry. Watch!" I dunked a fry in sauce, ate it, and then made a long mmm sound, and then smacked my lips gratuitously afterward, as they all laughed. They all followed my lead, imitating my mmm.

"Is that how it's done?" Harlan asked.

"Yes, verily! That's the way to do it!" I said, laughing.

"Kerry, you're wonderful!" Jennifer exclaimed. "It's too bad you're a Democrat!"

"I feel the same way about you, Jennifer. Except for being a Republican, you're perfect! You're so perfect, in fact, I think I'll start calling you Angel!"

"I second that idea," Harlan replied. Then Harlan turned to Jennifer, giving her an innocent peck on the cheek. "You're my sweet and beautiful Republican Angel!"

Jennifer was the type of female student I referred to as either a Betty BYU or as a Molly Mormon. Like most of BYU's female students, Angel was modest, far right in her politics, and majoring in Child Development and Family Relations or CDFR, as I liked to call it. Like most CDFR majors, Jennifer was only attending BYU to find a suitable Returned Missionary husband. And I suspected that she already had her sights set on Harlan.

In fairness to Jennifer, what BYU female student wouldn't find

Harlan an ideal choice? First of all, he was stunningly handsome; second, he was charming and debonair yet very masculine and manly in his demeanor; and third, he seemed to possess all the traits of a devout LDS man. He was an ordained Elder in the Melchizedek Priesthood and a Returned Missionary, just the type of man who would make an ideal LDS husband and father in the estimation of most young LDS women at the Y.

As the four of us discovered that night, Hawkins Drive-In was owned and operated by Brother and Sister Hawkins, a middle-aged couple who took an immediate liking to us. The Drive-In quickly became one of our favorite hangouts off-campus. We went there so often, in fact, that I started referring to Mr. and Mrs. Hawkins as our Ma and Pa.

In mid-November I was cast as Jesus Christ in *The Kiss: A Story of Those Who Betrayed Him,* a new play scheduled to open in early December. We began rehearsals immediately, even as Thanksgiving and Christmas approached.

******

Since we didn't have a fireplace at our home in Pocatello, each year I asked Santa Claus to bring us a fireplace for Christmas. Besides always wanting one, I thought it would make Santa's job much easier in delivering our presents if he could slide down a chimney rather than be forced to enter our house through the pipes of our old oil furnace in the basement. I faithfully wrote the same letter to Santa each year, and each year Mom and Dad explained that a fireplace was too big and too expensive for Santa Claus to bring in his sleigh, until I eventually stopped asking for one.

Santa never did bring us a fireplace, so I made do with the heat vent on the floorboard of our tiny bathroom. This was my place of safety and warmth, the cocoon I would retreat to after returning from delivering my papers on the winter evenings after school.

The Christmas holidays, and all of the holidays that I knew as a child, were joyous and magical, and there was much that was happy in our family life at home.

After the two car accidents in 1962, however, my family seemed to blow apart. It only made sense. When you repress a volcano, sooner or later you're bound to get a nasty explosion. Once the domestic explosions began, I hid myself behind the bathroom door as often as I could, curling myself into a ball on the ratty carpet in front of the heat vent, imagining it was a fireplace at someone else's house that was safer and less violent than ours.

When my oldest brother Dennis returned home at the end of the summer after running away with the circus at the age of 15, he started smoking cigarettes, drinking alcohol, and carousing with dubious friends. In our LDS world, such behavior was not to be tolerated. My parents put their foot down, as did Dennis—right into the kitchen wall!

Dennis and Denise were heading out the door to a high school dance one night when Dad stopped them in their tracks. Dennis was wearing tightly pegged pants, the style at the time, a style that my father considered immodest. "Where do you think you're going looking like that, young man?" Dad inquired harshly.

"To the dance!" Dennis chirped happily.

"Like hell you are!" Dad proclaimed. Having never been confident in himself—shame-based people never are—Dad had always reacted badly to any challenge to his authority. "No son of mine is going out to a public dance dressed like that!"

Dennis was immediately in Dad's face. "There's nothing wrong with how I'm dressed!" he yelled. "All the cool guys at school dress like this!"

Dad took his stand between Dennis and the door. "You're not going to the dance until you change into something respectable!"

"Like hell I will!" Dennis replied threateningly.

"Now, Allan," Mom interjected, trying to calm things down, "It's the way the young men are dressing now."

"That's enough, Millie Jane!" Dad snapped. "I am the head of this family!" Then Dad aimed his ire at his oldest son, Dennis. "As

49

for you, young man, you will respect my Priesthood authority and do as I say!"

"Go to Hell!" Dennis shouted directly into Dad's face.

"How dare you speak that way in my own home!" Dad fumed.

In her role as peacemaker, my sister Denise stepped in, as calmly and sweetly as she could: "Really, Dad, it's okay. It'll be fine. I'll keep an eye on him." But Dad ignored her.

Soon Dennis and Dad came to blows, and the glass of our storm door shattered. My brother Craig and I cowered in the kitchen corner behind and somewhat under the table, frozen in fear.

After that, our LDS home became an active war zone.

Dennis became so angry one night that he attacked my father in the living room. Mom tried to keep the two of them apart, but Dennis threw her across the room. Mom smashed into the piano, as Dennis and Dad tore into each other, fists and curses flying.

I was hiding behind the sofa in the corner, dumbstruck with shock, but I ran to my mother at the piano, attempting to comfort her and to hold her. Mom was inconsolable, as she wept bitter tears that had nothing to do with any physical pain. As I watched her face etched in heartache, I realized that my young heart was breaking, too. Forced to witness such violence, to watch my mother bleeding and bruised at my brother's hands, left me traumatized as much or more than if I were the one my brother had tossed against the piano. We all became damaged goods that evening, but the worst was yet to come.

A few nights later, Dennis used his 22-caliber rifle to try to kill my father. To save himself and protect the family, Dad bent the end of my brother's rifle. After struggling on the stairs coming up from our basement, Dennis chased Dad out into the front yard with his rifle in hand, while Dad took an ax from the shed and wielded it against his son. The shameful and shaming Wicked Witch of Mormon Oz rode high on her broomstick that night, and it seemed our home was flying inside a tornado. Since our house was prominently seen from all directions, as it sat on the corner of Poplar Street and Washington Avenue, it felt as though my family and I were forced to stand naked, exposed and on display, outside in our front yard, as all of our LDS neighbors looked on.

With our masks ripped from us, Mom told Craig and I to run up the block to fetch Officer Gerard, a cop who lived a few houses up Washington Avenue, to prevent a murder from happening on our front lawn. As Craig and I ran to the Gerard home, my heart thumped inside my chest. "Would Dennis and Dad still be alive when we returned?" I wondered.

Luckily, Officer Gerard was just returning home from work in his police car when Craig and I arrived. After my brother and I frantically pleaded for his help, Officer Gerard ran back with us to our home at the corner of Poplar and Washington. Still in uniform and with his gun still in his holster, Officer Gerard was able to convince Dennis to put down his rifle and to talk my Dad into putting away the axe.

Once the danger passed, my soul flooded with shame. What was wrong with my father and with my brother Dennis? What had gone so wrong in our supposedly perfect Latter-Day-Saint home? Was it my fault?

Whenever Dennis and Dad got into a fight, Mom would take my brother Craig and I down to our basement bedroom and tell us to hide behind our clothes in our darkened closet. "Stay here and hide, and keep quiet, just in case," Mom warned us both on many occasions. In truth, I spent many a night huddled with my brother Craig in the back of our closet, hidden under piles of clothes, barely able to breathe, consumed with terror, as we heard Dad and Dennis warring throughout the house.

We all walked on eggshells in our house whenever Dennis was around, knowing if we made a wrong step that either Dennis or Dad could blow up at each other over the slightest thing. And we each coped in different ways. Dennis caroused at night, played hooky from school, and drank even more; Dad attended even more church meetings; Mom swallowed her opioid painkillers like candy; Craig avoided home, hanging out with his friends; and Denise and I, seeking solace in food, both gained weight. But my parents, absorbed in Dennis's antics, didn't seem to take any notice. It seemed that they both had only two questions on their minds: "What had they done wrong in raising Dennis?" and "How had they failed Dennis?"

Mom spent her nights sleeping at the top of the stairs to prevent Dennis from creeping upstairs to murder his father, or Dad from sneaking downstairs to kill his eldest son.

When Mom had her frequent migraines, I would sit on the edge of her bed and hold her hand, reassuring her by saying, "Everything's going to be fine," while placing a hot towel on her forehead. As Mom's perpetual baby boy, I had an important role in my LDS family, to make certain that Mom's emotional needs were attended to. In fulfilling that job, I was expected to be everything for Mother that my Father could never be: A constant companion, loyal confidante, and a reliable source of emotional support. Mother kept our dysfunctional family functioning, and I kept her emotionally stable, already aware that the task fell to me.

As the domestic war between Dennis and Dad wore on, it took a tremendous emotional toll on me. A photograph taken of me that year by my father—when I first learned to ride a bicycle without training wheels—depicts a young, thin, and fairly athletic boy, shirtless, proud of my body and my newfound skill, wearing only jeans as I rode up and down the block on my bike with abandon. By the end of that year, I was overweight, fearful, enslaved by anxiety, and filled with shame.

******

Since Harlan had a bedroom with two single beds, the extra bed was mine to use whenever I wanted. When the first snow was forecast to arrive early in the morning on the first Tuesday after Thanksgiving, I slept over at Harlan's that Monday night.

Harlan was looking forward to a ski trip in the mountains on the weekend, and I was looking forward to building a snowman with Harlan early in the morning. So Harlan and I were both so excited for the first snowfall that we both barely slept that night.

When morning came, everything in view—the mountains in the distance, Harlan's backyard, and the frozen orchard and frosty pine trees beyond—was covered with a coating of peaceful white.

I was still looking out the window, when Harlan came up behind me to take in the view.

"It's really coming down, isn't it?" he whispered.

"Yeah," I replied with breathless excitement.

Looking from Harlan to the frosty wonderland outside, I added enthusiastically, "Let's go build our snowman!"

Dressed in gloves, warm clothing, my blue parka and boots, I trudged out into the deep snow, with Harlan just behind me.

It wasn't yet sunrise and the air was crisp and cold. My breath sent patterns of steam billowing into the early-morning sky.

Harlan's backyard looked peaceful. God's pure white blanket was undefiled by footprints, and what a sight it was! Snow had transformed the lawn into a magical winter playground. The pine trees were frosted white, their prickly bows laden with sticky glistening powder. Icicles, like shimmering prisms, hung from the ledges of the roofs. "Mom used to tell me that if I made a wish while the first snow fell, my wish would always come true," I said.

"Make a wish then!" Harlan replied, smiling broadly.

"All right." I shut my eyes and wished my secret wish.

"What'd you wish for?" he asked.

"I can't tell. If you tell, your wish never comes true."

In the midst of a perfect scene for a Christmas card, Harlan and I built our snowman, making it even fatter than I was at Alameda Junior High School. After we finished, Harlan threw a snowball, striking me squarely in the behind. I retaliated, but missed him by feet. "Missed me, Babe!" Harlan taunted.

"Now you know why I hate baseball!" I retorted.

"When spring comes, I'm going to teach you how to throw a ball!" he kidded. I threw another snowball and missed him again. "I'm over here, Kerry Babe!" Harlan taunted.

"Smarty-pants! We can't all be jocks!" I said, laughing. As if to prove that I knew something about playing in the snow, I dropped to the ground, laying out flat and spreading my arms through the powder. "Come look!" I stood up, brushing the snow off my coat.

"What is it?" Harlan asked, running up to me.

"I made an angel!" I exclaimed.

Just then I grabbed some snow and stuffed it down the front of Harlan's shirt and coat—then ran as fast as I could back toward his apartment door, sprinting through the snow as fast as my legs could carry me. Harlan chased after me. "Hey!" he shouted, "I'm not letting you get away with that!"

He tackled me an easy ten yards from the door, throwing me down into the snow and falling on top of me. Neither of us could stop laughing. Pinning me to the ground, Harlan pushed snow down the back of my pants. I screamed from the cold. "If you're going to play rough, you've gotta take your own medicine!" Harlan's lips pressed against my ear. "Ready to say you're sorry?"

"No!" I challenged, as Harlan's weight bore down on me.

"Well, I'm not going to let you up until you do," he said.

"All right," I gasped, with breathless giggles. "I'm sorry."

"No!" Harlan whispered heavily. "Say it like you mean it!"

His lips felt warm, even hot, as they pressed against my freezing red ears, as feelings of passion flushed my face. In horror, I felt my penis stiffen beneath me like a hard icicle glistening with desires I did not want to understand. "I'm sorry," I replied. Harlan couldn't have known that I wasn't apologizing to him, but to my Heavenly Father. "That's more like it," Harlan joked, laughing as he stood up. I lay motionless in the snow, feeling lost.

"Hey, Kerry, you all right?" Harlan pressed. Luckily, my large blue parka hid my erection. "Let me help you up," Harlan said, pulling me to my feet. Just then the sun rose above the mountains as the first snow of Utah Valley glittered like magic. "It's glorious, isn't it?" Harlan asked.

"It's beauteous!" I exclaimed, using Dad's favorite word.

That morning at 9:00am—as on every morning of every school day at the Y—the American flag was raised on the flagpole in front of the Administration Building on campus. When the "Star-Spangled Banner" boomed loudly from large speakers placed strategically around the campus and at its perimeter, all BYU students were expected to stop and stand at attention, whether on or off campus, and face in the direction of the flag while placing their hands over their hearts. I had always found this a stupid tradition, particularly if you were standing off campus in the middle of a snowy field with temperatures below zero, where you could not even see the flag— as was the case that morning. Yet, we stopped in our tracks, facing campus. I placed my hand over my heart, while Harlan stood at attention and saluted. Suddenly I was filled with pride.

When the anthem finished and after Harlan completed his military salute, we stood in the snow and turned to face each other. Looking directly into my eyes, Harlan suddenly asked me a very pointed question. "You don't know yet, do you, Kerry?"

"Know what?" I asked, taken back by his question.

"What you are," he stated flatly.

"What do you mean?" I asked defensively.

"Nothing," he said, lightening his tone. "I'm just fussing with you. Don't worry about it."

We stood in the snow facing each other in silence. This was an important moment, I knew, but I didn't comprehend why. We hesitated only a moment more, before continuing our trek up the slippery path to school.

The girls and I kept our promise on the weekend, and went skiing with Harlan at Sundance Ski Resort. Atop a snowy mountain on rented skis, I soon discovered what all beginning skiers discover: The only way down is on two skis. Harlan was patient with me, considering I spent most of my time falling down, far more than Angel or Bridget did. As for Harlan, he made skiing look effortless and graceful. It looked like he was born on skis.

Even though I proved to be a terrible skier and never attempted it again, I loved that first ski trip to Sundance, largely because I never saw Harlan happier.

Once we dropped the girls off, Harlan and I went to buy a Christmas tree, choosing a seven-footer for Harlan's apartment.

The following Monday for Family Home Evening, our BYU family met at Harlan's place for a tree decorating party. We hung rows of popcorn garland and ornaments made with paper, glue, crayons, and glitter. Harlan, being our family father, hung the lights on the tree with my help and that of my BYU brothers. When we were finished, glitter covered the floor of Harlan's living room, but the tree looked spectacular. After turning on the Christmas tree lights, we oohed and aaahhed, sang Christmas carols, and drank hot chocolate.

Later, as Harlan and I cleaned up after the party, he asked me if I thought the evening had gone well.

"Oh sure," I said. "Didn't you think so?"

"I hope so. I love them. I just have a hard time showing it." He paused and looked deep into my eyes. "I didn't used to be that way," he added, as his voice trailed off into silence.

"I know," I said quietly, thinking of what he had experienced both in Vietnam and during his mission. Harlan sat down on his sofa and nursed a cup Postum, the Mormon substitute for coffee, as I sat in the chair near him and sipped hot cocoa. The lights of the Christmas tree cast a romantic glow. "The tree's pretty, isn't it?" I asked.

"Yea, verily," he said, adopting my pet phrase.

"I love this holiday." I paused. "By the way, you haven't told me yet what you want for Christmas."

"I don't want you spending money on me," he replied. "You need what money you have to get presents for your family."

"Nonsense! Lucky for me there are four weeks 'til Christmas!"

******

As active members of our LDS ward, both of my parents volunteered when called to serve in various church jobs. Dad

56

served as Scoutmaster and later as our ward's Sunday School Superintendent. Mom served as Relief Society President in our ward, the highest position a Mormon woman can hold within the LDS Church.

Mom's need to be a perfect Mormon mother while being an ideal Relief Society President only compounded her stress. As head of the Relief Society, Mom was responsible for all of the preparations for our ward fundraising event at the Pioneer Day celebration on July 24th, the biggest event of the year, when people came to Alameda Park, one block from our home, to enjoy the scone booths, fish ponds, and cakewalks sponsored by the different Mormon wards in our LDS community.

The days leading up to Mormon Pioneer Day in July 1962—the same summer when I was nine—turned out to a nightmare. Like every other year, our ward was sponsoring the cakewalk. As Relief Society President, Mom had to make sure that hundreds of cakes were baked and ready for our ward's cakewalk on July 24th. This year, like every other year, Mom got stuck baking cakes for all of the women who had promised to help but didn't.

As usual, Sister Fenwick came to the kitchen door with her excuses and ten boxes of cake mix in hand. Mom sat the boxes on the kitchen counter. Suddenly, Mom seemed different, almost possessed. Something was very, very wrong. My instincts were confirmed soon enough, as Mom slowly and deliberately began pouring out all of the contents of the first box of cake mix into a big pile in the middle of our kitchen floor.

Sister Fenwick and I watched in horror as Mom continued to do the same thing with each box after that, slowly pouring out all of the contents, as she added to the growing pile of ruined cake mix on our dirty linoleum floor, until she had completed her task. No doubt, her histrionic behavior was due both to her opioid addiction and the emotional stress she was under at the time, and it was the first sign that Mom was having a breakdown, one that would soon force her to resign as Relief Society President. For me, it was the most horrifying moment of my childhood, since I always felt responsible for my mother's well being. Mom had seemingly just lost touch with reality. And it was entirely my fault; I had failed to hold her together. What would become of our family now?

"Sister Ashton," Sister Fenwick asked, "Are you okay?"

"I'm fine!" Mom answered robotically, sounding like the opioid addict that she in fact had become, as she used the broom to spread the cake mix out and cover our entire kitchen floor with it. "What makes you think I'm not fine?" she demanded.

I went to my battle stations. "Mom's just tired from having done so much baking," I muttered.

"Well," Sister Fenwick replied, "let me know if there is anything I can do to help."

I wanted to say, "How about baking some cakes? Or at least sweeping the floor!" But I didn't. Besides, Sister Fenwick, who was obviously quite frightened by what she had witnessed in my mother's behavior, had already run away as fast as she could.

Luckily, Mom was not so far gone that she couldn't recognize that she, and probably our entire family, needed professional help.

At Mom's insistence, our family went for counseling soon after that, but the first family session held in the counselor's office quickly became a screaming match between Dad and Dennis, and then it became violent, as Dennis struck Dad in the face and Dad struck back. As their violent confrontation escalated, Craig and I took refuge behind the desk, even as Mom and Denise and the Counselor tried to physically tear Dennis and my father apart. Now hiding under the desk and no longer behind it, I didn't move a muscle, too terrorized to risk even taking a breath.

Once we got home and Dennis retreated to his basement bedroom, slamming the door behind him so hard that the sound reverberated through the entire house, Dad announced, "If that's counseling, I want no more part of it!" But Mom—as sick as she was—knew that out family needed help, and that she in particular needed help, whether my father wanted to admit it or not. And she continued to seek counseling on her own over the next few years.

In time, Mom overcame her addiction to painkillers and healed from her nervous breakdown; she went to college, obtained her teaching degree, and became an elementary school teacher.

As Mom created a new life for herself, her relationships with her husband and with all of her children, particularly with me, became much healthier. And she provided the courageous example for me decades later, when I was facing the decision in New York City, to seek out a therapist for myself.

Not all of my childhood after the age of nine was terrible. Some of it, in fact, was so wonderful and loving that I wish I could revisit at least a few of the happiest of those days again.

For one thing, Mom and Dad took us on as many vacations as they could afford to. They took us twice to California, with stops at Yosemite, King's Canyon and Sequoia National Parks, my first visit to the ocean, and a memorable stay at Hotel Del Coronado, where my Dad's insurance company was holding an insurance conference for their employees and their families.

On our first family trip to California, I visited Disneyland for the first time, which left me delirious with joy. And we had two family visits outside the United States, a stopover in Tijuana, Mexico, and a visit to Banff, Canada.

Mom and Dad also took us to Yellowstone on frequent camping trips nearly every summer, something that all of us enjoyed.

Some of my favorite memories from childhood are of the ways in which Mom and Dad instilled their love of nature in all of their four children. I remember how Dad and my brothers and I would collect firewood for a campfire, while Mom and Denise prepared our dinner: Hamburger patties mixed with cut up fresh Idaho potatoes and vegetables, wrapped in aluminum foil to be cooked slowly on the edge of the fire. Later, after dinner, we would sit around the campfire, roasting marshmallows as Mom told us ghost stories, which made me cuddle up even closer to Mom by the fire.

My best and most vivid memories are of Idaho summer evenings spent at home on our front porch with Mom and Dad, looking up at the night sky filled with millions of stars, brilliantly clear from our altitude at over 3,500 feet in the middle of the

Rocky Mountains. Mom would have me pick out a star, and then she would make up a story about it, about the people who lived there and about their way of life.

My favorite stories were when Mom talked about Kolob, the planet where Heavenly Father lived with all of our Mothers in Heaven. "If you live righteously and obey all of Heavenly Father's commandments," she would remind me, "you too might rule your own planet one day, like our Heavenly Father does now."

But contrasting the many good times of my childhood were other harsher realities: Not just the domestic violence that we all had to contend with, but also the required attendance at endless church meetings, and not just on Sunday but also throughout the week. In my family, like most LDS families at that time, our lives began, circled and ended around the Mormon Church. My childhood was one long schedule of church meetings, school, chores, and working on my paper route. Once homework was done, there was time for little else.

By the time I had reached the age of nine, I knew that Sunday meant a grueling schedule, and that it always would. At 6am, I trudged out on my bike to deliver the Idaho State Journal. At 7:30am, it was time to clean and dress in Sunday best for General Priesthood Meeting which started at 8am for both the younger males of the Aaronic Priesthood and the older males of the Melchizedek Priesthood, while the ladies attended Relief Society.

Then came Priesthood Quorum Meetings for the men, and Prayer Meetings for the women, followed by Junior and Senior Sunday School. Church would break at 1pm, when we returned home for scripture study and dinner and to attend to our Priesthood duties, like going door to door to collect Fast Offerings.

We had to be back in our pews at 5pm for Sacrament Meeting. Then we would head home again at 6:30 so that Dad and my brothers and I could go Home Teaching, traveling from home to home once again, but this time to pray with our assigned families. At 8pm, our family would often to our Church Stake House for what was called a Fireside Chat.

Besides the Sunday schedule of church meetings from dawn until evening for all Mormons, our LDS community never missed an opportunity to cram our young minds with more religious dogma. Primary classes for the young ones came on weekdays after school, and Mutual Improvement Association for teens came on weeknights, where as a Mormon boy I was expected to participate in the Boy Scouts. I was also expected to win all of the awards that the Boy Scouts could afford a young man, since Dad was our ward's Scoutmaster.

There was no break from Mormon meetings even at school, where we were all expected to attend an hour of religious instruction at the LDS Seminary buildings across the street from my junior and senior high schools.

This was the yellow brick road that I was expected to follow in Mormon Oz. Stepping off the path even for a moment meant being ostracized and fielding untold questions and comments, like: "You weren't at the meeting; are you okay?" or "I noticed you weren't at the meeting; is something wrong?" or "We missed you today, Brother Ashton; were you sick?" and "Is everything all right?" The questions came at you from the Mormon Munchkins much the way Dorothy and her friends got clopped with apples or poisoned by poppies whenever they stepped off the yellow brick road. If ever I missed a meeting, Mormon Flying Monkeys attacked me from all directions, my LDS parents usually leading the assault.

******

Our final dress rehearsal for *The Kiss: A Story of Those Who Betrayed Him*, held in the first week of December in the Experimental Theatre located on the basement floor of the Fine Arts Center, went late into the night.

When rehearsal finished, I needed to pee and ran to the men's room at the end of the darkened hallway.

As I stood at the urinal taking a leak, I became aware that someone was looking at me through a crack from one of the stalls.

I assumed it was a fellow cast member from the play making a joke, so I spoke out loud, "I see you looking at me!" Even as I finished my business at the urinal, I addressed the Peeping Tom with added laughter and a question: "See anything you like?"

To my utter shock, a stranger opened the stall door. Naked except for his shoes and socks, he was sporting an erection.

"Yes," he replied lustfully, "I see something I like! How about you?" He stared at me in a direct and lascivious way. "So what do you think?" he asked directly. "Do you like my hard cock?"

I gasped. I had never seen a grown man naked much less an adult male who was showing off his erection in front of me. And I had never heard such filthy language, much less on the BYU campus. I was both turned off by his vulgarity and yet oddly stimulated by it at the same time. I had never experienced anything this sexual, unless you count what few childhood sexual explorations I had experienced with a cousin or with the boys who lived up the block. Shocked into silence, I said nothing. I simply stood there with my mouth open. But my penis was hard and throbbing, even as I stared at his protruding penis.

"I can see you like looking at my cock," he stated baldly. "You want to touch it?"

Still I said nothing, as the man continued stroking his hard penis, adopting an even more lustful expression on his face. In his early 30s, he was balding with short-trimmed hair and a gym-toned body far nicer than mine. Suddenly, he walked over to me and put his hand directly on my penis. I shuddered. I didn't know what to do. I had jerked off thousands of times prior to my 16th birthday, usually utilizing my parents' vibrator, but I had not masturbated since I was ordained a Priest in the Aaronic Priesthood when I turned 16. I was trying to keep myself worthy to be ordained an Elder in the higher Melchizedek Priesthood at 19, when I was expected to go to the Temple, make my covenants with God, and serve my mission. So I was more than a little shocked—and aroused—when he caressed my erect penis with his fingers.

I noticed right away that his erection was not as long or as thick as mine, but that his was perfectly straight, where mine took a slight curve to the left. Clearly, I was abnormal and inferior. I prayed that he wouldn't notice or make any comment about it!

When the naked man began poking his normal, straight erection into what I was convinced was my curved and abnormal one, all I could think about was my deformity. Consequently, I stood like a statue and said nothing. No doubt the naked stranger took my lack of protest as acquiescence. And before I could stop him or even react, he knelt down on the bathroom floor in front of me, and took my erection into his mouth. I was utterly flummoxed, but the stranger's hot mouth felt utterly … wonderful! "Oh, wow!" I exclaimed loudly. "What are you doing? I … I didn't know a man could do this to another man! I can't believe how good that feels!"

Even as I uttered these words aloud, I realized that I was even more deformed on the inside than I was abnormal on the outside.

As the naked man sucked on my erection, taking it deep into his mouth to the base, then pulling his mouth all the way back up to the head, I had never felt such pleasure! "I must stop this," I thought. "This is wrong! This is incredibly sinful! But how can I stop this man from doing what he's doing, when it feels this incredible? Not even the vibrator made me feel this good!"

And then it happened. I screamed loudly as my ejaculation exploded into his mouth. I thought he would spit it out, but instead, he swallowed it greedily as I squirted volley after volley, making him slurp and gulp to take it all down his throat. Once I finished ejaculating, he licked his lips clean and murmured, "Geez, Stud! That was a huge load! And it was sweet!"

It had all happened too quickly, all within a minute or so. Realizing that my first sexual act was a homosexual one, and not even with someone I loved but with a total stranger, I suddenly found myself drowning in a deeper pool of shame than I had ever known before. Even worse, ejaculating had only caused my penis to grow more rigid than before, as was often the case in my youth.

The naked stranger—still on his knees and looking up at me— was stroking wildly on his manhood. Observing the protruding and pulsating veins on my erection, he taunted me lustfully, "You want me to suck you off again, Baby? I'd love to take another load!"

His calling me 'Baby' reminded me of how Harlan called me 'Babe,' which only made me feel more ashamed. "If my first time was going to be with a man," I thought, "why couldn't it have been with Harlan? That would have been so much easier to understand and explain!" Obviously my body wanted and needed another sexual release, but disgusted as I was by the stranger's behavior and profanity, I backed away.

Still on his knees, the naked stranger then did the most outrageous thing—something I did not even want to try to understand. Splaying out naked on the white tile of the restroom floor in front of me, with his erection pressed against the cold floor, he crawled on his belly over to my dress shoes, and began kissing and licking them with his lips and stretched-out tongue. Looking up at me with the eyes of a submissive sex slave, he whimpered loudly, "Thank you, Sir." Then, reveling in a sexual degradation and an abject humiliation that I would only later come to need to express myself, he added, "Thank you for allowing me to serve you, Sir."

I was so disgusted with myself and with the wretch groveling on the bathroom floor beneath me, that I thought I might vomit. "You're disgusting," I retorted, tucking my still rigid penis inside my pants. Luckily, the winter coat I was wearing covered the shame of my erection.

I ran from the restroom and through the Arts Center, coming to the foyer where a few straggling students were hanging around the huge Indian statue. A student called out to me, "Hey, Kerry! Where are you going in such a hurry?"

I didn't stop to answer, but kept running up the two open flights of stairs, taking three steps at a time, making my way out to the parking lot. When I reached Oscar, I threw up by the side of the car. Once I was sitting inside my car, I lay my head against Oscar's huge cream-colored steering wheel, and wept, all the while praying for God's forgiveness.

The next morning I made an appointment to meet with President Wilkinson at his office in the Religion Building that same afternoon. I had no intention of confessing my sin, but only to get advice. I was ashamed, but I wasn't crazy.

As soon as I settled myself into President Wilkinson's comfy office chair that afternoon, shame swarmed inside me like a nest of angry bees. "President, I've been having lustful thoughts about someone," I admitted, feeling embarrassed. I was thinking of Harlan, not the stranger who had blown me the night before.

Wilkinson looked at me cautiously from behind his desk. "About some girl you're dating?" he asked finally.

"No, Sir," I replied, taking a deep breath. "It isn't a girl."

Wilkinson's mouth dropped open. He seemed shocked. "Not a girl?" he asked with faltering breath. "Who then?"

I knew better than to mention Harlan's name. "It's a male friend."

Wilkinson looked as though I had slapped him. "Have you acted on these feelings?" he asked dramatically.

"Of course not." Okay, I lied. But what else could I do?

"Well, that's good, Brother Kerry," he said, sighing with relief as he leaned back in his swivel chair. Discussing my shameful problem with the President only made me loathe myself all the more.

Looking through the booklets that the Mormon Church prepares for its Bishops on subjects such as this, Wilkinson said, "I can't comprehend how a man could make love to another fellow."

I looked down at the floor, ashamed to face him, as he began reading aloud from one of the pamphlets:

> "Some children are molested by strangers…or even relatives. This is shocking and may cause feelings of unworthiness in the innocent victim. Believing to be unclean, he is easy prey in later experiences."

He stopped reading. "Did any man molest you, Brother Kerry?"

"No! Never!" I replied adamantly, as he continued reading:

"Experimentation leads to habits that are at first physical, but later become deeply emotional, therefore much harder to change. A traditional explanation of homosexuality is that the child has a domineering mother and a passive father."

He stopped reading again, looking me directly in the eye. "Was your father passive, do you think, Brother Ashton?"

"I don't think so. But my mom is a pretty strong-willed woman."

President Wilkinson scratched his forehead while fiddling nervously with the buttons of his gray polyester-knit suit. "Brother Ashton, the Lord has entrusted your soul to my keeping, so I want to understand, but the idea of lusting after another man isn't normal!"

"But I can't stop myself," I replied. "Please tell me what to do."

Then he asked me if I was masturbating.

"No, Sir," I replied honestly. Though I had received a blowjob for the first time in my life the night before, I hadn't masturbated since my 16th birthday.

As it was, Wilkinson sent me away that afternoon with several church pamphlets to read. Later, alone in my apartment, I read through the pamphlet titled *A Letter to a Friend*, written by Apostle Spencer W. Kimball, next in line to become president of the church, and considered the foremost Mormon expert on homosexuality. I believed every word I read:

"Where would the world go if the practice as homosexuality became general? The answer: To the same place other unbridled civilizations have gone. If you have thought that through to its certain conclusion, you have Gomorrah, and you have Sodom. Rome, Jerusalem and Babylon followed, and London, Paris and Chicago are in their footsteps."

But Apostle Kimball had said that a homosexual could be cured, so I held hope in my heart that I could change with Christ's help.

The Kiss: A Story of Those Who Betrayed Him opened that night. I felt like a hypocrite portraying our Lord and Savior Jesus Christ on stage. But apparently the shame I felt only made my performance stronger, since my portrayal was very well received, which made me something of an instant celebrity on a religious campus like the Y.

******

Isolated and lonely in my early childhood, I had a vivid fantasy life. When I was little, I played with puppets, built my own puppet stage, and wrote plays for them to perform in.

As I grew older, I dreamed of acting and writing and singing and dancing, both on Broadway and on the silver screen.

Mom loved the theater and took me with her to see all of the plays produced at ISU.

Like Mom, I became a theater junkie. After finishing my paper route in the late afternoon, I would bike to the library to scan *The New York Times* for the latest news of Broadway. And when I wasn't at the library, I found escape at the movies.

My parents did not hide the fact that they owned a vibrator. In fact, they kept it openly displayed on their bed's headboard shelf.

I knew that Dad used the vibrator for Mom's frequent backaches, which she experienced more and more frequently after our family's first car accident. I, too, used the vibrator on Mom's forehead and back, attempting to relieve either her backaches or her stress, particularly during her nervous breakdown. But I also learned how to utilize the vibrator in a way that I knew was sinful.

The vibrator had a knob on the end built for various attachments. The attachment I loved the most was a round cone-shaped device that fit perfectly over the head of my penis. Whenever I used the vibrator from the age of eight until puberty, every time that I brought myself to climax—always without ejaculation—I fell to my knees and prayed to my Heavenly Father to beg for forgiveness, promising to never commit the sin again.

Inevitably, the next time I found myself alone at home, I would be back at it, with vibrator in hand, and always with extreme guilt.

The shameful sexual path I followed—as Mormon orthodoxy dictated—was already killing my soul.

If that were not enough, like all LDS faithful I was taught that if you commit the same sin more than once that you can never be forgiven, since Heavenly Father didn't look kindly on second-time offenders, whose repentance had proven to be insincere. On top of that, like all Mormons I was taught that if I repeatedly committed the same sin, I might hold my entire family back from rising together to the Celestial Kingdom in the hereafter. Even if the rest of my family attained the Celestial Kingdom, I could be sent to a lower Kingdom in the afterlife, either the Telestial or the Terrestrial Kingdom, where I would be eternally cut off from my family and from Heavenly Father. Not only that, like all Mormons, I was expected to confess my sins to my Bishop, face-to-face!

What was I supposed to do, with a penis that seemed to be hard constantly, a vibrator that felt so good, and a church that allowed me only one confession for such a sin?

Being ingenious and clever, I devised a plan to save my soul. I would put a large black X in a little black book, for each and every time I committed the sin. Then, when the day came that I was finally ready to tell the vibrator goodbye, I could go to the Bishop with my diary of sin in hand, and I could confess all of my transgressions at once. In one sweet moment, forgiveness would be mine, and I could still join with Mom and Dad and all of my family in the Celestial Kingdom, and perhaps even rule as a God on my own planet one day. I was elated to have found such a clever plan! I still felt elated when I took some of my paper route money and went to the drugstore and purchased the little black book that I could use to keep a private record of my sins. I even felt elated when I put my first few X's in my little black book, carefully noting the date and time of each offense. But over time, as my little black book quickly filled with X's, my elation faded. Clearly, my black book was one I couldn't show the Bishop.

Ironically, Mormons do not use the cross as a symbol—you

won't find a cross on any LDS building—but they certainly believe in hanging upon them. To be fair, so do most Christians.

One morning, Mom found my black book, and confronted me with it. "Kerry Lynn," she demanded to know, "what is this book I found hidden under your mattress?"

Traumatized, I felt my face burn red. "Oh," I stammered, "that's just a game I play with myself."

I was sitting in my fifth grade class at Roosevelt Elementary School in November 1963, when our teacher, Mrs. Jones, was called out into the hallway to speak to the principal. When she returned a few moments later, her face seemed drained of color and clearly she had been crying. I thought she was going to announce another bomb drill, where we were expected to hide under our desks, as though this would protect us when a nuclear bomb dropped. In anticipation of her announcement, we buzzed with excited chatter.

"Please quiet down, children," Mrs. Jones said.

We did as she asked, as American children still did in public school classrooms back then.

"I have a sad announcement," Mrs. Jones added. "President Kennedy has been shot. The President is dead."

A hush fell over the room.

"Given the situation," she continued, "class will be dismissed for the rest of the day and tomorrow."

I walked home in shock. Only ten, I did not fully understand what had happened. Mom had taken a day job as a waitress, so she was not home when I returned, but she called to tell me that she would be home in less than 20 minutes.

Over the next few days, my family and I watched with the rest of the nation over and over again on black-and-white TV, both the killing of our President and the murder of his purported killer. It seemed that all of the institutions that I had been taught to believe in and that I had put my faith in, were crashing down around me, both in our supposedly perfect Mormon family and in a larger sense, as a child growing up in America. For the first time, I felt shame for my country.

Later that year, I not only sought out but also received sexual humiliation for the first time. Having exposed myself to two neighbor kids while we were downstairs alone in our basement, watching cartoons, the two boys started laughing. The older one, Tony, slapped my erection with his hand, which only made my erection grow harder for some odd reason that I didn't understand. He laughed and kept slapping it, which only excited me more.

Soon, Tony encouraged his little brother Paul to slap my erection too, which only made my erection throb all the harder.

Shame colored my face and neck, but I felt as though I were finally receiving what deep down inside I felt I deserved. Once Tony wearied of the game, he told me to get dressed.

After that, whenever I saw either Tony or Paul at school, they would smirk at me. Sometimes they would talk under their breath to their friends, and soon their friends would look at me, startled, as their cruel laughter peeled through the halls. "You're kidding!" I heard one of their friends say once, "What a fairy!"

Shame and guilt filled my soul like poisonous fog.

******

While still performing in *The Kiss*, my BYU acting break-through came in mid-December when I was cast as Avrahm in *Fiddler On The Roof,* the biggest production of the year, which would open in mid-February of the next semester. I had hoped to be cast as Tevye, but getting cast at all was exciting, particularly once rehearsals began.

The director Dr. Harold I. Hansen was a well-known celebrity within the LDS world, having staged the epic Hill Cumorah Pageant in upstate New York, where Latter-Day-Saints believe that the Angel Moroni revealed to Joseph Smith the precise spot where the golden plates were buried—the same gold plates that were later translated and published as *The Book of Mormon*.

Meanwhile, Harlan worked out at the university gym at least three times a week, while I exercised only in the privacy of my apartment, and only sporadically at that. Harlan often asked me to go work out with him at the gym, reminding me that we could spot each other on the free weights, and that he could teach me how to work the machines. But the idea of undressing in front of him and of seeing him undressed, and indeed of "spotting each other," filled me with inexplicable terror. Inevitably, I always got out of it.

Once in early December, while I was visiting Harlan at his apartment, he went to his bedroom closet and returned to the living room with what looked like a painting, wrapped in embroidered linen. "This embroidery," he explained, "is one of the few things I have of my mom's."

Unwrapping the linen, he revealed a large framed painting. It was a portrait of a dove escaping in flight from a prison window. Something in the stretching of the dove's wings was frail and moving. "What do you think?" he asked sheepishly, seemingly embarrassed. "Do you like it?"

"Yes. It's strangely poignant and powerful. Who did it?"

He stared at me, his eyes fearful. "I did," he replied shyly.

I was flabbergasted by his revelation. "You're kidding!"

"It's my favorite," he offered, visibly ashamed in his revelation. "I did it in my senior year high school art class."

"You amaze me, Harlan," I said, "I had no idea you wanted to be an artist!" Then I remembered all of the times that I had seen Harlan drawing sketches in a notepad. I reproached myself for not connecting the dots.

"This is what I'm passionate about, not acting." He paused, taking a deep breath. "I just wish I could make a living at it."

"How long have you wanted to be an artist?" I asked.

"Always," he explained. "For as far back as I can remember. But my wanting to paint didn't fit in with Dad's expectations of me. It wasn't macho. That's why I joined the Marines and went on a mission; I did it all to please my father."

71

"Be an artist, Harlan," I replied. "Don't let anybody stop you from doing it." I paused. "And while we're on the subject, I think you should be majoring in Art, not Theater."

"It's been such a long time since I painted." His voice cracked with emotion. "I sold my easel and art supplies when I went on my mission. Then after Nam, I didn't want to paint any more. I don't think I have it in me anymore. I feel dead inside."

Harlan started wrapping his painting in the linen, preparing to return it to the bedroom closet where he had kept it hidden.

"You aren't putting it away, are you?" I asked.

"Yes," he uttered. "Why?"

"It's too good to put away! Why don't you hang it up here, in your living room? Your dove can't breathe in a closet," I pointed out. And neither can I, I thought.

He hung the painting in his living room, giving me the broadest smile I had yet seen on his handsome face.

Harlan and I spent the following Saturday at his apartment studying for our semester finals. As the record of Simon and Garfunkel's *Bridge Over Troubled Water* played, he began singing along, revealing a warm and melodious baritone.

"Very nice, Sinatra!" I said, looking up from the schoolbooks lying out on the carpeted floor in front of me. "Now, how about singing it as a duet, just like Simon and Garfunkel?" I asked, knowing I could sing well. We sang it twice, once in harmony.

"What a team!" I exclaimed. Harlan laughed. I believed in the Celestial Kingdom whenever I heard him laugh. "You know, Harlan, I love your laugh. It sounds like it comes from your toes."

"Maybe it does. I dunno," he replied, laughing again.

Then I asked seriously, "Where'd you learn how to harmonize like that anyway?"

"Danny and I used to sing in harmony all the time in Vietnam," he explained, before falling silent as I saw his face cloud over with a memory of Vietnam, of Danny, and of blood and death.

"Harlan," I asked, "can we talk about it? It might help if we

72

talked it out."

"No," he said, jumping up from the sofa and pacing the floor.

"I just want to understand," I explained.

"Until you've carried body bags over there, you can never understand!" He stopped at the door to put on his coat. "I'll be back soon," he added, closing the door behind him.

"And like a bridge over troubled water," I sang softly, *"I will lay me down."*

It was our last evening together before Christmas break, when Harlan and I sat in his living room enjoying the Christmas tree. "It's time, Harlan!" I said suddenly.

"What? What are you talking about?"

"You'll see! Just give me a minute!" I shouted as I jumped up and ran out the back through the snow to retrieve Harlan's present from Oscar's trunk. When I returned carrying a huge box wrapped in red-and-gold paper, Harlan nearly fell over in surprise. "Is that for me?" he asked.

"Of course it's for you!" I kidded. His smile made me want to put my arms around him. "Well, go on!" I prodded. "Open it!"

Unwrapping the paper carefully, when he saw the brand-new artist's easel inside, he gasped with childlike glee, "Babe, you shouldn't have! It's way too expensive."

"So I took a little out of my mission fund! Big deal!"

"Kerry," he protested, "you need that money for your mission."

"I wanted you to have it." I could feel a huge smile spread across my face. "Besides, that's not all I got you!"

"You didn't!" he exclaimed, giddy as a kid on Christmas morning. Leaving him in his excitement, I ran back to the car, bringing back with me an artist's canvas and a set of paints and brushes that I had kept hidden in Oscar's huge trunk. When Harlan saw the gifts, he protested. "Babe, this stuff is expensive."

"I don't care. Merry Christmas, Harlan!" I exclaimed.

Harlan put his arms around me and held me tight. "I got something for you, too, Kerry," he said huskily. "Actually, it's

73

something I made for you." He reached behind his sofa and pulled out a sketch that he had apparently worked on for weeks. Mounted in a gilded frame, it was a sketch of me.

"I'm not that good-looking," I responded quietly.

"I've drawn you the way I see you," he said. I began to blush. "So what do you think?" he asked. "Do you like it?"

"I love it," I replied. "Thank you, Harlan! No one ever did a portrait of me before. It's a wonderful gift!"

"Merry Christmas, Kerry," he said, "and Happy New Year!"

******

The next step in following the straight and narrow LDS path meant my ordination as a Deacon in the Aaronic Priesthood when I turned twelve. Given that, prior to my 12th birthday in 1965 and the interview with the Bishop that would determine my worthiness to be ordained a Deacon in the Aaronic Priesthood—the lesser of the two Mormon Priesthoods—Mom took me into the living room for a serious talk. "When Bishop Anderson talks to you today in private," Mom explained, choosing her words as though each was being processed through a giant and methodical sifter, "he is going to ask if you masturbate."

Her face was as red as mine. And I remember wondering at the time, "Why isn't my father the one having this conversation with me?" Wasn't that the way it normally worked? Why had Dad left this up to Mom? Regardless, Mother forged ahead courageously, albeit with some embarrassment.

"You have to know what the word *masturbation* means," Mom explained carefully, "so that you can answer the Bishop's question honestly." Mom's face had gone from red to purple, and there was perspiration on her forehead. "I know you don't do this, son," she continued, "but some young men ... play with their privates. That sin is called masturbation. It's a terrible sin because it breaks the vow of chastity. I know you haven't had problems with that sort of thing."

"No, Mom," I said hurriedly, with the anxiety of a liar. Now I knew that the dreadful sin that I had committed over and over again for years with the family vibrator had a name: Masturbation! Shame swept over my entire being.

Later that day, as I sat in the Bishop's office awaiting his questions, I twisted nervously in my seat. Wearing a suit and tie, with shoes polished, I hoped I looked presentable, particularly when Bishop Anderson leaned across his desk, eyeing me as though I were a heifer from his ranch.

"Brother Ashton," he said, "I must ask you a few questions to determine your worthiness for the Aaronic Priesthood. Do you pay a full tithing?"

"Yes, Bishop. I pay a full tithe on my paper route money."

"Have you attended all your meetings faithfully?"

"Yes Bishop," I said solemnly. "You know I have."

"Any problems with masturbation?" he asked, coughing.

There it was—the question Mom had warned me of in advance. How should I answer: With a life-destroying truth or a lie that risked my eternal salvation? I thought of all the times I had masturbated in secret and always with enormous guilt, each time promising my Heavenly Father to "never do it again". I thought of the hundreds, if not thousands, of black X's in my little black book of shame. Strange carnal desires gurgled within me like the laughter of Lucifer Himself. Even that morning, while washing my body in the shower, I had stroked myself with devilish delight. I felt my face blush crimson with the memory of it. Surely the Bishop would see the wickedness painting my cheeks harlot-red? At the very least, he would see me blushing, so I feigned innocence as best I could.

"Masturbation?" I asked, trying to sound as confused as I possibly could. "I don't know what that word means."

The Bishop moved about in his seat, suddenly uncomfortable. "Well," he said, fidgeting with a pencil on his desk, "masturbation involves the fondling of the … privates."

"With what?" I asked, registering a shocked expression.

The Bishop's face turned red; I was relieved that mine was not the only red face in the room.

"With your fingers or with your hand," the Bishop explained, quite flummoxed, "when you rub down there."

"Oh, no! I've never done that!" I said, taking a liar's way out.

At our ward's Sacrament Meeting held the following Sunday, Dad joined with the Bishop and his First and Second Counselors to ordain me a Deacon in the Aaronic Priesthood before the entire congregation. This was meant as a moment of honor, but I felt guilty, as though I were being publicly condemned, since I knew that I had lied to the Bishop and to God.

After Sacrament Meeting, my family gathered around the Sunday dinner table laden with the foods Mom had prepared in my honor, even as I felt mummified in guilt. I had lied to the Bishop—the same as spitting in God's face. But what else could I have done? If I had told the truth, I would have been the first 12-year-old boy in our 15th Ward to be refused priesthood ordination! That would have caused a scandal and horrible rumors. How could I have explained it to my parents? The only way to make things right again was to repent fully. I must never masturbate again, ever. Only then could I ever hope to know Heavenly Father's forgiveness.

That night I prayed for hours on my knees, begging the Lord to forgive me for lying to the Bishop, while solemnly promising to never masturbate again. But after my prayers were said and my sincere promises were made, when I went to bed that night, temptation came again.

In fantasies, I saw naked men with hard-muscled bodies rubbing themselves up against me. I often fantasized about such things before drifting on to sleep, though I never understood why. And this night, as every night before that, I succumbed again to sin, but this time my rigid erection felt not the wonderful touch of my hand but the excruciating pain of my fingernails, as I dug them into my erection, as I whispered my self-condemnation aloud: "You're a Deacon now, and it has to hurt! Dirty sins should hurt!"

******

As planned, Harlan and I took an acting class together the next semester. By then I had appeared in several productions on campus, but Harlan had yet to be cast in a play.

Over lunch, Harlan asked me what I thought of the acting scenes he had performed in class. "You haven't learned yet how to share of yourself on stage," I explained as gently as I could. "But when you flash that smile of yours when you're acting on stage, all the girls fall under your spell."

"You embarrass me when you say stuff like that," he said. "Besides," he added, "I would trade all of my charisma and all of my so-called good looks for one-tenth of your talent!"

Though Harlan's acting aspirations had yet to come to fruition, he had set up the artist's easel in his living room, and had already made great use of his new art supplies. It seemed that every time I went to his apartment, Harlan had either just completed a painting or was beginning a new one, and he was happier than I had ever seen him.

Between long and intense rehearsals for *Fiddler*, my writing, classes, and an active social life, I was very busy. Despite this and all of my promises to God, I started looking for another sexual encounter, while telling myself that I was just going through a phase, one that I would soon outgrow.

My second sexual adventure at BYU happened in mid-January in a basement restroom in the Wilkinson Center, after an intense rehearsal for *Fiddler* that had gone late into the night.

When I stood at the urinal playing with my erection, I noticed that the handsome student standing next to me was also stroking himself. I also noted that his erection was perfectly straight, too! This only confirmed my worst fears that my penis was deformed!

Regardless of what I felt was my deformity, he knelt in front of me and took my erection into his mouth. I was shocked into silence, particularly when he began slurping on my penis, going up and down in a slow but steady rhythm. After I ejaculated into his mouth, he stood up, exclaiming, "I can't believe you still have your hard-on!"

I felt shame at my oddity, if not my deformity. But despite my shame—or perhaps because of it—I asked him if there were safer places to find sex with men.

"Oh, you mean, the cruisy places?" he asked, tucking his penis inside his undies and zipping up his pants.

"Cruisy places?" I asked, utterly unaware of the term.

"You know ... where guys like me ... meet guys like you."

"Yes," I paused. "Where are the ... cruisy places?"

"All of the city parks in Provo have cruisy restrooms," he began, revealing a lot of information quickly.

"Really?" I couldn't believe what he was telling me.

"You wouldn't believe how many closeted gay students there are at BYU, and not just all of the students but many of the faculty, too. But most of them are too scared out of their minds to try anything on campus, the way you and I just did. Usually they go to the cruisy restrooms in the city parks."

"I have a hard time believing that. I mean, I thought I was the only one on campus. I mean, besides you and only a few others."

"Trust me, there are cocksuckers all over this campus!"

"So where do they all go?" I stammered. I was utterly turned off by his offensive language. I wasn't used to hearing it, and it bothered me terribly that I was still standing there, listening to him talk, yet I needed the information more than I needed to run away, absorbing all that he shared with me that night like a hungry and innocent sponge. "I mean, there must be other places they go than just to the park restrooms, where it's safer to ... hook up with each other?"

"Mostly to Salt Lake. There's a cruisy porn theater on State Street just north of Second South in downtown Salt Lake, and there's a gay bar in Salt Lake City, too. It's called the Sun Tavern. You can look up the address in the phone book. But the best places to find gay sex are in the rest areas on Interstate 15 by the Pleasant Grove exits, both on the south and north sides." He paused. "Both of the restrooms on each side of the interstate, going north and south, have glory holes!"

"Glory holes?" I asked, giving him a bewildered look.

"The holes in the wall between the urinal and a toilet," he replied. "You stick your finger or your cock through the hole to get a blowjob. I go there every week to get my fill of cock!"

Offended by his profanity, I rushed out of the men's room without thanking him for the information, much less for the blow job.

When I got down on my knees and prayed that night, I promised my Heavenly Father that I would never sin again.

As part of my sincere repentance, I gave up masturbation yet again. Having learned that I could make my persistent erections disappear by doing math problems in my head, I kept doing the math, telling myself that I could avoid masturbation altogether, as I had since the age of 16 when I was ordained a Priest in the Aaronic Priesthood. More than that, when I did allow myself to indulge in sexual fantasies, I forced myself to focus my thoughts on Bridget.

Having taken Bridget to the Mormon lover's lane one night, parking in the foothills above the Provo Temple, she rested her head on my shoulder as we looked at the view of the Provo Temple through Oscar's windshield. Bridget seemed nervous. If a Mormon girl said no too strongly, she risked losing her boyfriend; on the other hand, if she said yes, he might have his way with her, then never want to see her again because she was easy. No wonder Bridget was fidgety, but she had nothing to fear from me.

I sat with my arm around her, content to hold her in dispassionate silence as we looked at the Temple.

"The Temple's beautiful tonight," Bridget said quietly. I thought that Temples built in the 19th century were architecturally inspiring, but the modern Provo Temple reminded me of a very large, very white, prefabricated Spam can. "What is it, Kerry?" Bridget asked, interrupting my thoughts. "You seem distant tonight."

How could I tell her that I had brought her to lover's lane only to see if I could get turned on with her the way a normal man was supposed to? "I should never have brought you here," I replied. "I came here hoping to have my way with you!" Bridget gasped in surprise, before I could offer up my excuse. "But I love you too much to take advantage of you like that."

"Oh, Kerry," she uttered in admiration, "I love you!"

******

79

Mom's insistence on going to college infuriated Dad, but she went anyway. And just after my 12th birthday in late August 1965, Mom began her freshman year at Idaho State University, the same week that I began seventh grade at Alameda Junior High School.

When I began attending junior high, I entered an awkward adolescent period, having gained weight due to overeating—my main way of coping with all of the domestic violence at home. Before the violence began, I was quite physically active. Now I rarely if ever exercised or even road my bike, other than when I delivered papers on my route, as though I were afraid to move, for fear I would be yelled at, hit, or worse. I hadn't yet experienced a growth spurt, so I was both short and plump. And I wore only the hand-me-down clothes of my brothers. And because we could ill afford the price of a haircut, Dad always cut my hair, and in a way that the other students called "dorky." On top of that, I had horrid-looking, black-framed glasses that accentuated my chubby face. Needless to say, I was a good student and well mannered, but I was not at all popular with most of my classmates.

One day on the playground during recess at Alameda Junior High, I heard Rick—a kid we all thought of as a hood—call one of the other boys a *cocksucker*. Having no idea what the term meant, though I knew it had to be a terribly vulgar term, I somehow worked up enough nerve to ask Rick about it.

"Wow!" Rick hissed, "You really are the biggest dweeb!"

"I guess I am," I said shyly.

"I'll tell you what, Dweeb," he said. "It's simple. You know what a cock is?" I shook my head no. "All males have one; even you. It's hanging between your legs!"

"Oh," I said, as the light finally dawned.

He looked down at my groin. "That's your cock."

"Okay," I responded.

"A cocksucker sucks cock, which feels fantastic! Men love it."

I found his language offensive, and I was confused.

"If it feels that good and men love it," I asked, "then why do they use that word like it's such a terrible thing?"

"Only whores, sluts, and faggots suck cock," Rich snorted disdainfully. "You really are a nerd-ball, Ashton!"

My secret dream of becoming a cheerleader for the Alameda Junior High Bees was the first manifestation of my desire to perform before a crowd. If I had been selected as a cheerleader at Alameda, I would have become even more of a social outcast than I already was. Luckily, when I showed up for cheerleader tryouts, the Girl's P.E. Coach Miss Peterson—a butch lesbian if there ever was one—met me at the gymnasium door and talked me out of it. Even so, rumors about me began circulating Alameda's hallways, and in English class a teacher went further, defining the word *effeminate* to her students as "acting like Kerry Ashton." That story was often repeated after that in the hallways in between classes—and always to gales of laughter—by both faculty and students alike.

Idaho schools rarely closed for inclement winter weather; if they had, every winter day would have been a snow day.

Much of the snow on the ground that January morning of 1966 had already turned to ice. It began to snow early that afternoon and when we were released from school in the late afternoon there were already a few inches of new snow covering the treacherous black ice beneath. Many of the students had parents waiting for them in warm cars, but I knew I had to make my own way home, since Dad was out selling insurance as he always did at that time of day, and Mom was attending her classes at ISU.

It took a long time to make it home on foot in my snow boots, as I trudged through the snow on treacherously icy roads and sidewalks. It was snowing heavily by the time I reached home, and the temperature had dropped to 20 below zero. I didn't look forward to delivering newspapers on my paper route that night, but it was my responsibility.

Once home, I folded and covered each newspaper in plastic wrap for protection as quickly as I could, then packed all of the newspapers into the canvas bag I always used on my route.

After dressing as warmly as I could, I made my way outside to get on my new blue-and-white Schwinn bike that I had just received for Christmas two weeks earlier, and began bicycling on the snow-covered black ice, slipping many times as I made my way through blinding snow to my first customer's home.

Given the weather and the terrible condition of the roads, it took nearly two hours to deliver all of the newspapers. As I made my way from one customer's home to the next, I kept reminding myself that when I returned home, Mom would be back from her classes, and would be getting dinner ready in our warm kitchen.

I was happy and relieved when I made it back to our front yard, home safe and sound. But then, as I bicycled across the snow-covered ice in our front yard, I slipped and fell off my bike. As I tumbled to the ground, I rammed my face and mouth hard against the jagged metal edge of one of our old trashcans that had been left out in the front yard for garbage collection that morning.

Stunned and in shock, I tried to get up and lost my balance, falling again in the snow. Looking down, I saw blood pouring from my face onto the snowy ground. I thought that I had knocked some teeth out. Making my way to the icy back porch steps and the side door to the kitchen, I kept falling, even as more red blood dripped onto the packed white snow on the icy steps.

Finally, I managed to get the door open, and walked in. Mom, who was standing at the kitchen sink and preparing dinner, screamed as soon as she saw me, and dropped the boiling pot of water and potatoes that she was holding over the sink.

Still unknown to me, the ragged edge of metal had sliced completely through my lower lip and face, and the bloody flesh now hung to my chin. The sight had obviously unnerved my mother, as she rushed to me and took me in her arms.

"Kerry Lynn!" she gasped, apparently in as much shock as I was. "What happened?" I tried to answer her, but I quickly realized that I couldn't talk; for some reason, my lips and mouth were not working properly. "Come with me, Honey," Mom said gently, taking me to the kitchen sink and grabbing a kitchen towel to put over the wound. "Just hold that there, Sweetheart," she added. "I'm going to take you back into the bathroom to get you cleaned up, but whatever you do, don't look at yourself in the hallway mirror." She led me into the bathroom, washed the wound as best she could, then had me hold a warm washcloth to the wound, and rushed me out to the car and to the hospital.

Once in surgery, with me lying face up on the gurney, the doctor put a towel over my eyes so that I couldn't see what he was doing. Since my lower face was completely numb, I didn't feel much pain as he began sewing the wound shut. But I could still feel the pressure of the needle as he pushed it into my mouth and lips and face, and then pulled it back out again from one side and then to the other. Though he had covered my eyes, I could still see under the edge of the towel as I watched him slowly and meticulously sew my face back together, sticking the needle in and out, doing this over and over again with painstaking repetition. Watching as he sewed my face back together, I thought of the movie *Frankenstein*, and how the mad doctor had left huge scars on his monster's face.

When surgery was over, the doctor gave me a tetanus shot in my left arm. Unfortunately, I had an allergic reaction to the shot, and my arm began to swell.

After going home, as the numbness and shock wore off, I experienced terrible pain in my mouth, lips and face, but even more unbearably in my left arm, where I was given the shot for tetanus, which had now grown to the size of a basketball.

When I finally got the courage to look at myself in the bathroom mirror, I burst into tears. The huge gash in my swollen face cut through my lower lip and halfway down my chin. The stitches were grotesque, sticking a half-inch out on my face and lip and inside my mouth. But what hurt most was the shame I felt over having had such a stupid accident. Mistakes were not allowed in my childhood, where I felt I always had to be perfect. "It was an accident," I kept telling myself. "It could have happened to anyone." But having never learned how to forgive myself, I found little understanding or relief from the critical Mormon voices already internalized deep within me.

I stayed at home for over a week; I was simply too ill to attend school, particularly since the swelling in my left arm had swollen to gargantuan proportions, extending far into my left shoulder and upper back. I looked like a hunchback, and I still had a good deal of swelling on my wounded face.

When I returned to school the following week, stitches still stuck out on my swollen face, and the hump on my back and upper arm was utterly enormous. Already the brunt of jokes at Alameda Junior High, the kids at school now had new reasons to make up even nastier nicknames, calling me *Frankenstein, Quasimodo* or *Hunchback* in the halls as I made my way between classes. Such name-calling continued until the swelling in my arm subsided and the stitches on my face were removed. But the inner scars inflicted during that January of public shaming in 1966 at Alameda Junior High took far longer to heal than did the ones on my face.

******

In mid-January 1972, as Bridget and I sat by the Indian Statue in the Arts Center, a handsome young man with black hair and stunning blue eyes came up to us. At 5'8" and in trim physical condition, he was extremely good-looking, but in a boyish sense, not a manly one.

"Excuse me," he said, "I hope you don't mind me interrupting … but are you Kerry Ashton by any chance?"

I was taken aback. "Uh, yes, I am," I replied, noting that his boyish good looks had given me an unwanted erection.

"Oh, wow!" he said, giving me a huge smile, as the words gushed out of him: "I'm such a huge fan of yours! I saw you in *Starlight*, and then I saw you in *The Kiss* last semester. Your portrayal of Jesus was the most beautiful performance I've seen at BYU!" He finally paused, if only to catch his breath, before adding, "I guess I should introduce myself. I'm Jack Young. I'm a Communications major from Ohio. I'm a freshman like you."

There was intense heat in our handshake. His smaller hand

84

seemed to almost melt into mine, and with an electrical charge that was impossible not to notice.

I found out later that Jack was as big a Streisand fan as I was, and we began visiting each other frequently either in his dorm room at Deseret Towers or at my apartment to listen to Streisand records.

The more we saw of each other, the more I found him attractive, not in the way that I found Harlan intensely masculine and sexy, but in a cute and boyish way. And soon, Jack and his freshman girlfriend Debbie—a redhead with a sweet but fiery disposition—became part of our gang, and often went with us as a group to see films together.

However, when it came to R-Rated films, Harlan and I went to see those movies alone, since BYU, the church and the rest of our gang didn't approve.

BYU took a particularly virulent stand against the R-rated *Bless the Beasts and the Children*, banning the film in Provo when it was released, but Harlan and I made a clandestine trip to Salt Lake City on our own, to see it anyway. When we arrived at the movie theater in Salt Lake, hundreds of Mormons were gathered outside with picket signs that read, "Ban Porno!" or "R-Rated Films Are of the Devil" or "Smut Affects Our Children!" but we went inside and saw the movie anyway, despite the protesters.

A few nights later our group had dinner together at the Wilkinson Center cafeteria, with Bridget, Jenny, Jack, Debbie, Harlan, and I all gathered at a huge corner table.

"I don't understand this place!" I said, as I slurped my ice cream parfait. "Why would BYU ban a beautiful film like *Bless The Beasts and the Children*?"

All except Harlan eyed me suspiciously.

"How do you know it's beautiful?" Bridget asked.

Harlan spoke up first. "Kerry and I went to see it in Salt Lake."

Angel choked on her lemonade. "You went to see that filth?"

"Yes," Harlan admitted. "Kerry wanted to see it and so did I."

"I can't believe you two went to see that smut," Debbie stated.

"Debbie, I don't see how you can call it smut when you haven't seen it!" I replied hotly. "It was a good film. It wasn't pornographic."

"Well, there was that one scene," Harlan reminded me, "you know, when the kid ..."

"Oh, go on, say it! It won't kill any of us," I badgered. I was surprised to see Harlan blushing, a reaction I hadn't anticipated. All three girls looked to him for an explanation.

Harlan blustered out his response: "There's one scene ... in the film ... that implies ... that ... a boy is ..."

"Masturbating," I said, finishing his sentence.

Jenny's face turned the color of chalk.

"And that isn't lewd?" Bridget asked with disillusionment.

"It was tastefully done," I explained. "It was only implied."

"How can a sin like that be tasteful, regardless of how it is depicted?" Bridget asked with righteous indignation. "The Prophet says masturbation is a sin."

"Oh, Bridget," I retorted. "Stop acting like a Betty BYU!"

Behaving like Molly Mormons, all of the girls were incensed. Debbie retorted, "Kerry, I think that you and Harlan should start acting like the Priesthood holders that you are!"

"Now, Debbie," Jack interjected, "that's going a bit far!"

"Far!" Debbie shouted. "I'm just proud that you honored your priesthood vows and did not go see such trash with those two!"

"Well, I'm sorry," I replied, getting angry. "But I can't pretend that all's well in Zion when it isn't."

"Excuse me," Angel said disapprovingly, getting up to leave.

"What is it, Jen?" Harlan asked innocently.

"I think it's time that I went home," Angel replied.

Harlan stood to help Jennifer with her coat. "I'll walk you home."

"That's all right," Angel replied. "Bridget and Debbie and I can walk together!"

Harlan and Jack and I watched as our young ladies walked away in a true Molly Mormon huff if there ever was one.

When I went to bed that night, my erection ached for the touch of my hand, but I kept doing math in my head until I fell asleep.

Both my parents and grandparents came to Provo to attend the opening night of *Fiddler on the Roof* in February, presented on the massive De Jong Concert Hall stage in an auditorium that held thousands. Afterward, we all went to Hawkins for milkshakes to celebrate. They all thought that the production was wonderful and that I had given a great performance, but it was Jack and Mom who kept praising me the most. Naturally, I reveled in the attention.

Once *Fiddler* opened and my family returned home, I went to Salt Lake City to appear on a local talent show on KSL-TV, performing "If I Were A Rich Man" in my *Fiddler* costume.

During my TV interview afterward, the host asked, "Are you playing Tevye at BYU?"

"Yes," I replied. But as soon as the lie came out of my mouth, I felt ashamed that I was so needy of recognition and public approval that I would lie to get it.

People wrote in during the week to vote on each week's contestants, with the winner being announced on the following week's broadcast. Judging by the TV audience's reaction, it seemed that I would easily win. But when the winners were announced the next Saturday, I lost.

I learned later that Dr. Hansen, the director of *Fiddler*, who had seen me lie on television, had called the TV station in Salt Lake to have me disqualified. From then on, I became *persona non grata* to Dr. Hansen, who blacklisted me in every way he could think of.

A few days later, I published my first play *Buffalo Head Nickels* as a BYU freshman at the age of 18. All in all, it was quite a way to begin my second semester at the Lord's University.

******

In my Mormon childhood, there was rarely any discussion about sex. In the 50s and 60s there was little talk about sex anywhere in America, so we Mormons were not alone in this. But I believe that the sexual repression I knew growing up in Mormon Zion was of an even more intense nature than in most places in America at that time. Even at church meetings, if Bishop Anderson chose to speak from the pulpit about sex, it was only in the most veiled and subtle ways. "Wicked thoughts are as bad or worse than any physical act itself," he would say. Or he would intone, "We must avoid the sins of the flesh!"

When Elder K. Packer—one of the General Authorities of the church—talked about masturbation during a speech given at a General Priesthood Meeting during the Annual Church Conference held once a year in the Tabernacle at Temple Square in Salt Lake City, he avoided using the word masturbation altogether. Instead, he warned the young male members of the Aaronic Priesthood against "tampering with their little factories."

Elder Packer had apparently found the word *penis* too offensive, and chose instead to describe the male reproductive organs as "little factories," as though the only function the penis performed in Mormon society was in making LDS babies.

Alone in the house at the age of 13, I pulled out the dirty magazine that I kept hidden in my bedroom in the back of the closet. Leafing through the tattered pages, I examined each familiar pose in every photo with painstaking effort. The pictures I liked best were the ones showing men and women together. I found them frustrating, though. All of the photos showed the women's breasts and vaginas, while keeping the men's genitals hidden from view. That didn't seem fair to me somehow, and it left me feeling strangely cheated, though I didn't understand why.

Sufficiently aroused, I stripped off my clothes and ran into the hallway to get the vibrator—with my favorite penis-hugging attachment—from my parents' bedroom. I plugged the vibrator in and watched myself in the mirror as the vibrating cup sucked and worked on the head of my erect penis. Thrusting my penis in and out of the vibrating cone, I let myself pretend—but only for a few seconds—that I was penetrating a vagina, the way the men did in the photos I most loved in the dirty magazines I had collected and secreted away in my bedroom. "Someday, when I grow up," I fantasized out loud, "I am going to stick it inside a real woman!" After indulging in the fantasy for a moment, I chastised myself: "It's bad enough you're playing with yourself! Why make it worse by thinking such nasty thoughts! It's wrong to think about girls that way. It's a sin!" My Quorum Advisor had told all of us boys that in Deacon's Quorum Meeting.

I continued masturbating but forced myself to think of something other than girls. After several minutes, a new burst of energy and light overcame me, as I ejaculated for the first time. It was thrilling. But I was also terrorized. Knowing so little about sex, I thought that the new white fluid spurting from my penis was blood turned white by a curse from God. Convinced that Heavenly Father had at last unleashed His wrath upon me for my wickedness, I imagined my parents would return home to find me lying dead and naked on the floor, even as the white blood still spurted from my still erect penis, in volley after volley, like an unclean fountain.

I turned off the vibrator, got on my knees and prayed. "Please, Heavenly Father," I whispered desperately, "I promise I'll never play with myself again! Just please … don't let me die like this!"

Although my erection remained rigid after the white bleeding stopped, I stood up and wiped myself clean, before going back down on my knees to thank Heavenly Father for sparing my life.

When I soon made use of the vibrator again, the white blood started spurting once more! Now, I had really done it! God was striking me down dead this time, for sure!

Of course, once the bleeding stopped and my penis became flaccid, I found a dictionary and looked up as many words as I could think of, until I came upon the word *ejaculation*. The stuff shooting out of my penis wasn't white blood. It was semen!

The moment when a boy becomes a man should be a moment of celebration. But for me, it was a moment of terror. Had I known then what I know now, I would have grabbed my little factory with fervor, and squirted my first manly juices into the air with joy!

Weeks later, I felt both excited and apprehensive about my planned upcoming weekend visit to my grandparents' home. Knowing that my cousin Kevin would be visiting them on the same weekend, I took a *Playboy* with me, hiding it inside a game of *Monopoly* that I brought with me.

Alone with Kevin after locking Grandma's bedroom door behind us, I took out the *Playboy* from inside the *Monopoly* box.

Kevin's eyes bulged when he saw it, as a wicked smile spreading across his face. "Wow!" he said, "Where did you get it?"

"I bought it at the drugstore," I explained.

For a moment, I thought of how I had hung around the local drugstore for hours before I finally got up the nerve to buy it. Breaking from my thoughts, I asked my cousin a direct question. "You wanna look at it?"

"Sure," he said, his erection obvious under his pants as we both began stroking ourselves through our clothes.

"Want to take them out?" I asked, as I pulled down my zipper, exposing my erection.

He quickly followed suit. I had never seen another boy's erection before. My member was a bit thicker and longer than my cousin's, but I felt ashamed because mine had a curve and his was straight.

"Your thing curves! My brothers and I don't look like that! It isn't normal!" Kevin observed, as my self-esteem took a nosedive.

I tried to ignore his thoughtless remarks. "Want to touch it?" I asked. "I'll touch yours if you want."

"You first," he replied.

Reaching out, I touched the head of his erect penis. It was like nothing I had ever felt before. It felt both spongy and velvety. "Okay," I said. "Now it's your turn!"

"All right," he agreed as we stroked each other off until we both ejaculated. "Wow!" Kevin exclaimed. "My brothers and I lose our hard-ons after we cum, but you're still hard!"

Apparently I was even more abnormal than I'd first thought!

Puberty brought with it many anxieties. Not only had I become aware that my erection took an abnormal curve, as I entered adolescence my nipples grew larger and more prominent than those of most other boys. Convinced that I was deformed, I didn't know how to confront my fears, or to whom.

When I arrived at our dinner table one night wearing a tight T-shirt, Dennis exclaimed loudly, "Kerry Lynn, you've got bigger tits than Marilyn Monroe!" Bursting into tears, I ran to my bedroom, locking the door behind me. What was I to do? Besides having abnormal nipples, and not being athletic, I was fat! Feeling like a total loser, I cried myself to sleep.

After my brother Dennis married his girlfriend Deanna, she gave birth to their first child Doye Allan, on my 13th birthday in late August 1966. Doye was a miracle baby. Born several months premature, he spent the first few months of his life in a hospital incubator. Weighing only two ounces during his first few days, Doye was so tiny that I could hold him in the palm of my hand. Aside from this, he was Mom and Dad's first grandchild.

Having been born on my birthday, Doye and I had a special connection from the very first. But Dennis soon proved to be as violent and unstable a father as he was a brother. In fact, Doye was less than a year old when Dennis held him inside the toilet bowl and flushed, saying, "Since you keep shitting your diapers, let's flush you down the toilet, too!"

Having witnessed my brother's abuse and the look of horror on little Doye's face that night left me utterly shaken. Later, alone in my bedroom as I said my prayers, I wondered what hellhole Dennis had sprung from. He was raised in the same home that I was, but he behaved more like a spawn of the Devil than of Saints.

As a young man, I did my very best to please my parents and fulfill all LDS expectations, if only to help compensate for my brother Dennis's behavior.

As expected, I was ordained as a Teacher in the Aaronic Priesthood when I turned 14 at the end of summer 1967.

Of the three sons in our family, I was the most devout in performing my Priesthood duties. Whether it was doing home teaching or collecting fast offerings from the LDS faithful, I was relentless in performing the tasks assigned me as a member of the Aaronic Priesthood. When I stood to bear my testimony at Fast and Testimony Meeting, the fervency of my words usually left tears in the eyes of our ward members. I was a trained and skilled people-pleaser, after all.

1968 was a year of American political upheaval unlike any I had yet experienced. Race riots, civil rights marches, and unending protests against the Vietnam War were commonplace all across the country. Growing up in an all-white Mormon society in Southeastern Idaho, I had never met a black man in person, but I had heard Bobby Kennedy talk about Dr. Martin Luther King, Jr., when he spoke at his political rally held in the Idaho State University gymnasium earlier that year. After attending that rally with Mom, I believed that Bobby Kennedy and Dr. King could together bring about racial healing in our country.

When Dr. King was shot at the Lorraine Motel in Memphis on April 4, 1968, I was traumatized.

The next morning, as I walked the halls of Alameda Junior High School, I heard several students make ugly and racist comments.

"Thank God somebody killed off that uppity nigger!" one boy exclaimed, while his hateful friends laughed.

"I guess that'll teach those niggers to know their place!" another one said loudly.

Hearing those words forced me to face a harsh reality: I had grown up among white racists; they populated my school, my hometown and the Mormon Church. Only then did I remember how often my Mormon Bishop had explained from our chapel pulpit why black men were not allowed to hold the priesthood and could not be ordained, since their black skin bore the mark of Cain.

Running into the bathroom, I locked myself in the stall and bawled my eyes out, facing the reality of America's racism and the racism within my own religion for the very first time.

After Dr. King's assassination, I put my faith entirely in Bobby Kennedy, watching every one of Bobby's televised political events. But I wish I hadn't been watching on Wednesday night, June 5, 1968—only two months after Dr. King's murder—when Robert Kennedy was gunned down at the Ambassador Hotel in Los Angeles, as it saddened me no end.

Emotionally devastated, my heart broke for America. Who would save us now from ourselves? I could only hope that the nation would outgrow its shameful need for violence the same way that I had outgrown my chubbiness during a growth spurt that year.

Still 14 that summer, I rehearsed with 17-year-olds in the Idaho State University Summer Drama Institute as we prepared for our theatrical production of Moliere's comedy, *The Imaginary Invalid.*

Two of the older high school boys, Allen and Joe, who were in the show with me, took their girlfriends for a ride in Joe's new car one late afternoon, and they invited me to tag along. Allen and Joe sat up front. I was sandwiched in the backseat between the two high school girls. Once Joe parked at the top of the mountain overlooking Pocatello in the valley below, he suggested that the girls make me happy. Looking at each other with girlish delight, the two young women began kissing me all over as they rubbed their breasts up against my chest. Embarrassed and red-faced, I felt like a cuckold.

Though I had performed in church plays and in a few plays in Junior High School, this was the first time that I would act in a play for the general public, so I had no idea when I walked out on stage for the first time that the audience would howl with laughter.

Somehow I instinctively knew how to connect with an audience, not push myself at them but make them come to me. No one taught me this. It was a natural gift, one I discovered for the first time during that performance, catching me and everyone else by surprise. When I took my bow at curtain call, the audience stood and cheered. For a boy who had never received much attention, I was suddenly bathing in it, standing center stage and basking in applause.

After that, I fed hungrily on any public attention, and I did anything and everything I could do to earn it. But none of it was ever enough to quash the amount of shame I had already internalized.

I was barely 15 years old when I entered Highland High School as a sophomore that fall. I had drastically slimmed down by then, growing to over six feet tall, and the scar on my face was now barely noticeable. I was growing into a handsome young man, but inside I still felt like the awkward and chubby boy I was in Junior High.

As a new sophomore in high school, I couldn't wait to see Barbra Streisand's first film, *Funny Girl* when it opened in late

September 1968 in Salt Lake City, in what was then termed a Roadshow Engagement. This meant that the film would not come to Idaho for at least a year. But as fate would have it, my sister Denise fell down the stairs in a freak accident, and subsequently was taken to Salt Lake City for back surgery. When Mom and I went to Salt Lake to look after her, I convinced Mom to take me to see *Funny Girl* at the Century 21 Theater, a spectacular new movie palace with rocking chairs for seats.

After watching Barbra burn up the screen with talent, as Pauline Kael of *The New Yorker* had promised, I knew that I wanted to become an actor. But more than that, I dreamed of becoming a star exactly like Streisand. Mom sensed that something had changed within me as we left the movie theater that day. "You loved the movie, didn't you?" she asked.

"Oh, it was so good!" I exclaimed. "Barbra was magnificent!"

I was watching the Academy Awards later that winter on my portable color TV, alone at home in my downstairs bedroom, when Barbra won the 1968 Academy Award for her performance in *Funny Girl*. I jumped up and down excitedly in my tiny bedroom, and cheered out loud and applauded, suddenly awash with sadness and shame that I had no one at all to share this special and magical moment with me, one that I had predicted would come. Mom was at ISU that night studying for her upcoming exams, or she would have shared that special moment with me. And Dad was out selling insurance, as he usually did on weekday evenings. But why, oh why, was I so very much alone, and without any true friends to celebrate with, when such a special moment arrived?

I became a huge Streisand fan after Barbra won her first Oscar, as I anxiously awaited the release of each of her new films, TV specials, and albums. In fact, my memories of most of the years that followed are now filed in my mind according to what new Streisand film or album was released and popular at the time. And my memories of most of those years all have Barbra singing in the background.

******

I came running up the stairwell beneath the Indian statue in the huge foyer of the Fine Arts Center—our usual meeting place—and overheard Bridget, Harlan, Jack and Debbie talking above me.

"The art exhibit's pretty good, don't you think?" Bridget asked, forever the journalist.

"Trevor Southey?" Harlan asked. "He's a great LDS artist."

"Maybe someday your paintings will be on exhibition here," Bridget said.

"That'd be great, wouldn't it?" Harlan replied.

"Kerry says you do beautiful work now," Debbie interjected.

Harlan replied, "I think he has more faith in me than I do."

"You and Kerry," Jack observed. "are close like brothers."

"Closer than brothers," Harlan replied intently.

I didn't want to eavesdrop any more, so I ran up the remainder of the stairs to greet them. "Hi guys!" I called out enthusiastically.

"Hey, Babe!" Harlan replied, smiling happily.

"Hello there, Harlan!" I exclaimed.

"There you are!" he replied. "I was beginning to wonder if you and Jenny had eloped somewhere together."

"No way!" I retorted. "Angel's a Republican. I could never marry a Republican!" Both Bridget and Jack looked at me cautiously. "Angel's not here yet?" I asked.

"No," Harlan said. "I hope she hurries, since it's a Barbra flick!"

"This isn't just any Barbra flick," Jack said. "It's *Funny Girl*!"

"I don't know what you're worried about, Jack," Harlan replied. "You and Kerry have each seen it 17 times already!"

"But you haven't!" I remarked.

Harlan had missed the film when it was released in 1968, as he had missed so many things, while on his mission and in Vietnam.

"I'll tell you what," Harlan replied, "If Jenny's not here in ten minutes, we'll leave her a note and head over to the Varsity Theatre. That'll still give us plenty of time to get there." He had a point: It was only two minutes away, a short walk across the quad.

"Guess what?" I said suddenly. "I almost forgot my news."

"What?" Harlan joked. "Did the Prophet have a new revelation?"'

"Nope. I just joined the Young Democrats on campus!"

"That's the most radical group at the Y!" Debbie countered.

"I couldn't help myself," I replied. "Since 18-year-olds now have the right to vote, we need to get involved. Right, Bridget?"

"I suppose so," Bridget replied, knowing by then that it was best to avoid discussions about politics, as I usually got on my soapbox.

"We all have to do our part and vote!" I exclaimed. "And they gave me all of these McGovern buttons!" I added, opening up my coat to show all of the buttons I had pinned on the inside. "I'm giving each one of you a button later tonight after dinner!"

"I can't wait to see Jenny's face when you give her that button!" Bridget added ironically.

Just then, Jenny ran across the foyer from the opposite direction. "Sorry I'm late, guys," Jennifer said. "My Religion class ran late."

After the movie, we went to dinner in the Wilkinson Center.

As we ate, Jack and I pressed all of our friends into saying how good they thought the film was. Harlan liked the film and loved Barbra's performance, but to my disappointment he did not share my great love of Streisand's singing, as he found her style "overbearing." Harlan's blasphemy when it came to Streisand was something I simply had to learn to accept, and I did so begrudgingly.

Once we had finished our meal, I presented everyone with a McGovern button, telling Jennifer that she should consider voting for Senator McGovern since Nixon was a liar.

"How can you call President Nixon a liar?" Angel asked, throwing her McGovern button in the nearest wastebasket. "You don't even know him!"

A few days later, Jack and I sat at the base of the Indian statue in the spacious foyer of the Fine Arts Center, waiting for Bridget. As usual, I had told her to meet us at the Indian at 6pm and, as usual, she was late. Glancing up at the 15-foot dark bronze statue of an American Indian, wearing only a loin-cloth, moccasins and a head feather, I admired the contours of the statue's thighs and chest, imagining how Harlan or Jack might look in such an outfit. I decided that Harlan would make an incredibly manly and masculine Native

American, while Jack would be a boyishly adorable one.

Giving Jack a discreet once over as I often did, gave me another erection that I could not make disappear. Luckily, I was wearing my bulky winter coat, which covered my obvious state of arousal, when Bridget came running up to the two of us.

"Looking for me?" Bridget squealed, interrupting my fantasy.

"I sure am!" I exclaimed. "Where've you been, Sweetie?"

"Working late at the paper," she explained, out of breath. "A scoop on McGovern's campaign just came over the wire from AP. And guess what? I got to write the story!"

"Bridg! You're kidding!" I said. It was her first major story for the paper, a major breakthrough for her. "I'm so excited for you!"

"The other reporters must be emerald with envy," Jack replied. He had come to love Bridget almost as much as I did.

"I hope so," she replied, her lips curling into an impish smile.

"I'm so proud of you, Bridg," I added, giving her a quick hug.

"Thanks, Sweetheart," she said happily, having began to use the nickname when I had started calling her Sweetie.

"Come on, Sweetie," I said, "we have a date at Hawkins!"

The three of us ran briskly down the stairs to the parking lot filled with thousands of cars, all displaying the blue-and-white BYU sticker in the rear window. It was late afternoon. The late February air was crisp and cold, as the setting sun shone brightly on the snow-covered Mount Timpanogos in the distance, painting it pink and gold. We walked on through the slush of the parking lot to where Oscar was parked. The cold slushy water seeping through my boots made me wish I had gone to school at UCLA in Southern California.

Once we had driven off campus, I reached for Bridget's hand and held it tenderly. I was still paranoid even about holding her hand on campus for fear we might get ticketed by a university official for a "public display of affection."

As Bridget snuggled up to me, Jack looked away sheepishly, staring out at the snow-scape beyond.

Mr. and Mrs. Hawkins waved through the window as soon as they saw us pull up. They could recognize Oscar from a block away.

"Howdy, Ma and Pa!" I shouted, as we walked inside.

"So good to see you kids!" Ma Hawkins said, throwing her arms around all three of us.

"We were just drivin' around," I said, "and thought we'd stop in."

"Not up to any trouble, I hope," Ma kidded, brushing one straying grey hair off her forehead, as we sat down at the counter.

"So, what can we make for you young squirts?" Pa Hawkins asked, his huge belly protruding from his white T-shirt onto the red Formica counter. He seemed to enjoy flaunting the fact that he did not wear LDS garments underneath his shirts. Though Mormon, both Pa and Ma Hawkins acted like Gentiles. Regrettably their business suffered because of it, even though they made the best burgers and fries in the whole of Happy Valley.

"I want a blueberry shake," I said, "plus a double cheeseburger and fries." Pa and Ma could count on me for a large order.

"What do you want, Bridg?" I asked, turning to face her.

"I'm not very hungry," Bridget replied. She never was. "I think I'll just have a small 7-Up."

"And what about you, Jack?" Pa asked, as he made my shake.

"Give me the same as Kerry," Jack replied, smiling boyishly.

"Hey, Kerry!" Pa said, "Did you watch the game Saturday?"

"I went with Harlan," I explained, having attended the game in the newly completed Marriott Center Sports Arena.

"Great game, wasn't it?" he said, as he made my shake. "The Cougars have a dynamite basketball team this year."

"That's what Harlan keeps telling me," I replied. "I don't know much about it. I leave that to you sports fans!"

"Me, too!" Ma called out loudly from the kitchen where she was flipping burger patties over the stove in back.

"Here you go," Pa Hawkins said, handing me my shake. I felt grateful that blueberry shakes were not against *The Word of Wisdom*.

"Don't worry, Jack," Pa said, "Your shake's coming right up!"

"That's okay," Jack said. "I can slurp on Kerry's while I wait!"

I sat on the sofa in Harlan's living room, cramming for upcoming exams. Joining me on the sofa, he put his arm around me. "You're taking your studies too seriously," Harlan said. "You need to relax."

"I guess you're right," I whispered.

"Of course, I'm right," he said. Harlan rubbed his hand back and forth across my shoulder blades, giving me goose bumps. Even through my shirt, the contact of his hand seemed to melt my skin. "Whenever I used to get uptight in Nam," Harlan explained, "Danny would give me a back rub and then I'd feel like my old self again."

That Harlan could now speak of the war and his friendship with Danny without slipping into an emotional tailspin was only one of many indications that our relationship had been healthy for him. Yet, as I felt myself getting sexually excited, I had to wonder how healthy the relationship had been for me.

"Hey!" Harlan announced as his hand moved down to my bare arms, "You're getting goose bumps."

"It's chilly in here," I explained. Jumping up quickly and walking to the window, all the while hoping he hadn't noticed the tenting of my front pants, I took in the view outside. The setting sun colored the mountains in the distance a passionate purple.

Harlan walked over to join me, standing close behind me. "Beautiful sunset, huh?" he asked tenderly, almost apologetically.

"Yea, verily!" I responded quietly. "Just look at all those colors— the orange, red, and purple. It reminds me of one of your paintings, as though you painted the sky."

Even as I said the words, I looked into Harlan's soulful eyes, and reminded myself of God's words: "The wages of sin are death!"

Aside from Jack, I made three new friends that semester: The first, Stacey Taylor, a freckle-faced redhead, was a gifted singer, pianist, and a music and drama major, with a vivacious personality. Since she was also very fun to be with, we became close friends.

I also became friends with Dom Altman, a drama major who hoped to become a professional director one day, who was cast with me in the new religious play *Abraham and Isaac*. Dom had grown up on an Idaho farm in a small rural community. He was as tall as I was, but more muscular. Freckled like Stacey, Dom had bright red hair, huge blue eyes, and a handsome face.

The third friend I encountered late that semester was Oscar Wilde, when I heard my drama professor Dr. Charles Metten proclaim during a lecture, "Wilde was a gifted wit and playwright, but he was also one of the greatest degenerates of all time!" This made my ears perk up. Like the young Wilde, "I could resist everything except temptation." After the lecture, I ran to the library and started researching Oscar Wilde. The seed that was planted that night later grew into a life's work.

******

At Highland High School, I pursued activities that I knew I would excel at, like speech classes and theater and my studies, while avoiding athletics. Unfortunately, P.E. was required. Believing that my penis and nipples were abnormal, I dreaded the locker room.

During the fall of my sophomore year, I came down with a bad cold. Unable to contain my fears as I sat in the car while Dad drove me to see our family doctor, I suddenly blurted out, "Dad, I think my penis is deformed. It curves when it's erect."

"It curves?" Dad asked. His shocked reaction was highly disconcerting to me. Apparently, my father's erection was straight too! "That could cause you problems when you're married!" he stated erroneously.

"There's something else," I said. "My nipples are abnormal!"

"I've worried about that too," Dad replied. "I've wondered if it might be hormonal."

Dad had just confirmed my worst fears about myself. I was utterly mortified. In fact, there was little left of me but a rag and a hank of hair on the car's floor.

"Well," Dad said solemnly, "You better ask the doctor about all of it, while you're in there with him."

"Okay, I will," I replied.

Our family doctor seemed embarrassed by my questions.

"As to the nipples," Dr. Smith explained, "you have a mild case of *Gynecomastia*. When boys go into puberty, some develop larger

100

nipples. In your case, it's slight and nothing to worry about."

"Uh, okay," I stammered. I felt unsure.

Finally, I pressed him further, asking, "What about my penis? Do I have to get it hard, so you can see how it curves?"

"That won't be necessary," he said, choking on his words. Red-faced, he continued, "Let's just wait until you're married, to see if you have any problems with marital function."

A few days after that, I arrived home from a high school play rehearsal to find Dad apoplectic with rage. Dad came at me like a lunatic, clutching in his fist the new cache of adult men's magazines that I had collected over time and had kept hidden in my bedroom.

"Are these yours, young man?" he screamed. The veins in Dad's neck looked as though they might burst, as his other hand grabbed my arm in an unforgiving grip.

I did not know what to say. The Wicked Witch held me fast, with a burning broom of shame shoved in my face. I couldn't move.

Mom stepped in between us. "Those magazines couldn't be Kerry's!" she said. "Dennis or Craig probably hid them in his room."

"Well, whoever owns this filth has to answer to me!" Dad yelled.

When Dad finally released his grip on my arm, I ran out of the house as fast as I could, tears staining my face, but where could I run that would not bring me home again?

When I told this story to my therapist decades later, he noted, "That was a tight box they put you in, wasn't it?" Jim asked.

"What do you mean?" I replied.

"Your father attacked you for having a penis, while your mother defended you by saying you didn't—that she had cut it off!"

I started dating girls at the age of 15, during my sophomore year of high school, only because I felt that my Mormon society expected it of me. My modus operandi was to date a girl until I knew she expected me to kiss her, and then I would find someone else to date.

One of the girls I dated that first year in high school was more aggressive than the others in pushing for a physical relationship, attacking me one night while we sat in the front seat of Oscar in the school parking lot during a break from rehearsal for a school play that we had both been cast in. To save myself embarrassment, I quickly pushed her away from me, as we both tumbled out of the car. Once outside Oscar, I ran back to the school's auditorium as quickly as I could. My face flushed with shame and embarrassment.

When Mom graduated from college in the spring of 1969, I finished my sophomore year of high school.

Early in August, my sister Denise married Lee Simmons, solemnizing their wedding in a Temple ceremony held in the Idaho Falls LDS Temple. I could not attend the wedding itself, as I was not yet old enough to become an Elder or to take out my Temple endowments. To the shock of everyone in our family, particularly Denise and Mom, Dad was also prevented from attending the Temple ceremony, since he had told our Bishop that he did not feel worthy to receive the required Temple Recommend. What none of us knew then, and that Dad would only confess to me years later, he had good reasons for refusing to enter the Temple. Both Mom and Denise were heartbroken that Dad had refused to give his own daughter away at her Temple wedding, but they both chalked this up to Dad's low sense of self-esteem. In their eyes, Dad was a faithful Latter-Day-Saints and certainly no sinner.

Regardless, I vividly remember how happy my sister Denise seemed at her wedding reception held in the 15th Ward's recreation hall on the evening after she and Lee were married in the Temple that afternoon, and how beautiful she looked in her wedding gown, as she waltzed with Lee.

A few weeks after the wedding, and just prior to my 16th birthday in late August, I met with Bishop Anderson to determine my worthiness to be ordained a Priest in the Aaronic Priesthood.

Given that my little black book was now filled with thousands of black marks, I felt overwhelmed with shame. How could I show so many black marks to the Bishop? I simply couldn't. Instead, I lied to Bishop Anderson. It was the same as lying to God! To make up for my sin, I made a sacred covenant that day with my Heavenly Father that I would never masturbate again. I kept that solemn promise until I met a naked man in a BYU bathroom two-and-a-half years later.

I began my junior year at Highland High in the fall of '69, shortly after my 16th birthday, at the same time that Mom began her teaching career. I was so proud of Mom. And I was proud of Dad, who had overcome his fear of having his role of provider usurped, and had come to fully support Mom in her new career.

Barbra Streisand released her next album, *What About Today?* that fall at the beginning of my junior year in high school. I loved the album, and I played it incessantly on our family's stereo. When I showed Dad the album cover, he was appalled by a photograph of Barbra on the back that revealed a bit of her cleavage. In indignation, Dad proclaimed, "It's immoral how she's showing off her breasts!"

"What?" I asked innocently. Barbra's cleavage was the only thing that I hadn't noticed about the album. As Dad stalked out of the living room, I felt overwhelmed with despair. I knew Dad resented me for being closer to Mom than he was. I felt like every time he looked at me, he saw his own inadequacies. Somehow, I had to make room for Daddy. And so, taking a black magic marker in hand, I colored in Barbra's cleavage on the album's back cover.

Streisand's second film *Hello, Dolly!* opened in December 1969 to great reviews. I was thrilled, of course, by her second screen performance. Then Barbra's third hit film, *On A Clear Day You Can See Forever* opened in 1970. To my relief, the soundtrack album covers of both films met with my father's approval, so I didn't have to run for another magic marker to remove any offensive cleavage.

Since my brother Dennis was often on the road driving truck during my years in high school, I became extremely close with his wife Deanna, just as I became a surrogate father to his son Doye.

One afternoon in the summer of 1970, while I was visiting Deanna and four-year-old Doye, Dennis arrived home in a drunken rage. "What the hell!" he screamed. "I come home to find my little brother here, trying to fuck my wife!" The veins in his neck seemed they might be close to bursting. "And I can tell she wants it, too!"

Somehow I escaped and drove off to find my parents, as I knew Deanna and Doye were in danger. When my family and I returned, Deanna and Doye were both bloodied. We got them in the car and raced away, but Dennis sped after us, then passed us before slowing down in the passing lane, coming up beside us and then ramming into our car again and again, attempting several times to run us off the road. Then he backed off, pulling up behind us and then plowed into the back end of our car repeatedly. As he honked and cursed at us, we all looked at each other in abject terror. Clearly, he was trying to kill us all, and only gave up his pursuit when Dad drove to the Police Station in downtown Pocatello.

Deanna and Doye moved in with us later that night. All of us felt shell-shocked. I'm quite sure we all were suffering from PTSD. As for me, I felt personally responsible. Why had Dennis accused me of having sex with his wife? I knew Dennis resented me. And, in truth, I resented him. But why had he singled me out and tried to kill us all?

Before going to bed that night, I knelt and prayed to my Heavenly Father, as was my habit at that time. "Please, Heavenly Father," I prayed, "Help me not to hate my brother as much as I do tonight." I struggled to finish the prayer. "I want to love Dennis, but I need Thy guidance and Thy help in this, as in all things. I say these things in the name of Jesus Christ. Amen."

A few months later, Dennis and Deanna reconciled and they moved back in together. But his behavior grew worse over time, not better, and they eventually divorced, shortly after their daughter DeRae's birth. Dennis went on to abuse his second wife Kathy, then a third wife, and a fourth. Later, he assaulted his son Doye shortly after Doye's graduation from high school. Later still, Dennis was accused of sexually assaulting his daughter and a stepdaughter. The latter charges sent Dennis to jail in Colorado for several months, until Dad bailed him out by taking out a mortgage on his home.

******

Despite my best intentions, I soon began exploring the cruisy places in and around BYU that I was told about. I even got blown at a men's room in a park only two blocks from Hawkins Drive-In, where I ate afterward, not out of hunger but to assuage my guilt.

On a fateful Saturday in March 1972, I went searching again for anonymous sex. Since there was no action at the I-15 rest areas, I drove north to the seedy part of downtown Salt Lake near 2nd South, where I found the cruisy porn theatre I was told about.

The place smelled like a latrine. It was so dark inside that I had to feel my way to a row, taking a seat on the aisle. My shoes stuck to something sticky on the floor. As my eyes adjusted to the darkness, I realized that many men were walking up and down the aisle, almost as though they were searching for prey.

A handsome black man stopped to stand in the aisle by my seat. I was intrigued. Growing up in an all-white Mormon society, I had never met a black person, much less one who might be interested in me sexually. Extremely muscular and standing at least 6'8", with an iron jaw and a strong, masculine face, he looked very much like O.J. Simpson did in his prime, particularly since he was well-dressed in a business suit. Even his shoes were polished to a fine sheen. As he rubbed his crotch through his dress slacks, I could see the outline of his penis, which was far larger than anything I had yet encountered. This, I admit, intrigued me, too.

Catching me off guard, he bent down and whispered in my ear. "Want to go back to my place?" His breath felt hot and exciting against my ear. "I only live around the corner," he coaxed.

"I don't know," I whispered back.

Suddenly I heard the voice of my unseen spiritual guide—a voice I had not heard since the age of nine—warning me: "Kerry, do not go with this man. Tell him no."

But the handsome man stuck his tongue in my ear, making me nearly squirm out of my chair, so I ignored the warning. "I'll make it worth your while," the mysterious stranger promised, as he put his tongue in my ear and licked seductively.

"I don't know," I said again. "I just got here."

But finally I agreed, following him out of the porn theater, down the street, and into his flophouse hotel around the corner.

"It's much nicer on the third floor," he encouraged me as I gullibly followed him through the filthy lobby and up the three flights of stairs. When we arrived at his room and he opened the door, I could see that the place was disgusting, but I went in anyway, like a lamb to the slaughterhouse. The bathroom reeked of who knows what. The double bed was unmade. A lamp sat on a rickety nightstand. Locking the door behind him, his demeanor changed instantly. "Now, strip naked, you fat bitch!" he ordered.

I was shocked and a little afraid by the sudden change in him. "I ... I don't like profanity," I protested softly, already fearful.

He grunted in reply and looked down into my face. "I'm only going to tell you this once, cunt," he hissed. "I don't care about what you want. You're here to give me what I want. Understand?" I was afraid to say anything. Suddenly his powerful hand swung through the air, slapping me so hard in the face that I fell to my knees. "I asked you a question, bitch!" he said. "The bitch will answer me, or I will make it pay! Understand?"

"Yes," I muttered in shock, my face stinging in pain as I knelt on the floor. I had never been struck in the face before, and his profanity alone felt like an assault.

"Yes, what?" he hissed. Grabbing the shirt I was wearing, he tore it open, making the buttons pop off as he squeezed my nipples hard. "Yes, what, queer?"

"What do you want me to say?" I asked fearfully.

He twisted my nipples as pain overwhelmed me. "A man like me deserves respect from a faggot like you, so you'll address me as Sir when you speak to me! Got it?"

"Uh ... yes, Sir," I said softly, barely able to breathe.

"You have a lot to learn, but I'll turn you into a high-class whore in no time." He spit in my face and took his finger and slimed it with his own spittle, holding the finger in front of my eyes. "Now, be a good girl, and lick my finger clean!" I shuddered with fear. "Lick it clean or you're dead!" Suppressing my need to vomit, I licked his finger. Looking directly into my eyes, he added, "I had my doubts whether you and I were going to get along. But now I know we're going to get along just fine."

I just wanted the whole thing over, so I could get away. He

began stroking my burning cheek with his massive hand. It made me hate him even more, but I did nothing to stop him, hoping only to live another day.

Looking down from his height above me, he ordered, "Stand up and strip out of those clothes, faggot!"

"Yes, Sir!" I replied, complying instantly. Once I was naked, he looked me over, taking note of my limp penis. "The bitch is a little overweight and it has a fat ass, but that's okay. I like my girls with a few curves! And the bitch has big hot tits!"

I trembled in shame and terror, as he walked across the room, taking off his shoes and socks, stripping out of his clothes and folding them neatly in the corner before coming back to stand in front of me. His body was overly muscled. His chest, shoulders, and biceps were massive, as were his thighs. Far taller than me, he could have broken me like a twig, and I was 6'3".

As impressive as his physique was, it paled in comparison to his penis, gradually growing out of his groin like a tree trunk. Widest at the base, it became less thick as it neared the head, and his testicles were the size of cantaloupes.

He sat down on the chair in front of me and began stroking himself into a full erection.

"Kneel down on the floor between my legs!" he ordered. I knelt, even as my eyes grew wide as his penis grew to a monstrous size. It was perfectly straight, making me feel even more shame. "I bet you've never seen a cock this big, have you bitch?" he taunted. I could see that both of his massive fists could not reach around the width of its base. "That's why I call it my Cunt Destroyer!" He paused and took a breath before issuing his next command, "Stand up, cunt, and put your hands behind your back!" I complied quickly. "And close your eyes!" I hesitated, and he slapped my face again. "I said close your eyes, cunt!"

"Yes, Sir," I whimpered, closing my eyes in terror.

When he ordered me to open my eyes, I saw a switchblade knife that he held near my face. "This is my enforcer," he explained quietly. "I've already killed a few faggots, so if you don't obey me, you're dead!" Encircling my testicles with his left hand, he put the edge of his knife's blade under my scrotum and held it there. I froze in fear. "A faggot like you doesn't need balls," he said. "I'd be doing you a favor if I cut them off."

I began sobbing. "Please, Sir, don't hurt me."

"Oh, I'll hurt you! A bitch like you deserves to be hurt! In fact, don't turn away! Look me in the eyes while I hurt you!"

"Yes, Sir," I said, looking directly into evil.

Suddenly he squeezed my scrotum with his fist until I thought my testicles would pop. I wanted to scream, but I knew I mustn't. He would've left me there to bleed out on his filthy floor. Removing the switchblade from my scrotum even as he released his death grip on my nearly broken testicles, he grabbed hold of my limp penis, saying, "This must be the bitch's clit. Is that what it is, bitch?" I was too overwhelmed by shame to say anything. I felt his other hand place the edge of his knife at the base of my limp penis. "If that's a dick and not a clit, I better do the bitch a favor and slice it off! Is it your clit, faggot, or should I cut it off?"

"It's my clit, Sir," I rushed to say. I hated him forcing me to repeat his profanities. "But please don't hurt me, Sir," I pleaded.

"Get on your knees, you worthless twat!" he ordered.

"Yes, Sir!" I whispered, kneeling immediately.

"You ready to put my cock in that filthy mouth of yours?"

"I ... I don't know ... I've never done that, Sir."

He slapped me hard across the face, and put the edge of his opened switchblade knife against my throat. "You're either getting my cock or my knife, so which is it?"

"Your penis, Sir," I whimpered, as tears streamed down my swollen and bruised face.

"Kiss the head of my cock then," he ordered matter-of-factly. I was so scared and in such shock that I didn't respond. "Are you deaf?" he shouted. "Kiss my cockhead, but don't suck on it! I'm not sure your mouth deserves it, yet!"

"Yes, Sir," I whimpered, pressing my lips onto the head of his penis and giving it a quick kiss. I was amazed at how velvety the texture was.

"Good, bitch!" he said, placing his hands on my head. "Now, stick out that tongue and lick it all from top to bottom, and keep looking in my eyes, while you play with your clit!" I did as he ordered, but my penis was unresponsive. "Now, open that pussy mouth as wide as you can!" he snapped. "And get the entire head in your mouth!"

"Yes, Sir," I replied. I felt the edge of his knife at my throat, as he forced the massive head into my mouth. Suddenly I felt my lips split open on both sides as blood smeared my face.

Frustrated, he pulled his erection out of my mouth and slapped me. "What a lousy cocksucker! I thought a big girl like you could at least take all of my cockhead into its worthless mouth! You're just as bad as all the other cunts!"

"I'm sorry, Sir," I whimpered. "I've never done this before."

"That's okay," he sneered. "I can still fuck its pussy."

I stared back at him, not knowing what he meant.

"You have an asshole," he explained contemptuously, "and that's where I'm shoving my cock!"

I was horrified. "You'd kill me if you put that thing in me!"

He gave me an evil smile. "I either fuck the bitch or it dies!"

******

Starving for the attention that I now knew I could gain from performing on stage, I appeared in every high school play and musical. The two productions that stand out most in my mind are *The Music Man* and *Camelot*, both co-productions of our town's two rival high schools. With the talent and budgets of both schools combined, these shows were very popular in the community. In *The Music Man* in 1969, I was cast as Marcellus Washburn, and sang, danced and acted my way to my high school's Best Actor Award that year. According to the local paper, I stole the show.

Camelot was staged in the fall of 1970, during my senior year. Cast in the supporting role of King Pellinore, I made my entrance with a huge St. Bernard dog on a leash. Nearly as big as I was, the dog subsequently dragged me across the stage in any and all directions, wherever he wanted to go. Once I even have to follow him into the orchestra pit. During one performance, the dog, whom my character named Horrid, ran over to Queen Guinevere, lifted his leg, and promptly peed all over her gown. Everyone gasped in horror. But I did a double take, looked out at the audience and ad-libbed, "Sometimes Horrid is simply Horrid!"

My ad-lib stopped the show cold, with some people laughing so hard like my mother, that they peed their pants in the aisles.

In addition to acting in all of the plays and musicals, I won several awards in high school, and kept my trophies prominently displayed in my bedroom as evidence of my worth. Among them were awards for consecutive wins in the VFW Voice of Democracy oratory contest. Having written a suitably patriotic speech and one that I thought was a winner, I entered the speech competition early in my senior year, going to the local radio station to record my speech, since all entries were to be judged by a submitted recording rather than by live performance. Winning the City of Pocatello competition, then District and Regional Competitions, I first gave my speech live before an audience at the regional chapter of the VFW where I received a standing ovation.

Those who heard me give my speech that night predicted that I would easily win First Place in Idaho, and go on to Washington, DC, to compete for national honors.

My parents and I traveled to Boise for a banquet, where the Governor presented awards to the top seven finalists in the state.

Apparently, my recorded performance hadn't matched the fervor of my live presentation, because I took runner-up in the competition. Of course, my parents were proud of me. They couldn't know how much bitter shame and bitter disappointment I felt in taking second place. It wasn't enough to win second place in the entire state, and to have my picture taken with Governor Cecil B. Andrus. I had to win first prize. I had to go to Washington, DC and win national honors. Nothing short of this could quash my inner shame.

When my parents asked me that night how I wanted to celebrate, I asked if we could go see Barbra Streisand's new film *The Owl and the Pussycat*. My parents quickly agreed, thinking that we were going to see Barbra's fourth musical film. But the movie was hardly a musical. The film was rated R and spiced with language that my parents found offensive. Barbra played a prostitute in the film. I loved the movie, but my parents sat red-faced while the most of the Boise audience erupted in laughter.

I finally won First Prize in a statewide competition later that year. This time it was for the State's One-Act Play Competition, in which our drama department won the top award for our production of the first play I had ever written, a play I had titled *Buffalo Head Nickels*. Deciding to surprise me, my drama teacher Mrs. Kisling presented me with the award during a student assembly in our high school gymnasium. "Not only did Kerry write and star in this production," Mrs. Kisling explained, "he is the first and only student to ever win this award! Thanks to Kerry, we're not only #1 in basketball and football, but #1 in the Arts!"

When Mrs. Kisling called me to the stage to receive the award, I made my way down through the bleachers as the student body cheered. When I reached the microphone, she handed me the trophy, threw her arms around me and gave me a kiss on the cheek. This was all I had ever wanted: To be seen and to be applauded as special. Taking the microphone, I quieted down the crowd. "Wow!" I said, wiping a tear from my eye. "I never expected this!" I took a deep breath, imagining how I would make my acceptance speech when I won my first Oscar. "I could not have done this without Mrs. Kisling who encouraged me to write my first play and gave me the opportunity to stage it." The crowd burst into applause again. "I thank her and I thank all of you for this wonderful honor." I took the trophy and held it up high. "For Highland!" I added, as students cheered from the rafters.

When it came time to choose which university to attend, my choice was between Yale and Northwestern since both were known for their theatrical training. But my parents were adamant about one thing: I must not be exposed to too many "worldly influences," to use Dad's terminology. The choice came down to two: Idaho State University, our hometown college, or Brigham Young University, where I could receive a proper education rooted in Mormon doctrine. Happily, I received scholarships to both schools. Both Mom and Dad preferred that I stay at home and attend ISU. That way, they could keep an eye on me while saving on housing expenses. Though I could not articulate it at the time, even to myself, I knew I needed to break free from the overly protective clutches of my parents, so I chose BYU, a selection that still served to please both my parents.

Once my choice of university was set, the discussion of the profession I would choose came next. My choice was clear: I would become a professional actor and writer. Both my parents were fearful over my choice, declaring that I would need "something to fall back on," should my career not work out the way I dreamed it would. Mom very much believed in my abilities and thought I could and would make my dreams come true one day. But Dad, always more pragmatic about such things than my mother, had serious doubts about it. "Kerry," he admonished seriously, "I know you have talent but I can't see you making a living either as an actor or as a writer."

His bold statement, made to my face, cut deep into the hidden reservoir of shame and self-doubt within me. It wounded me. My face turned deep red. I couldn't let my inner frailty, my fear, and my lack of faith in myself be exposed, so I responded with the strongest statement I could muster:

"You're wrong, Dad. I swear I'll prove you wrong someday!"

After that, I couldn't let my father win. I had to prove him wrong. My very identity—the mask of false pride that I hid behind—depended upon it. I had to make my dreams a reality. I had to become a star! Only then would Mom and I win our battle with Dad.

In the end, I made a concession to my parents: Though I would pursue my degree in Drama, I would also pursue a degree in Education, so that I could teach drama classes if need be, to have "something to fall back on."

Being the only child still living with my parents at home, I furthered my reputation as a Saint by serving as president of the Highland High LDS Seminary during my senior year, then giving the main speech at my Seminary Graduation. By that time, I had won nearly every award and honor that the LDS Church bestows upon its youth, including a Duty to God Award and many Individual Achievement Awards. On the surface at least, I was the epitome of the clean-living and clean-cut young LDS male.

Only a few months after I graduated from high school, my brother Craig and his childhood sweetheart Peggy married in the LDS Temple. Craig wanted to ask a buddy of his to be his Best Man, but Mother insisted that he ask me, which is why I was appointed to a task that my brother did not want me to fulfill. It mattered little, since I could not attend the afternoon wedding held in the Temple, but could only attend the wedding reception held in our ward's reception hall afterward in the evening.

But throughout the summer, I was filled with the afterglow of my high school success. Knowing such success in high school, how could my college years be any less than triumphant?

******

"So which is it?" my rapist asked. "Do you want to get fucked or do you want to die?"

"Put it in me, Sir," I whimpered. "I don't want to die."

"Good girl!" he said. "Now, crawl over to the bed, bitch!"

"Yes, Sir," I replied, doing as he ordered.

He went to the bathroom and came out with lube greasing his penis, coming toward me on the bed as he ordered me to turn over. "On its back, up on its knees, cunt! And spread those thighs as wide as it can!" With the knife in his right hand, he came from behind me, between my thighs. "Stick that ass up in the air," he shouted, "and push its cunt out!"

"Yes, Sir," I whimpered, terrified.

He rubbed what felt like a quart of lube onto the lips of my anus, and then shoved a huge amount into my anal passage. I screamed. He pulled his fingers out of my ass and clamped his left hand over my mouth, as he brought the knife's blade to my throat with his right hand, cutting the skin. I could feel blood dripping from my neck. "Oh, my God!" I thought. "He's cut my throat open. He's killed me!"

He brought his mouth to my ear, whispering, "Don't worry, I only cut that throat a little; not even enough to scar! But if I hear another peep out of you, I will slit you open. It'll be messy, but I can fuck you just as easily with you dead. Now nod your head up and down like a good girl, if you understand!" With his hand still clasped over my mouth, I nodded. "Okay," he said, "I'm going to remove my hand, but if you make any more noise, you're dead! You got that?" I nodded again. He took his left hand from my mouth, but held the knife in his right hand at my throat. "Now," he whispered in my ear, "play with your little twat and get it hard! Make a sound, and you get a knife in your back!"

"Yes, Sir," I whimpered, trying in vain to obtain an erection. I heard him squeeze more lube from a container.

Without warning, he shoved two greased fingers into my anus. Only his threat of violence kept me from screaming. He twirled the two greased fingers inside me, and then added two more fingers and finally his thumb. The pain was excruciating, and it seemed there was no moment to relax my sphincter. I could feel my anal lips tearing, as I felt blood dripping down my crack. "Get that hole open, cunt!" he shouted.

The next thing I knew, his other massive hand began spanking my ass over and over again, distracting me from the anal pain. Suddenly, he unscrewed what looked like a silver bullet hanging on a chain around his neck, and shoved it toward my nose. "What is it, Sir?" I asked, believing I would never wake up again.

"They're poppers," he explained. "They'll help it relax!" He ordered me to breathe in the aroma deeply, as he shoved the silver bullet into each of my nostrils. Deciding it was better to be unconscious when he killed me, I did as he said.

I felt his fingers go up into me even further and wider, but the poppers stunted the pain. "If you think my fingers are big, they're nothin' compared to my Cunt Destroyer!" he said, moving his fingers in and out of my ravaged anus, as he made me take hit after hit of poppers. I felt gratitude for the amyl-nitrate, as it made the horrible pain slightly less excruciating.

Suddenly he tore his fingers from my rectum, my bloodied anal lips flopping open as he shouted, "Ready or not, here I come!" With that, he pushed his penis into me, as my anal lips snapped shut around it. He kept shoving amyl up my nostrils, while his massive hand spanked my ass again and again, making my cheeks sting with pain.

"If I were you," he said, "I'd stop worrying about that hole of yours and start worrying about the pain I can give you elsewhere!" He reached under me and grabbed one of my nipples and twisted it mercilessly.

As he pushed further into me, I prayed that he would kill me so the pain would end. But after burying himself inside me, he pulled out and pushed back in again and again. "That's it, bitch!" he whispered in my ear, "Take a real man's cock!"

Filled with shame, I blamed only myself. Why had I gone looking for sex? I deserved whatever happened to me! As the momentum of his thrusting increased, I felt my anal lips stretching and tearing as he went, while blood dripped down my legs. Yet afraid for my lie, I continued stroking my penis as he ordered me to. The intense rubbing against my prostate eventually brought me to an erection, much against my will.

He pulled me up onto his haunches and used his massive hands to pinch and twist my nipples. He reached down and began to stroke my shaft. "The bitch loves being raped, doesn't it," he whispered in my ear. "That clit ain't so little any more! But don't you cum, bitch! This is about my pleasure, not yours!" Somehow the combination of the poppers and his intense thrusting made semen leak from my penis. It wasn't an ejaculation: I took no pleasure in it; it was an involuntary release from the prolonged thrusting against my prostate, as though I was being milked like a cow, against my will. But my penis remained hard afterward.

When he saw the fluid leaking from my penis, he was furious with me. Slapping my face several times, he screamed, "You sneaky selfish cunt! I told it not to cum! This isn't about its pleasure! It's about getting me off! I've been a nice guy, throwing it a gentle fuck! Now I'm going to take my pleasure as I deserve, and rip it a new asshole!" And then he threw me onto the bed on my stomach. Holding the knife at my throat, it cut into my flesh. "If it makes a sound, it dies!" he growled.

"Yes, Sir," I whimpered into a pillow.

Pushing into me as far as he could go, he pounded his huge penis into me with a ferocity and violence that I never want to experience again. It seemed to take forever, but finally he grabbed my nipples and twisted them violently, screaming into my ear as he ejaculated inside me, "I'm cumming, bitch!"

Afterward, he lay on top of me for a long time, even as I felt his monstrous thing soften inside me. Slowly removing the knife from my throat, he pulled his penis from my bleeding hole, and sat up. He stroked my hair. "Did my bitch like that?" he asked quietly. I said nothing. "I asked it a question, bitch!" he said, slapping me hard across the face.

"I've never been ... penetrated ... before ..." I whimpered, all the while sobbing quietly, still numb and in shock.

"Don't tell me you didn't love it! You shot your cunt juice all over my sheets!" Turning my body over, he exposed my still erect penis. "Look at that!" he exclaimed. "The bitch's clit is still hard! So don't tell me you didn't like it, and don't call it rape, because you can't rape the willing!" I felt my face burn with shame. "Now, use that tongue and clean all that scum off my cock!"

"I don't think I can, Sir," I said, thinking I would rather die.

He slapped me so hard across the face that I fell from my knees to the floor. "You're not leaving my cock filthy after I gave it such a good ride!" he yelled. "Get that fucking tongue moving and lick my cock clean, or you won't live to see another hour!"

"Yes, Sir." I complied, licking him clean, even as the smell and taste of my own excrement and blood on his flaccid penis made me feel like I might have to puke.

"Good girl!" he exclaimed with a victorious smile, making me want to smash his face in. With his knife still at my throat, he had me stand. Backing away, he looked at me and laughed. "I usually kill fags, but I'm going to let it live, because I don't think it will tell anyone about what happened. It wouldn't want anyone to know what a pussy it really is!" I looked down at my limp penis. "I should kill the bitch," he smirked. "Lucky for you, I'm a nice guy!" He threw my clothes at me. "Now get out of here, faggot!"

I was still naked when he threw me into the hall, with my clothes and shoes in my hands as he slammed the door in my face.

I dressed as best I could, given that every part of my body ached, and began the long, painful trek down the stairs.

Walking down the three flights of stairs hurt like hell with every painful step. I was bruised and beaten everywhere, and my anus felt ravaged, but my mind and soul were in far more pain.

He was right: I wouldn't report the rape to the police or tell anyone, least of all my parents. I couldn't go to the hospital. There was nowhere to turn. I couldn't tell anyone! I couldn't tell anyone!

After the rape, I slowly made my way back to my car.

In shock, I fumbled with the car keys. Once inside the car, I struggled simply to close the car door behind me. As I went into shock, I felt as though I was not sitting in my beloved Oscar, but in a warped, surreal and unfamiliar place. "Just forget it," I said aloud. "It never happened."

When I returned home, I found that my roommate Mickey was out. Feeling grateful for that, I made my way slowly to the bathroom where I cleaned off the dried blood, tending to my bruised and swollen face, to the torn and swollen lips of my mouth and anus, to the bloodied cuts on my scrotum and neck, even as I repeated over and over again, "It never happened."

As difficult as it may be to believe, I quickly rid myself of any evidence and any conscious memory of my rape. Although my rectum bled for days afterward, I no longer had any conscious memory of why it should.

Although I succeeded in burying any conscious memory of the entire ordeal, I was victimized by it for decades afterward as it lay like a burning ember in the depths of my subconscious mind.

I started overeating and gradually gained weight, unconsciously soothing my wounded soul while finding a way to protect myself at the same time. If I made myself unattractive enough, no one would ever want to hurt me in that way ever again. Gaining weight was a scream for help. But no one, least of all myself, was listening.

As far as the rape was concerned, I would not listen to myself again for the next 40 years.

******

I moved to Los Angeles in February 1976. Not knowing a soul in L.A., and having little money, I slept in my car, camped overnight at state parks, and used park facilities to shower. Since I typed fast, I worked every day at temporary secretarial jobs.

My first few months in Los Angeles were disheartening, depressing, and terribly lonely. I kept working temp jobs as a secretary until I finally came up with enough cash to get myself a tiny studio apartment on Normandy Avenue in Hollywood. And little by little I feathered my nest. Eventually, I found permanent employment working as an office assistant and payroll manager for Job Shop, a temporary employment agency in downtown L.A., with the understanding that I would need time off for auditions.

Determined not to have sex with any man in L.A. until we made a commitment to one another, when I explained this to the first gay men I dated in Los Angeles, they laughed in my face. Still, I hoped to meet and fall in love with a man in a place in L.A. less shameful than the restrooms where I had met men in Utah, but I had yet to find that place or the man of my dreams. Instead, I soon discovered that gay men preferred anonymous sex.

In June of 1976 in Los Angeles, I marched in my first gay pride parade. It took a lot of guts back then to do so, even in a large city like Los Angeles, where one risked being pelted with tomatoes, rocks or worse. By that time you couldn't use the 'n-word' in public without serious social repercussions, but you could still call a lesbian a dyke or a gay man a faggot, and no one, except the dyke or faggot, would look at you askance. We were still just fags, the homos and queers that most Americans loved to demonize.

The streets along the parade route were lined with fundamentalist Christians, carrying signs that read "God hates Fags!" and "Kill the Queers!" And they shouted at us, hurling similar epithets.

My efforts to begin my career as a professional actor and writer in L.A. did not go well at first. Since I could not get in to see a single agent, I had yet to be submitted for any acting role. Everyone, it seemed, gave me the same advice, whether I asked for it or not: "To make it in this business, you've got to have a name!"

On top of that, I was in a huge catch-22: Not yet a union actor, I was not eligible to be submitted for any union job, and without the offer of a union job, I could not become a union member of either SAG or AFTRA, or of the Actors' Equity Association.

Then I hit on an idea: I would write and perform a one-man play. If I needed to have a name, I would make one for myself. And if the show received good notices, it would open doors. When I chose Oscar Wilde's life and works as the subject of my one-man play it was not surprising, given the research that I had already begun on Wilde at BYU. If anything, my brush with the Mormons at BYU had given me insight into what Wilde had to contend with in his battle with the Victorians. I believe this was partly why my performance as Wilde proved to be so compelling to audiences.

In addition to writing the script, I composed original music and lyrics for my one-man play, and I turned to Stacey Taylor, who was still living at home with her parents in Sacramento at the time, to do the musical arrangements. Stacey and her brother came to Los Angeles to record the soundtrack that I later used in performance, with Stacey on the piano and her brother on flute.

Prior to opening *Wild Oscar*—as my one-man play was originally titled—I was cautioned by many in the film industry that playing a gay character in Hollywood would be ruinous to my acting career. In fact, the first acting agent that I signed with after the play opened, cautioned me against coming across as gay. "Most of the male casting directors in the business are gay. But if they think you're in the same club, they won't cast you in a million years, no matter how good of an audition you give."

"Why?" I asked, wide-eyed and still naïve.

"They don't want to get the reputation that they are casting *their* boys," he explained simply. "Mind you, if they know you're gay, they'll expect you to give them certain favors. But if you come across as gay, if you're out of the closet, they'll avoid you like the fucking plague."

Looking back on it now, I did pay a high price for using a play like *The Wilde Spirit*—what I later renamed the show—to launch my Hollywood career, as it probably hurt my burgeoning acting career in L.A. more than it helped. But it was more important to me then, as now, to act in something meaningful than in something commercial. Things might have turned out quite differently for me as a young actor in Hollywood had I not ventured into what was then taboo territory. I could have played macho leading men since I had the looks for it back then and I came across as quite masculine, but I certainly didn't see myself that way at the time. If anything, I still saw myself as the overweight actor I was at BYU.

My grandfather Alvin Hamp passed away on May 13, 1977, less than a month before my one-man play was scheduled to open. Though I was in rehearsals and pre-production publicity and promotion, I went home to Pocatello to attend the funeral.

During the memorial service, I remembered how I had once confronted Grandpa in the kitchen of his home one early morning during one of my many sleepovers as a young child. "Grandpa," I had asked, as I watched him make his morning coffee while serving Grandma the tea she always drank. "How come you drink coffee and Grandma drinks tea? Aren't you Mormons like us?"

Grandpa Hamp had choked on his reply. "Of course, we are."

He had taken a careful pause. "We're just different kinds of Mormons than your Mom and Dad."

"But everyone at church says that drinking coffee and tea is a terrible sin," I replied, trying to reconcile the conflict.

"Well, maybe that's true, I don't know," he replied, coughing. "Do you think your Grandma and I are sinners?"

"No, I don't!" I said. In fact, I knew them to be good people.

"Oh, Alvin, dry up!" Grandma Hamp interjected. It was one of her favorite sayings, and inevitably whenever she said it, Grandpa fell silent. "Besides, Kerry Lynn, you're wrong about your Grandpa," Grandma added. "He's a sinner. He could never keep his thing in his pants."

I had no idea what she was talking about then, any more than I did as I sat in the ward chapel at Grandpa's funeral service, sitting between my mother and grandmother, holding both of their hands, and remembering him only as the loving grandfather I had always known him to be.

When I returned to Los Angeles the following day, I resumed rehearsals for *Wild Oscar*, scheduled to open in June.

How can I describe the magic that happened onstage at the opening night of my one-man play in Los Angeles at the New Playwrights Foundation on June 7, 1977? By that time, I had performed in hundreds of plays, both in high school and at BYU, and I had twice worked as a professional actor in summer stock, but I had never been the only actor on stage and the sole communicator of my own words as a playwright. The feeling was heady, but if anything, it was humbling.

I had a case of nerves prior to making my entrance, particularly since I knew that I was going out onstage alone to face both the public and the critics, and that as solo performer, playwright, lyricist, and composer, it was only my head on the chopping block if I failed. But after making my entrance, a very peaceful and serene feeling came over me. I have never felt a greater sense of personal power, that sense of doing what I was born to do and being full alive in the moment, as I did that night when I performed my one-man play for the very first time before the public. This became true of every one of the thousands of performances of *The Wilde Spirit* that I later gave over the course of the next 20 years, but it was never more apparent to me than on opening night, a night that I shall always remember and treasure.

Dad couldn't make it to opening night because of his work, but Mom was sitting front and center, and she led the standing ovation as I took my bows that night. A staunch Mormon who didn't care for the subject matter, Mom nonetheless fiercely supported my work and talent.

When we got back to my studio apartment in Hollywood, Mom confronted me directly. "Kerry," she asked, "why did you go into that … *ho-ho-homosexual* aspect?" The word *homosexual* stuck in her throat. I guess she saw the look of hurt that crossed my face, since she rushed to continue. "You know I loved the play. And you were wonderful in it! But why the … *ho-ho-homosexual* part?" Again, the word stuck in her throat! It was all she could do just to say the word aloud. "Couldn't you have left that out?" she pressed.

I was flummoxed as to how to respond. My mother had encouraged and understood my love of the theater. She had taken me to all of the shows at our hometown university, when no one else in my family wanted to. She alone had understood my desire to be both a writer and actor, and she alone had taught me to believe that I could accomplish anything I set my mind to. Furthermore, Mom was still in deep grief over the recent loss of her father. "Mom," I said, "you always taught me to tell the truth, and that is what I tried to do in my play."

"Yes, but why talk about his being … *homosexual?*" she asked. At least she hadn't stuttered on the word this time.

"I couldn't tell his story without including the facts," I said.

"But homosexuality isn't normal!" Mom replied solemnly.

Suddenly I knew that we were not talking about Wilde at all, but about me. How should I respond? I wanted to be honest but loving. Mom had come all the way from Idaho for my opening night. "Mom," I explained, "it was normal for him."

She eyed me up and down as mothers do. Finally she offered her verdict: "Maybe it was normal for him, but not for anyone else!" Meaning not for her baby, not for the star in her crown.

My one-man play received acclaim from most Los Angeles critics, and I moved the show from one venue to the next over the course of the next two years. One critic awarded me Best Actor and Best Director and picked mine as the Best Play of the Los Angeles season, an honor I shared with David Rabe for his new play, *In the Boom Room*, but this didn't mean much to the Hollywood elite.

Feeling disappointed with the results of my success, at least as far as my acting and writing career was concerned, I made the mistake of confiding these feelings to Dad during a long talk on the phone. "Well," Dad offered, "maybe if you wrote something that our Heavenly Father approved of, He would help open doors for you in Hollywood." Ouch! That comment hurt me deeply and shamed me to the core. But I said nothing.

At least I landed a booking at UCLA's Schoenberg Hall, which eventually led to professional engagements at university and college campuses all across America. And thanks to casting director David Graham, I got a gig as an extra on *Three's Company* during the show's first two seasons, helping me obtain my union cards in both the Screen Actors Guild and AFTRA.

Coming on the set in the TV studio on a Wednesday, with the regular cast having already rehearsed that week's show for the previous two days, I was welcomed by Jack Ritter, Joyce DeWitt, Suzanne Somers, and the rest of the cast. They and all of the crew helped me feel that I belonged. I acted like I belonged, but part of me felt terribly insecure. The shame within me, a deep shame I always tried to hide, nipped at me with vengeful questions: Did I really belong or would the cast and crew soon discover that I was an untalented fraud?

When David Graham later cast me in the TV pilot *Whodunit,* appearing opposite Eve Arden and Cesar Romero, I again wondered: Do I belong in this club? Am I enough? Such questions would plague me for many years to come.

Meanwhile, after Grandpa Hamp's death, my grandmother's health went steadily downhill, and I found myself back in Pocatello in October, to attend another heartbreaking funeral.

Dearly loved as she was, we all deeply grieved Grandma Hamp's passing, and she was dearly missed by all of us.

******

Harlan's 24th birthday arrived in March 1972. To celebrate, our gang went to a movie together and then to Hawkins Drive-In afterward to celebrate with root beer floats.

"Here's to Kerry," Harlan pronounced, "the best young playwright and actor in the whole of Mormon Zion!"

"To Kerry!" Bridget said, raising her float high in the air.

"And here's to Bridget Peters," Harlan said, "the gifted writer who has dated Kerry all these months without losing her temper or her virginity!" The girls gasped in righteous horror, but Ma and Pa Hawkins laughed.

"Why are you toasting me and Bridget?" I asked. "It's Harlan's birthday! Here's to Harlan on his 24th birthday!"

We all lifted our frosty mugs and drank to Harlan, even as the thought raced across my mind: Harlan was six years older than me; he was a man of 24, and I was still a boy of 18.

Harlan was caught by surprise, as we hoped he would be, when Jack and I ran out to the car, pulling out all of Harlan's birthday presents from Oscar's trunk, along with a birthday cake, which we lit outside before bringing in. We had previously asked Ma and Pa Hawkins to put the lights out when we brought the cake inside. So, placing the cake on the table in the dark with all of the candles lit, in front of Harlan, we all sang "Happy Birthday." And then Harlan made a wish before blowing out the 24 candles on his cake.

As we all applauded, as the overhead lights came back on, it was obvious to all of us that Harlan was quite overwhelmed by the warmth of our celebration and the obvious love he felt within that small dining room. "Wow!" Harlan gasped. "I wasn't expecting this! Thank you everybody!"

"We love you, Harlan!" I shouted. "Happy Birthday!"

Barbra Streisand's fifth film, the screwball comedy *What's Up, Doc?* opened to great reviews that same month. Like all of Streisand's films up to that point, it was a huge hit at the box office. Since Harlan didn't care for Streisand, I took Bridget to Salt Lake City to see the film before March ended, standing in a long line outside the theater to get tickets. A comic masterpiece, the film did not disappoint either of us.

During the early part of April, as the weather warmed and the snow melted, I took Bridget for a ride in Provo Canyon. The Provo River was brimming with fresh mountain water; dogwood and cherry trees were in bloom; the smell of evergreen was in the air, and Bridal Veil Falls cascaded from a sheer cliff. "It's beautiful," Bridget cooed. "Can we stop?"

"Yea, verily," I replied, steering Oscar off the road and parking. The waterfall fell from hundreds of feet above to the river flowing less than 20 yards from the car. Fruit trees sported pink blossoms in contrast to the green pines on the mountains. "Isn't it glorious?" I asked, as Bridget and I walked hand-in-hand across the bridge in front of the falls. I had never loved a girl as much as Bridget, but I had never kissed her. I knew that this was the moment. Yet, I hesitated. I wanted to be normal, but I hadn't even a vague idea of what to do with my lips. Using the movies as inspiration, I awkwardly pressed my mouth onto hers and prayed for passion.

It felt like I was kissing my mother, but Bridget moaned softly, apparently in heaven. Now that I had her in heaven, what was I supposed to do with her? Maybe I just needed practice, I told myself.

As I attempted to kiss Bridget in the same way Ryan O'Neal had kissed Barbra in *What's Up, Doc?,* I could feel Bridget's nipples stiffen, pressing through her clothing to push against my chest, yet I felt only embarrassment. Moaning with her, I feigned desire. And then the Great Epiphany happened!

As soon as I fantasized that I was kissing Harlan, not Bridget, I got an erection. Suddenly I understood. Even though I had long known I felt a sexual attraction to Harlan, I had passed it off as a phase that I would grow out of. Suddenly, I couldn't deny my true feelings for Harlan any longer. "I'm not going through a phase," I thought. "I'm in love with Harlan! I'm in love with him!"

Reeling from my epiphany, I tore away from Bridget. I knew I had to do something dramatic to alter the path I was on emotionally.

"Sweetie," I said tenderly, "we don't want to do anything we'll regret later. I want us to wait until later, when and if we get married."

"Are you asking me to marry you?" she asked, as tears welled up in her beautiful hazel eyes.

"No," I said, perhaps too abruptly, and then I rushed to explain. "I mean, not yet. I mean, you deserve to have a formal proposal, and I don't think either one of us are ready yet for such a big step. Besides, I don't want to get married until I've served my mission." I paused and took a deep breath. "If we do decide to get married, would you be willing to wait for me for two years while I serve my mission?"

"Of course I would! I love you, Kerry, with all my heart."

I took her in my arms and kissed her as passionately as I could.

Harlan asked me again in April if I wanted to go with him to the gym. Given my recent epiphany, this time I found no excuses.

When we left for the gym at dusk, a purple glow was on the snow-capped mountains, a scent of spring in the air.

When we walked into the locker room, the sight of naked men made me shiver. Harlan threw his gym bag on the bench, opened a locker, and began stripping out of his clothes. I stood frozen in place. "Aren't you going to get changed?" he asked, his voice sounding husky and every bit as steamy as the room itself.

"Yeah," I said quickly, opening a locker. "I'll hurry." I added, removing my shirt and hanging it in the locker. But feeling self-conscious about my body, I left my undershirt on. Unable to remove my eyes from Harlan's muscular back or broad shoulders that tapered to his slender waist, I felt an erection rising inside my shorts. Then, when he carefully lowered his garments—since they were considered holy and should never touch the ground—my face flushed red.

126

"How you coming, Kerry?" Harlan asked, trying to sound nonchalant.

"Fine," I replied hoarsely. Though I had seen him in only a quick and furtive glance, the sight of Harlan naked burned a permanent image in my brain that would stay with me forever. His body was hard, compact, and well-defined, but not overly muscular, with broad shoulders and a well-developed chest that tapered to a defined six-pack and tiny waist. Then, the brief glimpse of his naked buttocks, firm and smooth like molded sculpture, left me shaking and unsteady. Catching a similar glimpse of his genitals, I thought I saw evidence of a budding erection, even more prominent than my own, or had I imagined it? Scanning past his crotch to his muscular thighs and spread legs, I averted my eyes to the floor.

"You better hurry, Babe," he said, interrupting my thoughts.

"Yeah, okay," I muttered, stealing another glance as Harlan bent over to pull on his jock strap. Seeing how the white straps curved tightly around his ass, and how the white pouch stretched around the sack between his legs, made me feel as though I might orgasm involuntarily. As I folded my socks and stuffed them in my locker, my brain sizzled with erotic images that I did not want to accept.

As Harlan pulled on his trunks, he prodded, "Come on, Babe. We haven't got all night!"

"I feel sick," I uttered. "I need to go to the bathroom."

"You want me to help you in there?"

"No, you go ahead, start your workout. I'll meet you in a few minutes in the gym."

"Sure thing, Babe," he said, pulling on his sweatshirt.

As soon as he headed for the gym, I ran to the bathroom and locked myself in a toilet stall, pulling down my pants and underwear before sitting down. My erection ached for release, yet I knew if I succumbed to masturbation that I would soon commit more heinous sins, staining my sacred oaths as a priesthood holder. Fifteen minutes passed, as I stared at my erection with disdain.

Kneeling in the stall, I prayed fervently for my very soul. "Please, Heavenly Father, help me and give me the strength to resist temptation. I ask for these blessings in the name of Jesus Christ. Amen."

It took another 15 minutes of math and silent tears before my erection subsided. "Thank you, Heavenly Father," I whispered gratefully, finally getting off my knees and running back to the locker room to finish changing.

I felt relieved until I walked into the gym and saw Harlan bench-pressing, and my unwanted erection returned. No amount of prayer would ever change how I felt about Harlan or about the sight of naked men. When Harlan finished his routine and got up from the workout bench, I quickly explained, "Harlan, I'm still sick. I'm going to head home. But you stay and finish."

"You sure?" Harlan asked, wiping his hand on his sweatshirt.

"Yea, verily!" I retorted.

I dressed and ran from the locker room, remembering the two questions Harlan had once asked me as we stood facing each other in a snowy field one morning, almost in accusation: "You don't know yet, do you, Kerry?" he had questioned. "Know what?" I had asked in return. "What you are?" he had answered.

I ran into the bushes and vomited.

******

The first time I dabbled with S&M in L.A. nearly cost me my life. It wasn't that my sexual partner meant to hurt me; it was only that he was just as inexperienced as I was. Dressed in leather from head to boots, he ordered me to strip naked and handcuffed my wrists behind me. Sitting on my chest, with all his weight on top of me, he pressed my handcuffed wrists underneath into the hardwood floor, even as he shoved his large cock down my throat. I could feel the cuffs cutting into my wrists and I would have told him so, had his 7-incher not been shoved down my throat at the same time. The weight of his body blocked my air passages. With my mouth and throat stuffed with cock and his groin pressed tightly against my nostrils, I couldn't breathe. I was suffocating!

I panicked, trying to push him off me, but I was handcuffed. He was blissfully unaware that I would soon lose consciousness, as he closed his eyes in ecstasy until his orgasm. Only after he finally pulled his softening penis from my mouth, could I finally breathe again. "You nearly killed me!" I exclaimed, still gasping for breath. Once he saw that my face had turned blue and that my wrists were bleeding, he apologized.

One of the other anonymous sexual encounters I experienced a little while later during my time in L.A. helped me heal at least some of my accumulated inner shame. It happened in the men's room of the YMCA in downtown L.A., very near Macarthur Park. The man I met there—a short but extremely handsome Hispanic— might have been sent from Heaven itself to intercede on my behalf, because after our sexual liaison was finished, he made a point of saying, "You're so fucking hot! You have the hottest nips, and you have a beautiful cock! I love that curve! It's so sexy." His compliment caught me by surprise. Could my so-called physical abnormalities actually be assets? "Thank you," I replied. "That means more to me than I can say. I've always been ashamed that my erection curves, and that my nipples are abnormally large."

"You're kidding!" he said, flashing me an enormous smile. "If I had a chest like yours, I'd walk around everywhere with my shirt off! As for your cock, not only are you a bit longer and thicker than average, it has a beautiful shape! What more could any man wish for?" Then he noticed that I was still erect after having cum. "And look at that! You're still hard! That's amazing!"

"Sometimes I have to cum more than once before I can lose an erection," I admitted sheepishly. "I'm ashamed of that, too."

"That's nothing to be ashamed of! God made you a stud!"

"I don't think so," I replied. "I'm just weirder than most men!"

"Do you have any idea how many men would kill to have that kind of virility, me included?" He gave me a big smile, adding, "Don't ever forget how handsome and special you are!"

And then he left, closing the door behind him.

"Thank you for saying that," I said aloud, to an empty restroom.

In that moment, I finally realized that my nipples, my virility, and the slight curve of my erection were no longer things that I needed to apologize for. These were gifts that I became increasingly grateful for from that time forward.

One night in 1978, I got picked up in a Los Angeles leather bar by a handsome, leather-clad bodybuilder. He took me back to his Los Feliz apartment and tried to introduce me to kinky sex, but I wasn't up for it. "You seem uptight about sex," he observed.

"I guess I am," I said. And then I told him about myself.

Later he pulled a book off the shelf, signed it, and handed it back to me. "Here," he said, "It's my gift to you."

It was *The Sexual Outlaw* by John Rechy.

John Rechy was only the first of several gay celebrities who sought to help me heal my inner shame through a sexual encounter. Another was James Leo Herlihy, author of *Midnight Cowboy*, who encouraged my writing career while attempting to discourage me from worshipping his fame and success. I couldn't understand what he hoped I could see at that time—that I had self-worth regardless of success or failure in my career—since I was still too filled with shame to understand anything, other than my blind ambition to become famous.

Like many young and physically attractive hopefuls, I also had to contend with sexual harassment in the meat market that was the film industry of that time, just as many young women and young gay men still do today within the Hollywood system. One Casting Director, the Head of the Casting Department at a major film studio—a truly ugly man both inside and out—promised to make me a star if only I would have sex with him. I didn't, so I'm not.

******

On a warm sunny afternoon in April of 1972, as Harlan and I washed our cars in his backyard, I announced my recent decision.

"Harlan, I've decided not to go on a mission this year."

Harlan dropped the bucket of water in his hands. "What?"

130

"I want to wait a while, at least another year and then decide."

"I hope it isn't because of what I told you about my mission experience," he said, sounding rather guilty.

"It has nothing to do with you or what you said," I said, lying utterly. "It's my decision. I'm not sure I'm ready to serve a mission."

"Have you told your folks?" he asked.

I shook my head no.

"I don't blame you a bit. Your parents are going to have a cow!"

"I know," I replied, feeling the weight of my decision. "Geez!"

I met with President Wilkinson soon after that and explained my reason for not wanting to go on a mission.

"I'm still having sexual feelings for other men," I admitted. "I want to get a handle on that before I serve a mission."

"I understand, Kerry. That shows integrity," Wilkinson replied. "We'll put your mission call on hold until you're ready."

"Thank you, Sir," I said. "I appreciate your understanding."

While taking the final exam for my religion course at the end of my first BYU semester, I tried to concentrate on questions about *The Book of Mormon*—about the Prophets Mormon and Moroni, and both the Nephites who once populated the Americas. But I kept thinking of how Harlan might look dressed in the uniform of a Nephite soldier. I recalled how virile he had looked bench-pressing, his strong arms glistening with sweat as he moved the weights up and down, matching his strength against the weights and winning gracefully. Then I fantasized how Jack might look dressed in only a Nephite loincloth, quite confused by the intense sexual attraction I felt to both men but in very different ways.

I contemplated tearing my exam to shreds, but I didn't.

Good, people-pleasing Mormon boys never do things like that.

Spring arrived at the end of our freshman year. Within a few weeks, Mickey went to England, to spend two years there, converting lost souls to the church. Bridget returned to Salt Lake City to live with her parents and to work at the public library that summer to earn more money for school. Jennifer headed south to Mesquite, Nevada to work at her family's store and gas station. Jack

Young went back to his small hometown in Ohio. Harlan stayed in Provo. And I returned to Pocatello to work a summer job, feeling trapped inside my Mormon sugar bowl existence.

When Mormon men turn 19, they are expected to be ordained Elders in the higher Melchizedek Priesthood, go to the Temple to make sacred covenants with God, and go on a mission. On my 19th birthday, I declined to do all three. My parents were stunned, of course, and more than a little disappointed in me.

Harlan had asked me if I would consider moving in with him at the beginning of our sophomore year in the fall. It only made sense; I often stayed overnight at his place anyway. Yet the thought of being in the same bedroom with him, being so close to the temptation of him constantly, filled me with a horrible self-awareness. "I dunno, Harlan," I had replied squeamishly. "It may not be a good idea."

"You practically live here already," he had reminded me. "You don't even have to pay rent; you can live here for free."

"I can pay my share. That's not the problem."

"What's the problem then?" he had asked, seemingly afraid I might answer him with the truth. I looked into his eyes, my body and soul needing him, and I wanted to cry. I wanted us to live together, too. But I knew I had to say no, so I lied.

"My parents already paid a deposit with my landlady. I can't back out now; it wouldn't be fair to her."

"Guess I'll just keep you as a part-time roomie then," he had said.

At the beginning of our sophomore year, Harlan and I were again assigned to the same BYU family that we were part of as freshmen, though our BYU brothers like Mickey—who had left to serve missions—were replaced either by new freshmen male students or by RMs like my new roommate Doug, a short but likable Elder who was quiet and shy, quite short, and a few years older than me, and who had just returned from his mission.

One of my first artistic efforts that semester was directing my first published play, *Buffalo Head Nickels*, as a project for a directing class, and presenting it in October at the Arts Center. When the show was presented in October, my parents attended, driving down from

Pocatello to see the show. In fact, Mom and Jack started the standing ovation at curtain call.

On Sunday, Mom and Dad went with me to church on campus. After Opening Exercises finished on Sunday morning, President Wilkinson stopped us in the hallway on our way to Sunday school classes, to chat with us. "Geez!" I thought, "if he tells my parents anything about my problem, I'll kill him." I tried to sound cheerful when I said, "Good morning, President Wilkinson!"

"Good morning, Brother Ashton!" he replied. I responded quickly, introducing him to my parents, as they exchanged greetings and friendly Mormon handshakes. "It's a pleasure to meet you both," Wilkinson proffered. "Your son has mentioned you both so often."

"Only saying good things, I hope," Dad joked awkwardly.

"Oh, of course," President Wilkinson replied. "He loves you both very much."

Needless to say, I was relieved when my parents left for home that afternoon. I didn't want them hurt by whispers in BYU's halls.

Whenever I attempted to sleep that semester and closed my eyes, I would either see Harlan standing naked before me like an idol demanding worship, or I would see Jack, boyish and cuddly and naked, kneeling before me. Believing that I would break my vows of chastity and masturbate if I closed my eyes, I tried to sleep with my eyes wide open. Racked with sexual tension, I often lay awake all night. By late October, I was masturbating nightly, inevitably fantasizing either about Harlan or Jack.

Even worse, I felt overwhelmed by a new and mysterious desire to serve men orally, something I did not know how to handle. In a particularly self-destructive act, I even wrote my phone number on the wall inside a bathroom stall in a Fine Arts Center men's room, with the words, "Call for a good time!"

One night, as I sat studying at my desk, the phone rang. When I answered, I could hear someone breathing lustfully on the other end. "Hello?" I asked. "Is anyone there?" Finally the voice on the other end said, "I'm calling for … a good time."

My penis instantly stiffened in my pants. "Yes," I replied, breathless with excitement. "I'm up … for that."

"Me, too," he said. "Can you meet me in the Fine Arts Center parking lot?"

"Yes," I said. "How soon?"

"Half-an-hour," he replied.

The man was parked in the Harris Fine Arts Center parking lot, precisely where he said he would be. I got in the car, and we talked for a bit. He was a balding, older gentleman that I recognized as Dr. Owen Banes, a Music Professor on campus. He recognized me too, from my stage performances that had attracted a lot of attention.

Dr. Banes warned me about the Standards Office. "They're like the Gestapo! They can be merciless if they catch you."

At the professor's insistence, I walked into the Harris Fine Arts Center and removed the graffiti I had left on a men's room wall, while Dr. Banes waited for me in his car in the parking lot.

As I made my way from the professor's car to the Harris Fine Arts Center, I had no idea that two undercover BYU Security Police-men had Dr. Banes under surveillance, or that they were watching from an unmarked car at the other end of the nearly empty lot.

When I returned to his car, Dr. Banes drove me back to his place. Unknown to me at the time, the unmarked car followed behind us. The undercover BYU Security Police even took photos of us as we stood together on the professor's front porch, as the professor struggled to find his key in the dark. Once inside his darkened living room, Dr. Banes fell to his knees, greedily providing me with oral service. It felt wonderful, but it did not meet my deep, newfound craving to serve a man in precisely the same way.

******

While in L.A., I joined *Affirmation*, a new organization founded as a social and support group for gay ex-Mormons. As new members joined, however, a schism developed between those like myself, who wanted it to remain a supportive social organization, and those who wanted our meetings to become church services where we could worship in a traditional Mormon manner. Cutting to the core of the conflict, I asked one of our new members a direct question: "Why would you want to be a member of a church that is anti-gay in every respect?"

I was delighted when Dom and his wife and baby moved to Los Angeles, and Dom joined our local chapter of *Affirmation* while I was still a member. But the conflict between those who still identified as Mormon and those who did not became so dire that I finally left the organization.

Affirmation has since grown into a global organization with chapters all around the world, but this conflict still exists within the ranks of its members, between those who want to identify as LDS and those who need to classify themselves as ex-Mormon.

Unfortunately, Dom divorced his wife soon after moving to L.A., and he and I became roommates, sharing a two-bedroom apartment together in West Hollywood.

In the three years I spent in Los Angeles I moved from being destitute and sleeping in my car to becoming star and author of a celebrated play, but with not much to show for it other than two union cards and three critic's awards.

Deciding that Los Angeles had been the wrong place to start my career, I made plans to move to New York City.

Dom came to a similar conclusion, and we decided to move together to Manhattan in January. Selling Oscar to raise money for the move, I stored my things in L.A., and spent Christmas in Idaho with my parents. By that time, my family knew that I was inactive in the LDS Church—the Mormon term for apostasy. My parents reacted during that Christmas holiday as I expected they would, by fasting and praying, by putting my name on the Temple prayer list, and by trying in every way to coerce me back into the fold.

Before I flew east to join Dom in Manhattan on January 9, 1979, Dad insisted on giving me another Father's Blessing, laying his hands upon my head and praying for my poor, demented soul.

Two weeks after Dom Altman and I moved into our new Manhattan apartment in January 1979, Dom realized that New

York City was not for him and he returned to Los Angeles.

Feeling lonely and abandoned, I moved from the larger apartment that Dom and I had rented together on West 29th Street to a tiny studio apartment that I could barely afford, in a rundown, 4-floor walk-up on West 54th Street.

Stacey Taylor, along with a couple of other BYU friends, soon followed me to New York and our friendship continued to blossom. Stacey lasted longer than Dom, living in Manhattan for more than a year before returning to live with her parents in Sacramento. After that, we gradually lost track of each other.

Thanks to my 9th grade typing class at Alameda Junior High School, where I had learned how to type over 120 words per minute without error, I found immediate work as a "temp" secretary at hundreds of different corporations in the city, through various temporary employment agencies in midtown Manhattan.

Being a temp meant taking on the worst jobs that no permanent employee wanted to do; it meant usually being treated as a less-than, and as the ultimate joke in Manhattan employment, joining the legion of chronically unemployed actors in the city, the ones who did the typing, answered the phones, and made and served the coffee, who waited on the tables and did the dishes.

I hated working as an office temp and I felt deep shame about it, seeing each day that I was forced to work in an office as another sign of my failure to make a living as an actor and writer. But it kept the wolf from the door. And it gave me the option to take time off for auditions and interviews, and to quickly leave the job if I found any work as an actor. But I subsisted only on peanut butter and crackers for my diet and walking across the city to auditions to save money on the fifty cents for a subway token, just so I could avoid temp work as long as possible.

In one of my first career moves in New York, I convinced the owner of a cabaret on West 23rd Street to allow me to perform my one-man play on his intimate stage, and I managed to get Byron Belt, a critic for Newhouse newspapers, to attend a performance.

Byron loved my performance and admired my writing, and

came backstage afterward to tell me so. Byron became one of my best friends, introducing me to many wonderful experiences, taking me to see operas at the Met, ballets at New York City Ballet, and to dozens of Broadway shows, as he knew I could not afford such experiences on my own. In fact, most of my letters home that year mentioned Byron.

When Christmas approached that year, I had no idea how I would get from New York to Pocatello for the holidays, since I had no money to make the trip. Grudgingly, I accepted Mom's suggestion and hitched a ride with my truck-driving brother Dennis, who picked me up in front of my apartment on 54th Street.

Dennis cussed out the "goddamn faggots" at every truck stop during our trip home, but I am glad that I went home with him that year, as it would be the last Christmas I would spend with Mom. When I arrived at the new home on Elm Street in Pocatello, where my parents had recently moved, I felt grateful just to be home.

Later, as Mom and I decorated the tree in her beautiful new living room, she brought up a delicate subject. "You mentioned Byron a lot in your letters," she said cautiously, pausing to exhale a slow breath. "Is he … *ho-ho-homosexual*?" she asked, the word homosexual still seemed to stick in her throat.

"Yes," I admitted, "he's gay."

"I thought he might be," she replied, after several seconds of silence. Then she asked another question. "Are you and he close?"

"Yes, Mom, we are," I said quietly. "He's one of my closest friends in New York."

Foolishly, I left it at that. Mom was inviting me to tell her about my sexual identity, but I was not yet ready to talk about it.

In the spring of 1980, I got a job in Manhattan working as an office boy at The Lantz Office, owned by Robert Lantz, known to virtually everyone in show business as Robby.

Robby had a talent roster that read like the Who's Who of Show Business; he received more calls in one day than most receive in a year, but he returned every call. I worked for Mr. Lantz for only six months, but I met and dealt with hundreds of his famous clients. Every time I encountered a celebrity, I compared myself to them, and always came up short. In my eyes, I would never be enough, not until I became as famous as they were.

Despite the famous clientele that Mr. Lantz represented, my job in The Lantz Office was hardly glamorous. I typed letters, answered phone calls all day, took and left messages, made coffee, ran errands, and typed endless messages on the telex machine. I was simply the office boy.

After awhile, none of the calls from celebrities threw me, until I answered the phone one afternoon and heard an unmistakable voice speaking on the other end of the line.

"Hello," she said. "Is Robby there? This is Barbra Streisand calling." The Goddess that I had worshipped since I saw *Funny Girl* at the age of 15 was on the other end of the line, and she was speaking directly to me! Trying to remain calm, I replied, "I'll see if Mr. Lantz is available."

I put Streisand on hold and in my excitement ran into Robby's office, interrupting his international call with Elizabeth Taylor. "What is it?" Mr. Lantz asked, looking up from his desk.

"I have Barbra on the phone," I stammered.

"Barbra?" he queried, as if there was more than one. "Oh, Barbra! Okay. I'm on the phone with Liz. Ask her to hold or I'll call her back."

"Yes, Mr. Lantz," I replied. My face turned crimson as I ran back to the phone at my desk.

It was no secret to anyone working in the office that I adored Barbra. So everyone working in the office had gathered around my desk to watch how I handled the call.

I picked up the phone, and spoke as calmly as I could. "Miss Streisand?"

"Yes?" she replied sweetly. Barbra had been on hold for at least three minutes, but she seemed understanding about it, far more than most of the celebrities I dealt with on the phone every day.

"Mr. Lantz is on an international call," I explained calmly, trying to act professional. "Would you like to hold?"

"I'm on the set and between takes, so you can put me on hold, as long as it isn't too many minutes."

When Mr. Lantz was still unable to speak to her in a few minutes, I picked up the phone again. "Ms. Streisand?" I asked.

"Yes," she replied, not putting on airs. She didn't need to. Being authentic was more than enough to get what she wanted.

"Unfortunately Mr. Lantz is still unavailable," I explained. "Would you like to leave a message or continue to hold?"

"Please tell Robby that I'm calling about *Yentl*," she said simply. "I want Alan and Marilyn Bergman to write all of the lyrics for the songs. Ask him to call me tonight at home if he can."

"Yes, Miss Streisand. I'll see that he gets the message."

"Thank you so much," she said politely. And then we each hung up the phone on both ends of our conversation.

The office employees who had gathered around my desk applauded. "You handled that beautifully," Bob Bishop, our Office Manager, said.

Barbra Streisand taught me that day that when one has real power, one doesn't need to be a bitch; one only needs to be authentic. After my encounter with Babs, I yearned to be authentic, too. More than that, I yearned to be famous and powerful like her.

******

A few weeks after encountering Professor Banes at BYU, I drove to the rest areas on Interstate 15 near Pleasant Grove, looking for a man to service orally, for what I believed would be my first time.

Finally a man drove into the rest area parking lot on a Harley-Davidson motorcycle. After he got off his motorcycle, taking off his helmet and hanging it on his bike, I began to salivate. Dressed in boots, leather chaps, and a leather jacket, he had black hair with a beard to match. Giving me a knowing glance as he walked to the restroom, I got out of my car and followed him into the restroom.

When I entered the bathroom, he was already standing at the only urinal next to the glory hole in the only stall wall. Casually looking over his shoulder and obviously jerking off, he smiled at me lasciviously, as though he knew precisely what I was looking for. Walking into the stall and locking the door behind me, I pulled down my pants abruptly and sat down on the toilet. Once I peered through the glory hole, I saw that his lengthy penis was not only erect but also very straight! As if I needed more evidence that my erection was abnormal! Yet this information only made my desire to service him even stronger: After all, he was a real man, and I was an aberration, one intended by nature to serve my betters.

I knelt and stuck my tongue through the glory hole as far as I could, literally begging him to allow me to take his penis into my mouth. He responded by teasing me, holding and playing with his erection just beyond the reach of my tongue. When he finally pushed the head toward my lips, I felt like an addict who had finally found his fix. His erect penis felt like heaven in my mouth.

Though I believed that I had never done this act before, it felt as though I were reenacting a past event.

I felt like I was doing a good job, despite my inexperience, until he pulled his erection out of my mouth, and tucked away his prize.

Seeing him leave, I got up from the toilet and ran after him, catching him outside. "Don't you want me to finish?" I entreated. "I'll swallow it for you."

"I bet you would," he replied, "but you're a lousy cocksucker!"

I was repulsed by his profanity, but I wanted to learn from my mistakes. "What did I do wrong?" I asked. "Please tell me."

"If I had a few hours I'd show you, Kid," he explained. "But I'm headed to San Francisco, and I have to make up time as it is."

"Please!" I begged. "I'm new at this. I want to learn."

"You're Mormon, aren't you?" he asked, softening his tone. I nodded affirmatively. "So was I," he replied. "That's why I'm in a hurry to get the fuck out of Utah!"

I tried my best to overlook his profanity. "So, will you teach me?" I begged. "Please?"

"I'll tell you what, Kid," he responded, "let's get in that classic Chevy of yours and I'll give you a few lessons."

Once we were inside my car, he began my lessons.

"The first thing you need to learn, Kid, is how to address any man you are lucky enough to serve. In a situation like this, where you're going to be sucking a man's cock, you should always address the man as "Sir," unless the man tells you otherwise. A true cocksucker needs to know how to obey and worship any man that he is allowed to serve and to please."

"Yes, Sir," I replied obediently.

"You have the right attitude, Kid, but you need to learn technique," he said. "Now, unzip my fly and take my cock out, but make sure that you keep eye contact with me the whole time."

When he said these words it felt familiar, as though another had instructed me in a similar but far more frightening way once before, but I couldn't place the memory. "Yes, Sir," I replied, obediently doing exactly as he suggested. Once I had his erection in my hand, I said, "You have a beautiful penis, Sir."

"Thank you, but don't call my cock a penis," he rushed to explain. "That's a cock, Kid!"

"I don't like using swear words like that," I said. "It's vulgar."

"Then you should quit right now, because you're too fucking conservative to learn what I can teach you," he scoffed loudly. "Now be a good boy and suck my cock!"

"Yes, Sir," I replied. Not thinking twice, I went down on him voraciously, but he stopped me.

"Kid, don't eat a man's cock like you're gobbling down a cheeseburger!" he said quietly, but in a tone that indicated he was losing his patience with me. "Worship that cock with your mouth and your lips!" I looked up at him quizzically. "Being allowed to suck a man's cock is both a privilege and an honor," he explained. "You should perform the act in a way that is both sacred and profane, all at the same time. Few men want a saint sucking them off. Most of us want cocksuckers to act like worshipping whores."

"Yes, Sir!" I said, slurping and licking, as I looked up into his eyes without breaking our eye contact. Suddenly I felt him jump.

"Jesus!" he exclaimed. "Watch the teeth, Kid!"

I took my mouth off his penis. "What did I do wrong now?"

"Don't let your teeth cut into the cock! Most men don't like being bit, anymore than I do!"

"I'm sorry. But how do I do it so you don't feel my teeth?"

"Wrap your lips down around your teeth," he instructed. He had me practice the technique, but he had a large erection and I kept gagging whenever he thrust deeply into my mouth. "You have to learn how to control your gag reflex," he insisted.

My leather professor trained me for hours until sunrise, when he finally realized the time. "Oh, wow!" he exclaimed. "I've gotta get outta here and hit the road."

"Thank you for teaching me," I exuded.

"You're a true cocksucker now, Kid," he replied. "I'm proud of you!" Then he hopped on his motorcycle and drove away.

******

It was two weeks after the Streisand episode, that Bob Bishop ran over to me where I was typing on the telex machine in The Lantz Office, and said in his most gentlemanly voice, "Kerry, these are contracts for Elizabeth Taylor's Broadway appearance in *The Little Foxes* that require her signature. I need you to take these to Miss Taylor's suite at the Lombardy Hotel. Miss Taylor needs to read these and sign all three copies of the contract. If her assistant Chen Sam is there, you'll deal with Chen directly. Either way, once Miss Taylor signs the contracts, leave one copy with her or with Chen, and bring the other two copies back to the office."

It was a summer afternoon but not at all humid, always a nice surprise during a New York summer. As I walked to the Lombardy Hotel nearby, I remembered how I had idolized Elizabeth Taylor, Bette Davis, and Julie Andrews in my youth, until Barbra took their place. I remembered how excited I was when my parents and I went to the Sunset Drive-In Theatre to see *Cleopatra*, watching from the back seat of our blue Ford Tempest as Elizabeth road into Rome on a sphinx.

Arriving at the door of Miss Taylor's hotel suite, I felt small and unimportant. But I rang the bell anyway.

A moment passed and then Elizabeth Taylor answered the door. Not the butler or the maid. Not her assistant Chen Sam. It was Elizabeth Taylor herself, in little makeup, and dressed in an elegant but comfortable white pantsuit. I was amazed by her beauty, and particularly mesmerized by her violet eyes.

"Hello," she said graciously, "You must be Kerry."

"Yes, Miss Taylor," I replied. "It's a pleasure to meet you."

"Thank you, Kerry," she said. "Please come in."

"Thank you, Miss Taylor," I said politely.

"Oh, just call me Liz," she said, giggling.

"I couldn't," I replied. "Mr. Lantz wouldn't approve."

"I'll tell you what, Kerry, I won't tell Robby if you don't!" Laughing, she motioned me to the sofa in her living room.

"Okay, Liz," I answered cautiously.

"What can I get you to drink?" she asked.

"Just some ice water, please," I replied.

"Would you like a snack?" Liz asked. "You must be hungry."

"Uh ... yes," I admitted. "I am, actually."

"Of course you are!" she said. "How could you not be? I know I could eat a horse!" She giggled. "And if you mention a word of this to Joan Rivers, I'll sue!" Although Miss Taylor had lost most of her excess weight and looked fabulous, Joan Rivers had continued to make fun of her. "Excuse me while I get your water and find something for us to snack on," she said, as she left the room, returning moments later with iced water and a plate of nuts.

"We're out of almost everything!" she explained. "In fact, I just sent Chen out to buy some snacks. But at least I managed to find us some cashews to chew on!"

"Great! I love them!"

"So do I!" she squealed. "Too much, I'm afraid!"

"Thank you, Liz," I said, eating some cashews. "You seem to know just how to make a person feel at ease."

"I had to learn how to do that at a tender age," she said.

Reclining on the sofa, Miss Taylor explained, "I had to simply to survive my childhood. At this point, all the fame and nonsense bores me to tears!" She let out a cackle—the same cackle heard in *Virginia Woolf*, in *Cat On a Hot Tin Roof*, and in many of her other great screen roles. As I learned that day, the cackle was authentic both to the star and to Elizabeth Taylor, whom I was growing to like. "Now," she said, turning on the lamp on the end table, "excuse me while I read the contract." After reading it, she laid all copies on the table. "No problems here," she said, giving me a smile. "Have you a pen, Kerry?"

"Of course," I replied, pulling a pen from the satchel and handing it to her. Once all three copies were signed, I scurried away. But Miss Taylor gave me more than some ice water and cashew nuts. Without knowing it, she taught me that no soul is more important than another. It was yet another lesson in confronting and lessening at least some of my inner shame.

I was not surprised when Liz later became AMFAR's ambassador, using her fame to force President Reagan to acknowledge for the first time that gay men were dying of AIDS. Not only was she a great star, she was a great human being.

******

On Halloween night 1972, our whole gang dressed up in costumes and went to the school dance. I went as a vampire with bloody fangs and a menacing black cape. Harlan dressed as a cowpoke in spurs and a huge cowboy hat. Bridget went as a witch on a broomstick. Jack went as a circus clown, and Debbie came as Snow White. But Jennifer outshone us all. Using her nickname as inspiration, she came as an angel with a halo encircling her head.

Bridget and I watched the cowboy dancing with his angel from the sidelines. "Vat do you think about Jenny?" I asked, doing my best Bela Lugosi impression.

"She looks like she just got off the train from the Celestial Kingdom," Bridg replied. "I hope you're not going to bite her neck later on tonight!"

"Not at all. That is vat I have planned for you!" I said, as I came toward her with my fake teeth, as she scurried away laughing.

I couldn't help thinking how handsome and sexy Harlan looked as a cowboy. The costume accentuated his masculinity, especially when contrasted with the petite and wholesome angel in his arms.

Suddenly, I found myself wishing that I had dressed as the cowboy's angel, not as a vampire. I also thought Jack looked quite sexy and cute in his clown outfit. It seemed to bring out the best of his boyish good looks. And Debbie, whom I still didn't know very well, looked adorable as Snow White.

"I have an idea!" I announced later that evening, as we sat outside the ballroom in between dances. "Why don't we trick-or-treat the President's Mansion?"

"The president of the university?" Jennifer asked shyly.

"Why not?" I asked. "He lives right here on campus, not even that far away. What could be more convenient?"

"I don't think it's a good idea," Angel said, obviously quite concerned. "What do you think, Harlan?"

Harlan offered her a wide grin. "What can it hurt? I think it sounds fun. Besides, when Kerry sets his heart on something, you might as well go along!"

I laughed. "Besides, Angel, why shouldn't the president see us as we really are?"

Bridget cackled. "Are you saying I look like a witch all the time?"

"Not at all, my little pretty!" I exclaimed, doing an impression of the Wicked Witch of the West.

After University President Dallin H. Oaks answered his door, I spoke in a Transylvanian accent, saying, "Excuse me, but could you direct me to the nearest blood bank?"

"It's trick-or-treaters!" President Oaks announced excitedly, turning to his wife in the presidential living room. Apparently, none of the other 26,000 students had paid them a visit that night.

"Pardner, you best hand over some treats!" Harlan said in a well-done cowpoke drawl. "Or we'll have to play a trick on ya'll!"

President Oaks laughed in a good-natured manner. "Well," he said, "let's see if we can't roust up some treats for you kids!"

Harlan and I laughed, Bridget guffawed, and Jennifer quivered with obvious embarrassment, even as Jack the clown, boyishly athletic as he was, did a cartwheel on the presidential lawn, and Debbie's Snow White curtsied.

"You all right, Jen?" the considerate cowboy asked.

"I'm fine, I guess," Angel said. "I'm just too shy for this."

President Oaks returned with some candy bars in his hand. "There you go, Kids!" he said, distributing the candy among the four of us, obviously enjoying our visit. "Thanks for the visit!"

"You're welcome, Sir," I replied respectfully.

Then the witch and the angel, the clown and the princess, the cowpoke and I, disappeared into the fog of Halloween night.

When I visited Harlan at his apartment on Friday, November 3, I found him working on an oil painting.

"Wow!" I said, "That's beautiful work!"

"Really?" he exclaimed. "I'm glad you like it." He paused a moment. "You know, when you got me all of the art supplies for Christmas, it made me feel like I could start painting again. I owe all of this to you, Babe." We looked deeply into each other's eyes for a brief but intense moment. His manly eyes fondled with my feelings in ways Bridget's hazel eyes had not even begun to do.

"If you keep this up," I joked, "you won't have any space left on your walls by the end of the year!"

Harlan smiled, as he sat on his couch. "Think I should stop?"

"No way. I want to see every wall papered with the works of Harlan Alphonse LeClair! That goes for the ceiling, too! So, you better keep right on painting for all you're worth!"

Harlan's smile broadened even more as I joined him on the sofa.

By that time, I was completely in love with Harlan, of course, and I fantasized about making love to him almost constantly. But in the way I saw things then, Harlan couldn't possibly be gay; he was a Marine, for Heaven's sake! But Jack was quite another story. I had a strong suspicion that Jack might be in love with me. At least he gave me every indication that he had those sorts of feelings about me, short of taking me in his arms and asking for a kiss.

Having had only a few sexual experiences up to that time, and all of them in public restrooms except for a horrible and violent rape in a flophouse hotel that I had managed to erase from conscious memory, none of these experiences had been acts of lovemaking. I desperately needed to find a way to bring love and sex together. And I came to think of Jack as someone with whom I could finally make that happen. At least Jack Young wasn't a stranger in some public men's room. He was someone I knew and loved, or at least he was someone I cared about a great deal. And, unlike Harlan, I thought of Jack as having gay tendencies.

Since I knew that my roommate Doug would be away visiting his family the following weekend, I invited Jack to spend Sunday night with me at my apartment, and to have a sleepover.

On the night of November 5, 1972, Jack and I stood in the middle of my living room, eyeing each other with inevitable lust across the red shag carpet. As our eyes met, my heart thumped in my chest.

I quivered with excitement as he walked toward me, looking up into my brown eyes as I looked down into his soulful blues.

"I love you, Kerry," he whispered intently. "God help me, but I do." With exquisite deliberation, Jack moved his lips closer to mine. I closed my eyes and waited in anticipation until our lips met.

It was the first time that either of us had ever kissed another man, at least in a romantic way. I had, of course, had several sexual experiences by then, but kissing was an entirely different, and far more intimate and meaningful than any act of sex I had yet explored.

A sensitive exploration at first, our kiss stirred me to new heights of ecstasy. As passion flared, our lips became hot and wet with lust, his lips crushing mine with bruising impact.

Before I knew it, we had both stripped out of our clothes except for our underwear. I felt self-conscious. Slim and far tinier than me, Jack had a tighter, fitter body than my larger, flabbier one. I prayed he would find me satisfactory.

"Oh, Kerry," he gasped. "You're beautiful!" But I had a hard time accepting his compliment.

Jack pressed hard against me, holding me tight against his smaller but more muscular frame. As I felt his erection thrusting against my groin, I voiced the fear that had surprisingly overwhelmed me all at once. "Jack," I whispered, "I don't know if we should do this."

Jack's lips found mine, reassuring me. His mouth moved to my ear, nibbling at it deftly. "I have to have you, Kerry," he whispered. "I'm so in love with you, I can't stand it anymore."

Soon his tongue lapped a wet trail from one ear to the other then down my neck and across my hairy chest.

He removed his undershorts, tossing them on the floor opposite us, and rejoining me on the bed, as flesh touched flesh. Lost in his own lust as he moved his hand down across my chest, passing the quivering flesh of my stomach to gently slip his fingers beneath the waistband of my shorts and remove them. Kneeling, he took my penis into his mouth. It wasn't just sex; I was finally making love.

After he swallowed my ejaculation, Jack stood and began beating himself off, but I knelt in front of him and brushed his hand away gently. "Let me do that for you, Jack," I whispered hotly. "I want to show you how good it feels."

Jack soon ejaculated, moaning happily as I drank from him.

Afterward, Jack became remorseful. The signs of our sin were everywhere, on the sheets and in the sticky stains on our bodies. Apparently guilt-ridden, Jack asked if he could take a shower alone.

After Jack finished in the bathroom, entering my living room wrapped in a towel, I excused myself to go take a shower myself. Not only did I need to clean up, I needed the private time to think. Like Jack, who I felt quite sure had washed and scrubbed as hard as he could, no amount of cleaning my body over and over again could wash away the truth.

******

A few weeks after I met Elizabeth Taylor, Bob Bishop came to see me in the telex room at The Lantz Office. "We have the contracts ready for Bette Davis, for that made-for-TV movie, *Family Reunion*," he said. "I need you to run these over to her at her suite in the Lombardy, have her sign them, give her one copy, and bring back the other two."

"Yes, Bob," I replied quickly. "Shall I finish the telexes first?"

He looked at me with a wry expression and a bit of a gleam in his eye. "No. Go now. One does not put off Bette Davis once you have been summoned. I will take care of the rest of the telexes."

I filled the satchel with contracts and headed out.

I had always wanted to be an actor, and part of the reason for that was because of Bette Davis and her career. So I was more than a little intimidated after checking in at the Lombardy Hotel's security desk, to approach the door of her hotel suite.

After knocking on the front door of her hotel suite, I felt like an empty sack, needing to be filled up by the attention and adoration of strangers. Yet I was on the verge of meeting Bette Davis, the greatest film actress of all time. How would I get through the afternoon without peeing my pants?

When an itsy-bitsy elderly woman answered the door, I was taken aback. Bette Davis hadn't bothered to clean up, nor had she bothered to dress, as she was only wearing her bathrobe. But why should she? She was just answering the door to get some contracts from an office boy nobody. Nor had she bothered to send the maid to the door, or her personal assistant, whose name I knew then but have long since forgotten. They were out that day, so Miss Davis just came to the door herself, in her bathrobe, with a drink in one hand and a cigarette in the other. "Oh, it's you!" she said matter-of-factly. "You've got the contracts?" I nodded in reply. "Good!" she exclaimed as she exhaled a huge amount of cigarette smoke directly into my chest.

Physically, Bette Davis was a midget. But even though I stood framing her doorway, she blew her cigarette smoke all over me, as though I were her ashtray. I was still a good Mormon boy who had never smoked. I hated smoking and thought it the vilest of habits. Yet I accepted her exhaled smoke as though it were the only air I cared to breathe.

"Well, don't just stand there! Come in!" she ordered, with an air of authority. I felt at that moment the way Miriam Hopkins must have felt in *Old Acquaintance*, when Bette Davis took Miriam in her arms and shook the hell out of her. Indeed, had Bette Davis ordered me down on the floor to lick her feet, I would have dropped instantly to my knees and started licking.

Truly, she was horrible and superb and divine. With her hair unkempt, wearing no makeup, in a bathrobe, with scotch in one hand and a dangling cigarette in the other, Bette Davis was an authentic dragon, breathing fire all over me, and I melted into a puddle in the middle of her doorway. I don't know how my legs carried me into the suite, but I somehow managed.

"Would you like a cocktail?" Miss Davis asked, as we entered her spacious living room.

Although I was living my life as an out and proud gay man, I still observed the Mormon *Word of Wisdom*, abstaining from all forms of alcohol, cigarettes, coffee, and tea. Having been offered an alcoholic cocktail by Bette Davis, I was in Mormon Hell: Who owned my soul, Bette Davis or Heavenly Father?

"No, thank you," I replied.

"You don't drink?" she asked in shock, nearly spitting out the liquor she had swirling in her mouth.

"I don't drink alcohol," I explained shyly. "I'll have water."

"You don't drink alcohol?" she asked again. That was when I realized that she had already drunk a lot of alcohol that afternoon.

Insinuating herself into the sofa, she threw the contracts down on the coffee table. "Oh, that's right!" she exclaimed. "You're that new Mormon kid that Robby hired, aren't you?"

"Yes, Miss Davis," I replied, ashamed of my LDS past.

"I don't get Mormons at all, not a goddamn bit," she said, not wanting or waiting for a reply from me. "They don't drink. They don't smoke. What a bunch of tight-assed, religious fanatics! Just keep them away from me! And don't let 'em tell me how to live!"

"Yes, Ma'am," I said, hoping that she would offer me a seat.

150

Sloshing down the rest of her drink, she grabbed one of the copies of the contract. "Goddamn it!" she exclaimed. She seemed befuddled about something. Then she affirmed it, asking, "Where are my glasses? How can I read this contract without my glasses?"

We began searching frantically for her glasses until she said, "Fuck it! If I lost 'em, I lost 'em. I'll send someone out for another pair!" I stood motionless. "Tell you what," she said, "just read me the goddamn thing so I can sign it."

"You want me to read the entire contract out loud?"

"How else will I know what I'm signing?" she explained.

"Yes, Miss Davis," I said, a bit uncomfortable. "I understand."

I took the contract from her hands, and I began to read it aloud. This was my chance to please her, to perform for her.

I hadn't read much of the contract when she interrupted me, saying, "You're an actor, aren't you?"

"Um ... yes, Miss Davis, I am," I admitted sheepishly.

"And you're a pretty good one at that, judging from the way you read that boring crap! You make it sound exciting!"

I was pleased that she had taken notice of my presentation. "Why do you say that, Miss Davis? This isn't a reading or an audition," I said, doing my best Eve Harrington bit.

"Of course it's not!" she snapped. Without warning, authenticity had suddenly entered the room. After a lifetime of being inauthentic, I did not know what to do or say. "But I hear it in your voice," she explained, "and in how you hold yourself." She paused to look directly and deeply into my eyes. "You even make that boring shit interesting. Besides, I sense it in your need!"

"My need?" I asked, vulnerable and authentic for once.

"Oh, I don't mean it in a bad way. You have the hunger," she explained. "It was the same with me when I was your age." I was speechless. "Come over here and sit by me," she ordered. I obeyed and sat next to her on the sofa. "What's your name?" she asked.

"Kerry Ashton," I replied simply.

"Is that your real name? It sounds like a theatrical name."

"It's real. My mother liked the sound of it, so here I am."

"Is that Kerry with a C or a K?" she asked, reminding me of how Harlan had once asked me the same question.

"With a K," I murmured.

"Interesting. I was thinking Cary like Cary Grant."

She took a moment to look me up and down and sideways. "You're not as great a looker as Cary Grant, but you're quite handsome. And your name will look goddamn good on a marquee, if you ever get to where you want to be."

"Yes, Ma'am."

"And where is it that you want to be? Stage? Film? What?"

"All of it, Miss Davis. I've always dreamed of having a career like yours," I said. "And thank you for the compliments about my looks. I've never thought I was very handsome."

She laughed heartily. "You have got to be kidding? When you walked in here today, I thought you looked like a Greek God! In fact, I thought you looked a bit like my ex-husband Gary Merrill! And he was quite a looker in his day!"

Her comment caught me up short.

"Well, Kerry with a K," she added seriously, as she put her hand in mine, "I never thought I looked like anything either when I was your age. I had the worst self-esteem. They couldn't make me watch my dailies. Jack Warner never understood that. 'Why can't that cunt watch dailies?' he'd ask. He thought it was because I thought too much of myself! How wrong they were! You know why I refused to watch the dailies?"

"No. Why?" I asked breathlessly, hanging on her every word.

"Because I thought I looked like hell!" she said, bursting out with raucous laughter.

"Really?" I asked.

"I never thought I was pretty like the other Hollywood babes!" She poured herself another scotch and took a slurp. "Now, when I watch my films, there's no question that I was the best looking dame in Hollywood! But I sure as hell didn't know it then!"

She must have seen the look of recognition on my face, because she squeezed my hand intimately and patted it. "You're a good-looking young man, Kerry with a K, though you may not know it yet. All I knew then was that I loved the work!"

"The work?" I asked.

"The work is everything," she retorted. "You have to work!"

She took another gulp from her glass and lit another cigarette, taking a deep drag of smoke. "I just have one question for you, Kerry with a K." She paused, then pounced: "Why the hell are you working as Robby's office boy?"

I was caught off-guard. "Well, I have to make money somehow," I stammered. "I figured I would make connections at The Lantz Office that might help me get a leg up in the business."

"Precisely!" she snapped. "And that is a very big mistake!"

She took another gulp from her glass and puffed away on her cigarette, looking into my very soul.

"If you want to be an actor," she continued, "you have to work as an actor, not as an office boy! If you work as an office boy, the world will see you as an office boy. You have to know who you are and be who you are. That's all!" She drew another drag on her cigarette, and blew all of the smoke directly in my face. "That's my advice to you, if you want it!"

She took a deep breath and said, "Now, can you finish reading that goddamned contract, so I know what the hell I'm signing?"

After I read the rest of the contract aloud, she signed all three copies. I gave her back her copy and put the other two back in the leather satchel. Then she saw me to the door. As we prepared to say goodbye, she took another puff on her cigarette but this time she made sure that the smoke didn't go into my face. "It was a great honor meeting you, Miss Davis," I said, shaking her hand.

She nodded, but grabbed me by the arm as I prepared to walk away. "Kerry with a K, please remember what I said and think about it: If you want people to see you as an actor, you have to work as an actor, not as an office boy."

"Yes, Miss Davis, I will," I replied, "And thank you again."

The next day I handed Mr. Lantz my resignation letter.

******

Jack and I lay together all night in my single bed in my living room, but neither of us slept. Like sinners waiting for God's wrath in the morning, neither one of us said a word.

When morning came, our erections jabbed each other in accusation. We hadn't just had sex; we had kissed and made love, which ironically made our sin seem far more evil and profane.

Jack got out of bed and ran to the closet, throwing on the blue bathrobe he had brought with him. I sat on the bed with the covers pulled up to my neck, not daring to move, as Jack sat on the sofa.

Finally Jack spoke. "I can't believe I did this. I've made a mess of everything for both of us."

"No, Jack," I explained. "I wanted this to happen."

There was a tortured expression on his face as he sat in silence, like a bomb set to explode. Had I met Jack under different circumstances, we would have made love until our genitals were sore and our stomachs were hungry, then eaten breakfast. But we were not in L.A. or a Promised Land in the East; we were at BYU in the very heart of LDS Zion.

"I have to confess," Jack announced suddenly.

"Confess?" I asked in a disbelieving voice. "If you do that, my Branch President will want to see me, too!"

Jack ran around the apartment like a man possessed, grabbing up his clothes and putting them on as fast as he could. "I'm sorry, Kerry," he reiterated, "but I have to confess."

Fear coursed through me as Jack slammed the door behind him. I wanted to escape, but where could I go or to whom could I turn?

I thought of calling Harlan or Bridget, but how could I tell them about my sins? Anxiety propelled me to the dresser drawer where the church pamphlets Wilkinson had given me were safely hidden. I read the words aloud like an epitaph: *"The sin of homosexuality is carnal and sensual and devilish!"*

The words swam in my head until I needed to throw up.

After vomiting in the toilet, I flushed it away quickly, just as I had flushed away any and all memories of my rape. I looked at the razor on the bathroom sink. It was capable of a quick deep cut. If I used it on my wrists, I would not have to face President Wilkinson or expulsion from school. I could flush my sins away. I brought the razor to my wrist and held it there, as I stared at the reflection of my tear-stained face in the mirror.

Suddenly, the phone rang. I dropped the razor and ran to the phone. It was President Wilkinson calling.

"Hello, President," I said, fear grasped at my throat.

"Brother Ashton," he replied firmly, "I'm sure you know what I'm calling about. Can you be in my office in a half-hour?"

"Yes, Sir, I'll be right there." I felt my head whirling with despair as blood drained from my face. In shock, I slowly hung up the phone.

There was no way out. I was trapped.

It was snowing heavily as I ran across the snow-covered campus of early November 1972 in record time, my long dress-coat flapping like a flag in the wind. The bitter cold air slashed against my tear-stained face, making it throb with pain, but even if my face turned into jelly, it didn't matter any more.

"Sinners should suffer," I told myself mockingly.

Even my breath in the clean cold air reminded me of the foul stench of my sin. I had reached the Religion Building at the south end of campus when my foot slipped on a patch of ice, hurtling me into a treacherous embankment. A sharp edge of ice cut my trousers and slashed my knee like a knife. Red blood dripped on white snow, like evil dripping on purity, like the stench of sin on the Lord's clean campus. I pushed myself up and continued running.

"Dirty sins should hurt!" I reminded myself as I ran into the religion building on my way to President Wilkinson's office.

After knocking on President Wilkinson's office door, I heard him shout, "Come in!"

When I walked inside, I found him sitting behind his large, cluttered desk in his cramped office, wearing a grave expression on his face, not noticing my ripped trousers or my bleeding knee.

"Hello, Brother Ashton," he said quickly, trying to sound

pleasant. "It's very cold out, isn't it?" he asked.

I nodded, afraid to speak.

"Please take your coat off, Brother Kerry, and make yourself comfortable." I hung my coat on the rack, but I couldn't make myself comfortable. "Sit down, Brother Kerry," he added.

I sat down in the hard-backed brown chair facing him at his desk.

He eyed me with severity, as though he wanted to slap me. "According to Jack's confession to his Branch President," Wilkinson said quietly, "you committed horrible sins last night with Jack Young. Is this true?"

"Yes, Sir," I mumbled helplessly.

"These sins are an abomination before God! Only through a complete and full repentance can you ever hope to know the forgiveness of our Heavenly Father!"

"I know," I uttered weakly, feeling nauseous again.

"The Lord tells us that in order to repent we must confess the sin fully and completely. Brother Young did this. I assume you will, too." He looked down at the pamphlets on his desk, seemingly embarrassed. "Tell me what happened last night, Brother Kerry."

"I invited Jack to my apartment last night to sleep over," I explained. "The next thing I knew we were … kissing each other."

"The way a man might kiss a woman?" he asked.

Tears fell from my pink penitent eyes. "Yes, Sir."

President Wilkinson cleared his throat. "Then what happened?"

"We … made love."

"Let's not call it that. The sins you two young men committed together last night had nothing to do with love."

"You're wrong, President. Jack is in love with me. I'm not sure if I'm in love with him, but I do love him as a close friend."

"A close friend!" he retorted. "What you and Jack did together wasn't about love. Jack says that he took advantage of you."

"Jack wants to take all the blame, but we both sinned."

"Did Jack perform fellatio upon you as he confessed?" he asked.

His questions cheapened what I needed to believe had been a loving experience. "Yes, Bishop." Sweat poured from my armpits.

156

"And you ejaculated into his mouth?" he asked pointedly.

"Yes, Sir," I said meekly, wanting to crawl out of my skin.

"And then you performed fellatio on Jack?" he asked.

I nodded, fully ashamed of myself.

He pressed still further. "And you took his ejaculation into your mouth, and swallowed it?"

"I hate myself!" I shouted. "I don't want to live if I'm like this!"

President Wilkinson seemed touched by my repentant attitude, and stood up from behind his desk and walked toward me.

"You may be spared excommunication, Brother Kerry," he explained. "But that is for an LDS Church tribunal to decide. At the least, you'll be disfellowshipped. You won't be allowed to partake of the Lord's sacrament, and you will be stripped of your Priesthood until your repentance is complete. Of course, it is not merely a church tribunal that you must worry about, but the Office of University Standards."

My blood ran cold. "What do you mean?"

"You and Jack violated standards. Naturally, the Standards Office had to be informed. Jack already met with Brother Clarke earlier today. In Brother Young's case, he chose to drop out."

"Jack dropped out of school?" I asked. "Already?"

"Yes." He let the word seep into my brain, before he continued. "As to whether or not you can remain in school, I have scheduled a meeting with Brother Clarke at 2pm tomorrow."

"What can I do? If my parents find out, I'll kill myself!"

President Wilkinson walked slowly back to his desk. "Kerry," the President said gently, "Suicide would only make matters worse for you in the hereafter. A young man like you has everything to live for. Once we get this problem licked, you'll have a mission and a marriage to look forward to." He paused, as he sat back down in his chair behind the desk. "If you can agree to meeting weekly both with me and with a psychiatrist on campus, we will both try our best to convince Clarke not to expel you." Tears of gratitude fell from my eyes, as Wilkinson continued talking. "I scheduled an appointment for you with Dr. Hugh Parker at 8am tomorrow morning," he explained. "He is a psychiatrist at the BYU Health Center on campus who is not only eager but quite willing to work with you." He paused a moment to look around the papers scattered on his desk. "Where did I put his business card?" He found the card under some papers. "Ah, here it is!" He handed me the card, and I put it in my pocket. "If you meet Dr. Parker in the morning and agree to meet with both of us on a weekly basis," Wilkinson continued, "we will both join you tomorrow at your 2pm meeting with Brother Clarke."

I would have knelt to kiss his hand, if not for the gash in my knee. "Thank you, Sir," I said, weeping uncontrollably. "I want to change now more than ever."

President Wilkinson leaned back in his brown-vinyl swivel chair. "Brother Ashton, the Holy Ghost informs me that you are one of our Heavenly Father's choicest souls. That is why Lucifer has tried so hard to seduce you to his side." I wasn't sure, but I thought I had just been paid a compliment. "Of course, you and Brother Young must never communicate again after today," he continued. I felt my heart break. "But if you wish to say goodbye to Jack, as you say that you two were close friends, you can go with me now, since I'm driving over to Jack's dorm room to meet his Branch President, who will be taking Jack to the airport." Wilkinson fiddled with the papers on his desk. "Now, I think you and I should kneel in prayer."

We knelt together, but the pain in my knee made me gasp. Wilkinson looked down, his eyes widening at the discovery of blood.

"Brother Ashton!" he uttered. "What happened?"

"I fell on the ice."

"It looks like you need stitches," he said, genuinely concerned.

"Oh, it's okay," I replied, feeling that I had earned the pain.

"Nonsense!" he insisted, "You'd better let me drive you over to the Health Center before we head over to Jack's dorm."

After getting my knee attended to at the campus Health Center, Wilkinson and I drove on to Deseret Towers, to say goodbye to Jack.

When President Wilkinson and I walked into Jack's dorm room, Jack was sitting on the bare mattress of his bed, his suitcases packed and waiting by the door. A man I had never met sat at Jack's desk.

"Kerry," Wilkinson said, "This is Branch President Landau."

President Landau looked up at me, saying, "Good afternoon, Brother Ashton. I've heard a lot about you from Brother Young. I only wish we were meeting under different circumstances."

"Yes, Sir," I said sheepishly.

I looked at Jack, sitting in grief and silence on the edge of his mattress, with his head bowed in shame. He could not look me in the eye. "Why did you drop out, Jack?" I asked finally. "You could have stayed on at school like I'm doing."

Jack finally looked at me and explained, "Branch President Landau thought it best, and I agreed." Jack's boyishly handsome face was filled with sorrow. Seeing the pain in his stunning blue eyes only made me hate myself all the more.

"Did you say goodbye to Debbie?" I asked, knowing how hurt she would be when she heard about his dropping out of school.

"Yes," he replied. "She doesn't understand, but I couldn't tell her the truth about us. That's just the way it has to be, I guess."

Jack stood and walked toward the door, pulling on his coat.

"Kerry," Jack said softly, "I hope you'll be able to forgive me someday for the mess I made of your life. I do love you, Kerry."

Emotion clotted my throat, making it difficult to respond.

President Landau grabbed a suitcase as Jack grabbed the other two. "Good luck, Kerry," Jack said. "You have so much talent. I know you're going to be a huge success one day."

President Landau tugged at Jack's arm. "Jack," Landau said, "we have to go or you'll miss your flight to Ohio."

"Jack," I said, as he reached the door, "I love you, too." Jack nodded in my direction as Landau pulled him from the room. I turned to President Wilkinson. "Well, that's it then," I said.

"Yes," President Wilkinson replied. "Now then, Brother Ashton, if anyone asks you about Jack dropping out, mum's the word. We must avoid a scandal on campus at all cost."

"Yes, President," I whimpered.

"It should go without saying," Wilkinson warned, "If I ever hear of either you or Jack contacting each other again, I will have to recommend your excommunication from the church and expulsion from BYU."

"Yes, Sir," I replied. "I understand completely."

We stood side-by-side looking out the window. From where we stood on the seventh floor, we could see most of the expansive campus below us. "Come on, Kerry," Branch President Wilkinson said finally, "let's get you home. I want you to rest that knee."

******

On my last day working at The Lantz Office in 1980, Mr. Lantz asked me to meet with him privately in his office.

When I walked into Mr. Lantz's private chamber, he was sitting behind his elegant desk that looked like a piece from Versailles. As always, he behaved in an elegant and charming European manner. "I wanted to speak to you, Kerry," Robby explained. "We're all very fond of you here, you know."

"Thank you, Sir. I'm fond of you, too, Sir," I replied. "I am fond of all the people that work here."

"I'm curious," Mr. Lantz said. "Did anyone mistreat you here?"

"No, Sir. Not at all," I said. "If anything, everyone in the office has been lovely to me." I was telling the truth. I had enjoyed working at his office and meeting Bob Bishop, Hortense, Irv, David, and all the other folks who worked for Robby. "And I learned more about show business in the last six months than I did in the whole rest of my life."

"Kerry," he said, "I want to make you an offer. I would like you to consider becoming a junior agent in my office."

Whoa! I hadn't seen that coming!

Robert Lantz was offering me an opportunity that meant making millions of dollars and having a life of comfort and fame. Becoming a junior agent in The Lantz Office was like being a very big and famous agent anywhere else. He was offering me the opportunity to act as agent to some of the biggest stars, writers, and directors in the industry, with a percentage of all those incomes going into my pocket. As an agent at the Lantz Office, I would move from nobody to a huge somebody within a heartbeat. He had offered me the Holy Grail: I knew it, and he knew it. He smiled and waited quietly for my answer. "Well, my boy?" he asked finally.

"Sir, I am terribly flattered," I replied sincerely, with an authenticity that startled me. "But I have to decline. I came to realize some things a couple of weeks ago, after talking with a friend, who is a well-known actress." I was proud that I had not mentioned Miss Davis's name. "I realized after talking with her, that I have to work as an actor and writer, not in an office."

Mr. Lantz shook my hand, saying, "Very well then!" he said, as I felt the door to an opportunity of a lifetime closing as the seconds passed. "Best of luck to you, my boy," he added, as he saw me to the door. He only did this with people he respected.

The next day, I was back walking the pavement, trying to get in to see the acting agents who did not want to see me, but I felt like I was an actor again, not an office boy.

Not long after leaving Robby Lantz's office, I met Stephen Sondheim through a mutual friend. Sondheim, in turn, invited me to his fashionable East Side townhouse in midtown Manhattan one evening for dinner.

I found Sondheim's townhouse both elegant and stunning. And he helped me feel at ease, giving me a tour from bottom to top, even as he insisted that I call him Steve. He took me into his den on the second landing in the front, where a huge poster of his Broadway musical *Follies* hung on the wall, and into his huge office and study in the back, where a wall of windows overlooked a lovely garden. And he showed me his grand piano in the study, where he composed his music. He even introduced me to his beautiful white cat, a gentle creature that had obviously known only love and tenderness.

Steve's personal chef prepared our dinner before leaving, and when we were ready to dine that evening, Steve served our food in the den. Later, Steve took me into his bedroom on the top floor, where we made love for quite a few hours. In turn, Steve explored my body with a sensitive touch that I have only rarely experienced.

After making love, Steve invited me to spend the night. But I declined. I was already feeling ashamed that I had let myself be used like his boy toy.

Though we never got together again, Steve and I stayed in touch on the telephone for several months afterward. I had high hopes that we would soon have another date, and perhaps enter into a long-term relationship. If only Steve and I could have had a relationship on equal footing. But how could a struggling young actor and playwright get on equal footing with Stephen Sondheim?

Still hopeful that our relationship might evolve into something more than a one-night stand, I called Steve in early September 1980 to let him know that my mother had been diagnosed with colon cancer, and that I was flying out to Salt Lake City. Of course, he said that he hoped my mother's health would soon improve.

I was surprised when I arrived at the Salt Lake City airport late that afternoon to see Mom sitting in a wheelchair on the tarmac, waiting with Dad and the entire family. Looking gaunt, Mother nonetheless stood up from her wheelchair to give me a kiss. "My baby's home!" she said, as we kissed and hug.

Mom later made a special request of everyone. "I want to go to Temple Square this afternoon, while I still can, with my family."

"Of course, Mom," I said. "Anything."

And off we all went to Temple Square in downtown Salt Lake, where the towering spires of the Mormon Temple hovered above us.

"I love Temple Square," Mom said. "It is so good to be here with all of my family." This was a sacred place to all Mormons, the heartbeat of the Mormon Church, where the Lord had established His Promised Land. Mom turned to all of her children. "I know that the church is true. I hope you all can say that, too." Her grip on my hand was particularly firm.

A gutsy, courageous woman, she would not go gentle into that goodnight.

Mom's exploratory surgery at the LDS hospital began early the next morning and went on for many hours. Her doctors removed as much of the cancer as they could, but gave her less than two years to live, assuming chemotherapy proved successful.

After Mom recovered from surgery, she was moved to a more comfortable room in the hospice ward of the hospital.

My oldest brother's way of coping with the stress was to boss all of us around, and to drink heavily. And when Dennis drank, he abused his second wife Kathy, just as he abused her boys and his own children. That week I got a call at the hospital from Kathy. Dennis was on another drunk, and he was being abusive. Against my better judgment, I drove to their home. When I arrived, a drunken and violent Dennis backed Kathy and I into a corner, sat in a chair in front of us, and threatened us both with a broken beer bottle for the next several hours. When I finally got Kathy and the children safely out of the house, my nerves were frazzled. As usual, Dennis was aware only of his pain: It was not our mother who lay dying in the hospital, only his. No one's pain mattered to him, other than his own.

Despite my oldest brother's violent behavior, Mom's health improved and the rose returned to her cheeks. But the prospect of chemotherapy and a death sentence still loomed.

Once Mom was doing well in hospice, I made plans to head back east, as I had professional bookings to perform both at Cornell and George Washington University. On the day of my flight home, Mom and I talked giddily about her coming to visit me in New York after she completed her first round of chemo.

But when it came time to say goodbye, Mom asked everyone to leave the room so she could speak with me alone.

Mom was yellow with jaundice—a result of her liver being ravaged by both cancer and chemotherapy. Thin like a skeleton, with tubes stuck down her nose and an intravenous needle connected to a vein in her arm, she barely resembled the vivacious and beautiful woman I remembered. Even her hair, once a beautiful dark brown, was gray and thinning.

Mom held me close to her in the bed and stroked my hair, telling me how much she loved me, and what great things she expected of me in the future, and how she was looking forward to visiting me in New York. Then she got down to her real purpose for asking to speak with me alone. "Sweetheart," she said, "I love you so much. I can't stand the thought of you remaining inactive in the church. You must promise me that you will return to the church and keep your Priesthood commitments."

Conflict tore my heart apart. "Mom, I love you," I reiterated gently, "but I can't make that promise. I don't believe in Mormonism any longer."

"But you must return to the faith," she said, "so that you can enter the Celestial Kingdom in the afterlife."

"That's your belief, Mom, not mine," I explained gently. I tried to add some levity. "Besides, I'm not so sure I would like the Celestial Kingdom if only Mormons are there." I took in a deep breath. "I'll be better off," I continued, "if I end up in the Terrestial or Telestial Kingdom or in Purgatory!"

Mom gasped, her eyes wide in horror. "Don't even say that, Kerry!" she exclaimed, looking at me intently, as her eyes filled with tears. "You must come back to the Mormon Church and honor your Priesthood. That's all I ask of you." She squeezed my hand. "I can't go into the next world knowing that I will never see you again, that you'll be cut off from me forever!"

"At least I'll be among my own kind," I retorted.

Tightening her grip on my hand and summoning considerable strength, Mom's plea was intense and emphatic. "Kerry Lynn, you must promise me this! Otherwise, you'll never be able to join us as a family in the Celestial Kingdom!" Mom's voice was shaking both with weakness and emotion, but she continued speaking to me with all the firmness of her convictions. "Kerry Lynn," she added emphatically, "I can't die knowing I'll never see you in the hereafter."

"We'll see each other again, Mom. Don't worry," I reassured her. "If Heavenly Father is just, He won't keep us apart."

"I can only count on that," she said, "if you do as I've asked."

I tore myself away. "I have to go, Mom, or I'll miss my flight. We can talk about this when you come to New York." I hugged her and kissed her, and added, "I love you, Mom."

"I love you too, Kerry," she replied. "Always remember that."

As I left the hospice ward, I felt the eyes of my Mormon family staring at me from every corner of the hallway—the pleading eyes of my father, the prayerful eyes of my sister Denise and her husband Lee, of my Mormon brother Craig and his sweet wife Peggy, of my oldest brother Dennis and his tortured wife Kathy. As one who had ventured beyond their mountains and their LDS beliefs, I again felt like a Saint shamed by my Latter-Day-Saint family. I could almost hear them thinking, "Will he remain in Satan's grasp?"

After I completed my professional engagements at Cornell and George Washington University, Dad called me on the morning of November 4, 1980 to tell me that Mom had taken a turn for the worse. Minutes later, I was hailing a cab.

******

It was Tuesday, November 7, 1972, and Election Day at BYU.

I began the day by keeping my early morning appointment with Dr. Hugh Parker at the BYU Health Center, as my young life and future as a BYU student depended upon it.

Dr. Parker's office looked like a shrink's office should. It even had a reclining couch. As for Dr. Hugh Parker himself, he was an attractive middle-aged man, clean-shaven with raven black hair. Married with four children, he seemed to be a good LDS man.

Dr. Parker began our first session by asking me questions about my tryst with Jack. I answered all of his questions as best as I could. Then Dr. Parker asked, "Do you sincerely want to change your sexual orientation?"

"Yes, I do, Dr. Parker," I said, stretching out on his couch. "More than anything else." After that, Dr. Parker asked me questions about my parents and my upbringing. As I talked, he took careful notes. When I stood up from the couch at the end of the session, Dr. Parker gave me a friendly handshake.

"Brother Ashton, this is a good beginning," he pronounced.

As they had each promised, Dr. Parker and President Wilkinson were both by my side later that afternoon at 2pm when I met with Brother Clarke at the Standards Office.

This time, Clarke's secretary was young and pretty, probably a student doing work-study. When she entered Clarke's inner office, informing him that all three of us had arrived, Parker and Wilkinson reassured me that everything would turn out fine, even as the secretary came back into the room with a pert grin on her face. "You Brethren can go in now," she said. "Brother Clarke is ready to meet with the three of you."

Brother Gilbert Clarke hadn't changed at all, his thick gray eyebrows rising slightly as he perused my file in front of him on his otherwise immaculately clean desk.

"I'll be brief, Brother Ashton," Clarke began. "The outrage you perpetrated with Brother Young the other night makes me ill to even think about." He eyed me with severity, adding harshly, "By all rights, I should expel you today!"

I panicked. "Please, Brother Clarke," I blurted, feeling genuinely repentant. "If I'm expelled, my parents will find out. I won't be able to face them! I'll have to kill myself!"

"Young man, you should have thought of that before you broke the moral and ethical standards of this university," he said.

President Wilkinson interceded on my behalf. "Brother Clarke, I can tell you that the young man is extremely repentant. He needs our compassion and our help, particularly now more than ever, not our condemnation. We have a chance here to save this young man's soul. If we don't, we might lose him forever."

"Besides, Brother Ashton wants more than anything to change," Dr. Parker proffered. "Why else would he seek my help?"

The three of them battled it out, deciding my fate, as I sat there like a wilting flower. "I want to believe you, Brethren, and naturally I want to do best by Brother Ashton since you both believe he is sincere in his repentance," Clarke replied, thinking long and hard as he eyed me squirming in my chair. When Brother Clarke spoke again, it was with a kinder and far more compassionate tone, addressing himself to the two Brethren defending me. "Since we only have a few weeks until the semester ends, I will allow Brother Ashton to stay in school." I breathed a huge sigh of relief. "But only if he meets with both of you weekly," Clarke continued. "Meanwhile, you both must report to me weekly as to his progress."

After Wilkinson and Parker agreed to Brother Clarke's terms, Clarke turned to me. "As for you, Brother Ashton, you must understand that should you commit any infraction like this again while a student at BYU, I will expel you. Is that clear?"

"Yes, Sir," I said gratefully, "Thank you, Sir."

Thus, I began what President Wilkinson and Dr. Parker termed my Rehabilitation Program. Essentially, it was the same Conversion Therapy process that most young LGBTQ people still undergo today, only the techniques used back then were much harsher than most of the techniques used today, particularly where the use of Electroshock Therapy—a part of what was then termed Aversion Therapy—came into play. What I did not know at the time was that Brother Clarke's procedure in cases such as mine, where a student seemed sincerely repentant, was to trust but verify the veracity of a student's repentance. Unknown to me, Brother Gilbert Clarke had already contacted the BYU Security Police and ordered me put under surveillance.

Later that afternoon, undercover BYU Security Police followed me when I went to the polls for the first time, voting for Senator McGovern for president. And they followed me in an unmarked car as I drove back to my off-campus apartment, and then later followed me that night when I visited Bridget and Jennifer and Harlan at Bridget's apartment, to watch the election returns.

"I'm so depressed," I admitted, slumping down in Bridget's sofa, as I watched Nixon defeat Senator McGovern in a landslide.

"All that's left of me now is a rag and a hank of hair," I exclaimed sadly, munching softly on the popcorn that Bridget had made us.

"Cheer up!" Jennifer commented. "The best man won!"

"Oh, Angel," I replied, "Why do you always have to be so Republican? Why don't you go have your hair done instead?"

"It's not the end of the world," Bridget pointed out, as she cuddled closer to me on the sofa. "The country wants Nixon; you have to go along with what everybody wants."

I brooded. "The country's full of ignorant jerks who don't know any better." I exhaled deeply before adding, "Bridg, I'm sorry I'm in such a bad mood. I feel like I'm becoming a stranger at BYU."

Unaware that Nixon's reelection was not the deepest reason for my despair, Bridget put her hand in mine. "I love you, Sweetheart," she said. My words in reply came easily: "I love you too, Sweetie."

A few days later, as a way of dealing with the recent stressful events, I began writing a new one-act play, hoping to submit it to The Mormon Festival of Arts Competition. If my play was chosen as one of four winners, it would be presented the following March, at the annual Festival in the Fine Arts Center.

Then in mid-November, Harlan, Bridget, Jennifer, Stacey, Dom Altman, and my roommate Doug and I all gathered in the living room of my apartment to listen to the newest Streisand album *Live Concert at the Forum*—a benefit concert for Senator McGovern's bid for the presidency. "That's Barbra?" Harlan asked in astonishment. Her new sound was much more to his taste.

"She's changed her image again!" I replied. "I wish Jack were here. He'd love this!"

"I still can't believe that Jack just dropped out of school without saying goodbye to any of us," Bridget noted. "It makes no sense."

I turned numb.

Later that night, after everyone else had left the party and my roommate Doug had retired to his sleeping alcove, Dom Altman finally found the courage to confide in me his deeply held secret. "Kerry, I ... I've heard rumors around the Drama Department about you," he mumbled in a whisper, "that you might be ... homosexual."

"And?" I was ready to deny any and all of his accusations.

"I just ... well, I don't know how to say this," Dom sputtered, "other than to just say it. I suspect I might be homosexual, too."

The relief I felt was palatable. I could breathe again. "I'm glad you confided in me," I responded, still in a whisper so that my roommate Doug, sleeping in the alcove, would not hear, "and that I have finally found someone at BYU that I can confide in. In so many ways, your coming out to me is like an answer to a prayer. I've felt so alone on campus for so long."

"I've never acted on my gay impulses, Kerry," Dom confessed, "but I'm terrified I will soon. It's all I think about."

"I've been getting a lot of help from my Branch President."

"Really?" Dom queried. "Is his counseling helping?"

"I'm not sure yet. But he's been counseling me for quite a while now. It probably will help in the long run. You might want to confide in your Branch President, too."

Neither Dom nor I thought of each other as sexual prospects. Rather, we each had finally found a BYU friend to confide in.

Eventually, Dom took my advice and sought out counseling with his Branch President. But Dom was given the same advice that I was given, and soon Dom was looking for an unsuspecting girl to marry.

My repentance on November 7, 1972 was sincere. Honestly. And as I look back on it now, it was a miracle that I wasn't immediately expelled that very day. After such a near brush with disaster, one would think that I would have kept my nose clean. But that was not how things played out. As I only came to understand decades later, the subconscious memory of my brutal rape was far more in control of my destiny at that time in my life than I was, driving me mercilessly toward more sexual encounters. Like an addict prowling for his next fix, two weeks later, on Monday, November 20, two days before Thanksgiving break, I cruised the men's room in the Fine Arts Center basement where I had my first sexual encounter.

It was entirely quiet in the restroom, since it was late morning and between classes. There was no one, naked or otherwise, waiting in a stall or standing at the urinal.

I entered one of the two empty stalls, pulled down my pants and underwear, and sat on the toilet as I began playing with myself. It felt so good to be stroking again, going up and down, riding my palm, as I had done thousands of times before my 16th Birthday.

Suddenly I heard the creak of the outside bathroom door opening. Then I heard footsteps in the corridor between the public hall and the restroom, then the creak of the inner door opening as a man entered.

My erection jumped and throbbed in my palm, as I heard the guy walk into the stall next to mine. I heard the door close behind him as he took a seat. Then, as I heard him unzip his fly, I bent down to peer under the wall that stood between us. I could see he was wearing wingtip shoes and dress slacks and nice dress socks. And then it happened. He began tapping his foot, subtly and slowly at first, stopping for a while and then tapping it again on the bathroom tile.

He was waiting for me to signal him back. I tapped my foot in response, slowly and carefully at first, giving him the signal that it was okay for him to be more assertive. He tapped his foot again in response, more loudly this time, as if he were saying, "Come and get it! It's feeding time!" I signaled back: Tap! Tap! Tap!

He moved his shoe closer to the edge of the stall wall between us, just as I moved my foot closer to his, until our shoes touched.

From under the stall, he passed me a pencil with a note that he had written on some toilet paper. "What are you into?" it said.

I wrote back: "I like to suck or get sucked," and handed the note back to him under the stall wall, along with his pencil.

A moment later, he stood up, and pulled his pants up even as I heard him zip up his fly and buckle his belt. He left the bathroom quickly. Soon I heard a walkie-talkie in the outer hallway and the sound of boots marching across the bathroom tile to my stall door, where I was sitting on the toilet. And then I heard a man's voice speaking loudly. "Come out of there!" the man said, not in a belligerent way but in a way that made me know he meant business. "This is BYU Security Police!" he explained. "You are under arrest." My heart sank and I froze in fear. After giving me a few seconds to respond, the officer knocked on the door again. "Sir, you need to come out of there!" he said, still maintaining a polite demeanor. "I don't want to tear this door off its hinges, but I will if I have to."

"Yes, Sir," I whimpered. "I'll be right out."

When I opened the door, a tall and quite handsome BYU Security

Policeman in full uniform stood outside the toilet stall.

"Sir, you are under arrest for lewd conduct in a public restroom," he said quietly. "Please put your hands up against the wall."

I obeyed immediately, as the officer frisked me before handcuffing my wrists together behind my back, all the while reading me my Miranda rights. When he finished, he asked if I had understood everything he had just read. "Yeah, I guess so," I replied.

"Good," he responded. Not saying another word, he escorted me in handcuffs out of the men's room and down the hall, then up through the stairwell as many students I knew watched with gaping mouths. Finally, he took me out through the glass doors of the Arts Center, marching me to the adjacent Administration Building next door, then down the driveway to BYU's Security Headquarters.

Though the police officer could not have been more professional in how he treated me, handcuffed as I was behind my back I felt every step of my 'perp' walk, as though I were being taken in chains directly to Hell.

It was a walk of shame I shall never forget.

Above: The author in the center on his fourth birthday, with his family in 1957. Seen from left to right: Kerry's oldest brother Dennis, his father, his brother Craig below him, his mother, and his sister Denise, with her doll. Below: The author at far right at age five, on Christmas morning 1958.

Above: The author at age six with his mother in 1959. Below: Kerry at age seven on Christmas morning 1960, with his beloved china closet and tea set.

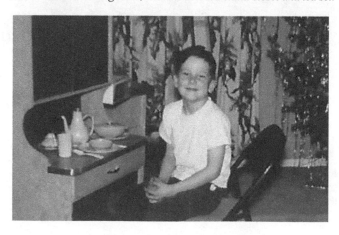

Above: Kerry at age nine, with his father in 1962. Below: The author's family in 1963, when the domestic violence was escalating. Seen on top row from left to right are Dennis, Denise, Craig, and the author at age ten; his parents are at bottom left.

Above: Kerry in 7ᵗʰ grade during his awkward phase at age 12 in 1965.
Below: At 17, with his parents at his 1971 high school graduation.

Above: The author with his parents on Friday, April 18, 1975, the day he graduated from college, at age 21. Below: In a disco in 1975 in Provo, after the author lost 75 pounds. (Photograph by Kent Tyler Smith. Used by permission.)

Above: The author at age 23, in L.A. in 1977 with his '56 Chevy named Oscar.
Below: At age 23, with his parents in Los Angeles in April 1977.

The author in his Hollywood hey-day in 1977, a month prior to the premiere of his one-man play. (Photograph by Kent Tyler Smith. Used by permission.)

*Above: The author at age 26, at Mormon Temple Square in Salt Lake City with his
parents, on the day prior to his mother's surgery for colon cancer in 1980.
Below: The author with his mother on the last day he saw her alive.*

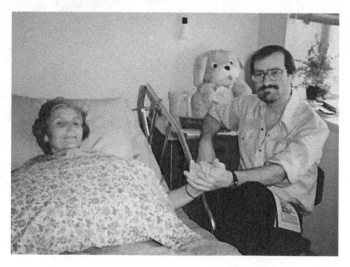

Above: The author at age 28, at the height of his acting career in New York in 1982.
(Photograph by Denise DeMirjian. Used with permission.)
Below: The author in his leather gear, taken in NYC in 1992, at age 38.

*Above: The last photo taken with the author and his father, September 1994.
Below: A publicity still of the author at age 42, appearing as Oscar Wilde
in the Off-Broadway production of THE WILDE SPIRIT in May 1996.
(Photograph by Kin Chung Kong. Used with permission.)*

Above: The author in 2002 while battling cancer at the age of 51 and weighing 345 pounds, sitting outside his Pocono Mountains log cabin in Northeast Pennsylvania. Below: Feeling much better at Grand Teton National Park in 2013, at age 59.

Above: The author on a Paris balcony in May 2016 at age 62.
(Photograph by Victor Ramirez. Used with permission.)

183

PART TWO

The cab ride to LaGuardia on November 4, 1980, was frantic.

Stuck in a traffic jam, I suddenly felt Mom's spirit with me in the cab, as though she were holding me close, the scent of her perfume pervading the air. And then I felt her spirit move through me before passing on. I knew then that she had just died, that her spirit had come to me to say goodbye.

As I found out later, Mom had died at that precise moment. It was the second profound spiritual experience of my life, one that prompted me toward a new and deeper spiritual path quite apart from my religious upbringing, but one I refused to respond to for several years thereafter. If anything, I was angry with God. If there was a God, why had He taken my mother, and robbed us of our time to even say goodbye?

Knowing there was no point in rushing now, I felt numb as I got on the plane. As it happened, it was Election Day 1980. And when the pilot announced that Reagan had been elected president, the Republicans on board celebrated, while I told myself, "Both Mom and my country died today."

Dad and my entire family were waiting for me when I arrived at the Salt Lake City International Airport. Mom had obviously died. They all would have been with her at the hospital if she were still alive. But none of them said a word to me. The Salt Lake airport was at that time undergoing a complete remodel. We walked in collective silence as a family, down and through one makeshift corridor and winding hallway after the next, until we finally arrived in a large corporate conference room with a long table extending from one end of the room to the other. Dad and the rest of the family sat at one end of the table. I sat at the other end. We faced each other in silence. Finally Dad said, "Kerry, your mother's gone."

My heart felt like stone. "Of course, she's gone!" I said quietly. "If she were still alive, all of you would be at the hospital now!" I paused, before three painful questions burst out of me, as I began shouting: "Why would all of you choose to tell me this way in a conference room as though this was some corporate meeting for stockholders? Why didn't you just whisper it in my ear and give me a hug? Are all of you crazy?" Having said this, I ran from the room.

Not even knowing how I got there, I sat on a bench outside the airport's main entrance, when Denise found me.

Coming up to the bench, she sat down beside me, gently taking my hand. "I'm sorry," she said in her usually sweet and understanding way. "Dennis insisted this was the best way to handle things. He thought you might make a scene if we told you in public."

"Of course he did! Dennis always tries to control everyone in our family, and he always will! But why didn't you or Dad stop him?"

"We should never have let him do it his way," Denise replied with gentle understanding. "Don't blame Dad. He's so lost now."

"I know," I replied, calming myself down. "We all are."

I didn't cry for the next three days. I didn't cry when Denise told me that a negligent nurse had allowed Mom to fall while taking her walk, and that she had grabbed Mother on the port in her arm, causing a blood clot in the artery leading directly to Mom's liver. I agonized over the incompetence that had robbed Mom of precious time, but I didn't cry. Even when picking out the casket and flowers, I didn't cry. Even on the day before the funeral, as Craig and Peggy, and Dad and I were sitting at the dining room, deciding what songs should be performed at the funeral, I still didn't cry.

Walking over to Mom's piano bench nearby in he living room, to look through the sheet music that Mom had always kept there, I came upon a homemade card, in red and white. I didn't recognize it at first, so I pulled it out and unfolded it, and then I knew: This was the Valentine that I had made for my mother when I was a little boy; it had hearts all over it that I had drawn by hand. I had no idea that she had saved it for all those years, much less that she had stored it in the piano bench. Suddenly the tears came, in a gushing flood, and I began to faint. Dad, who had kept his eyes on me, perhaps expecting something like this, ran from the dining table and caught me just before I collapsed onto the living room floor. Taking me in his arms as he did when I was a little boy, Dad kissed me on the cheek and stroked my hair. "It's going to be okay, Honey," he said tenderly. "We're going to get through this."

Dad cuddled me on the floor for several minutes, while I bawled like a baby. In that moment I knew that Dad loved me, that he had always loved me, and that he always would love me. Dad was a member of the greatest generation who fought for our nation's freedom. But I never saw my father as a hero, perhaps because he never told any of his war stories. If anything, I thought Dad spent too much time pretending to be something he wasn't. But in that moment of crisis, Dad became my hero.

We all went as a family to the funeral home that night. I hadn't seen Mom since I had kissed her goodbye in her hospice room a few weeks prior, so when we went to the funeral home that night, and I saw Mom lying in the lavender casket that we had chosen for her, displayed like a wax figure, I was horrified.

It was emotionally taxing on all of us to stand for hours near her casket, to greet all of her current and former students and their parents as well as all of our friends and neighbors and ward members, as they paid their respects.

The next morning the family held a private viewing at the funeral home. When the casket was sealed for the last time, I suddenly broke down in tears, sobbing uncontrollably. Nothing it seemed could stop my flow of tears.

My brothers and I acted as pallbearers that day, carrying Mother's casket from the funeral home to the mortuary limousine and then into the LDS ward chapel where Mom and Dad had attended church meetings after moving to their new home and a new ward. With each step, my heart ached.

Grieving friends, relatives and neighbors—many of them lifelong members of our 15th Ward congregation—attended the funeral services, packing the chapel to capacity. Once the funeral service began, it became instantly clear that I was far too emotional to deliver the eulogy. Instead, Deanna, Dennis's ex-wife, read the eulogy I had written for my mother, while I sat in the pew and wept. Sitting at the end of the long bench with my Mormon family, I stared at the sealed casket and the many flowers from loved ones and friends, as one LDS speaker after another found their way to the pulpit. For much of my life, I had believed in the Celestial Kingdom where all faithful LDS receive their reward for a lifetime of piety. As a child, I thought of the Celestial Kingdom as Emerald City, where the yellow brick road led directly to the throne of God. I tried to imagine Mom in the Celestial Kingdom, somewhere over the rainbow. But what if Heavenly Father turned out to be a charlatan like the Wizard of Oz himself?

At the cemetery, as my family and I stood at the graveside and Mom's casket was slowly lowered into the ground, I broke into uncontrollable sobs once more.

After all the prayers were said and the dedication of the grave was completed, it came time for us to leave. My sister Denise took me by the hand, saying as gently and lovingly as she could, "Come on, Kerry, it's time for us to go. The Relief Society is waiting to serve us lunch back at the ward recreation hall."

"I can't leave yet," I replied. "You go on. I'll join you later."

Remaining at the graveside long after the rest of my family had left, the gravediggers finally arrived to fill in the dirt over Mom's casket, but stood at a respectful distance as I continued grieving by her graveside. Taking the red rose from my hand—one that the Funeral Director had given me earlier—I tossed it on top of Mom's lavender casket in the ground. Leaves danced about my feet in mockery, taunting me to weep. I kept hearing the words that Mom had said to me, "That's all I ask of you." I heard her voice saying those words over and over again and again, even as the wind tore at my hair and the rain fell.

Then, as I turned from the grave and slowly walked away, I heard from behind me the thump, thump, thump of dirt being shoveled and tossed on my mother's casket, as though they were throwing the dirt directly into my mother's face. The sound of it made me begin weeping again. "Mom," I said aloud, as I walked back in the rain to my rental car, "I hope you can understand now why I could never return to the church. Wherever you are, I hope you understand."

******

Once we arrived at the campus Security Police Headquarters in the basement of the Administration Building, I was taken out of handcuffs and directed to a small room, where I sat for an hour or so.

When Detective Hall finally entered the room, he explained that Utah's sodomy laws prohibited fellatio and its solicitation. He told me that I had the right to call an attorney, but that it would go easier on me if I didn't. "You have committed a felony," Hall explained carefully. "And we have you dead to rights. We don't even need a confession. We have this note you wrote." He took out the rolled up toilet paper, showing me my handwritten note that said, "I like to suck or get sucked." I felt like I might throw up. "A felony means a police record that can never go away," Detective Hall explained. "The conviction will follow you for the rest of your life. But if you cooperate and waive your right to an attorney and provide us with a full confession, I will prosecute your crime as a misdemeanor. You won't serve jail time. Your arrest will be a matter of public record, and you will have to face a judge in a civil court, but if you plead guilty to a misdemeanor, the judge will show leniency, and you may be able to have your police record expunged later on, after a year, if you keep your nose clean." My heart felt like a leaden rock. "It's up to you," he continued. "If you call an attorney, I'll throw the book at you. If you confess, you'll only be guilty of a misdemeanor."

"What about BYU?" I asked. "Am I going to be expelled?"

"That's up to Brother Clarke and the Standards Office."

In the end, I provided Hall with a written confession. Mug shots were taken and I was fingerprinted, each finger pressed into black ink like the curse of Cain.

I was given the date of December 7th to appear before a judge at the courthouse in Provo, where I would plead guilty to a misdemeanor. "You must show up for your trial date and cooperate with University Standards and church authorities," Hall explained, "or we will issue a warrant for your arrest."

"Yes, Sir," I said, wincing with shame. "I understand."

188

A policeman I hadn't met yet stepped into the interrogation room just as Detective Hall and I completed our talk. Hall turned to him, saying, "Okay, Officer Dooley, please escort this young man to the Office of University Standards upstairs. Brother Gilbert Clarke is waiting to see him."

The Detective's words stuck in my heart like a thorn, as Officer Dooley escorted me out respectfully, taking me three flights up the darkened back stairwell to the Standards Office, until I was standing before Brother Clarke sitting behind his desk, with my head bowed and penitent. "Officer, please wait outside, until I call you back in," Brother Gilbert Clarke said softly.

"Yes, Brother Clarke," Dooley replied quietly as he left, closing the door silently behind him.

"Sit down, Brother Ashton," Clarke stated quietly. I sat down in the hot seat, facing him. "It was only three weeks ago that you sat there in that very same chair, acting repentant after committing outrageous and outlandish acts of perversion with Jack Young, yet here you are again! I can see now that I was wise to put you under surveillance and to encourage BYU Security to test the veracity of your so-called repentance."

"Yes, Sir," I muttered. I had no excuses left.

"I have contacted both President Wilkinson and Dr. Parker. Despite their disappointment in you, they still believe that your soul can be redeemed, though I can't for the life of me understand why. Because of this and as we are less than three weeks from final exams, I am going to let you complete this semester. However, you must continue seeing President Wilkinson and Dr. Parker until semester's end on December 21st. Then, at that time you will be expelled."

"Do my parents have to be told about this?" I asked.

"They'll have to be told that you're being expelled. As to the reasons why, I will leave that up to you."

"Yes, Brother Clarke," I replied solemnly.

"Worse than dealing with me or facing you parents, however," Clarke continued, "you must answer to our Heavenly Father. President Wilkinson is expecting you in his office in ten minutes."

"Yes, Sir," I whimpered.

"Once Officer Dooley escorts you to President Wilkinson's office, you will be answerable to him and to Dr. Parker for your actions until December 21st. So behave yourself until then."

"I understand, Sir," I replied, as tears streamed down my cheeks.

"Officer Dooley?" Clarke called out, loudly enough for the uniformed policeman to hear him through the door. "Could you step back in here, please?"

"Yes, Brother Clarke," Dooley replied, reentering the office.

"Please escort this young man to President Wilkinson's office in the Religion building," Clarke ordered.

"Yes, Brother Clarke," Officer Dooley replied, guiding me out of the office and then walking with me to the south end of campus.

It was 3:50pm. Afternoon classes at BYU had just let out and thousands of students were walking on the sidewalks to their next classes, when Officer Dooley and I walked across campus. Dooley was dressed in full police uniform, so this was a second and much longer 'perp' walk across campus that I shall never forget. At least, they hadn't kept me in handcuffs. Even so, many students averted their eyes, not daring to look a criminal like me in the face, as we passed them by on the crowded sidewalks. The public shaming that I felt at that time was excruciating, but something I felt I had earned.

I remember feeling confused at the time that Officer Dooley seemed almost apologetic, even sorry that I had been caught in such a compromising and embarrassing situation. Indeed, he seemed to have more sympathy for me than I did for myself. Upon reaching President Wilkinson's office in the Religion Building on the far south side of campus, Officer Dooley knocked on the door. "Come in," Wilkinson shouted.

Officer Dooley escorted me into the room to stand before Wilkinson. "You're excused, Officer," Wilkinson acknowledged pointedly. "He's my responsibility now."

"Yes, Branch President," Dooley replied, then left, closing the door behind him as quietly and gently as he could.

"Sit down, Brother Kerry," President Wilkinson said kindly.

I sat down in the seat facing him. "Well," he said, looking over the report on his desk, "you certainly stepped into a mess this time!"

"Yes, President," I replied, wanting to hide under the chair.

"Only three weeks ago we managed to talk Brother Clarke out of expelling you from school. Now you only have yourself to blame! And this, after Dr. Parker and I vouched for your behavior! Now you face a church tribunal on the 5th and criminal court on December 7!"

I felt overwhelmed with emotion. "Please, President, I want to repent, but the harder I try, the more I sin." What was I to do? I thought. "I can't face my parents. I'll have to kill myself. It's the only way out," I responded hopelessly.

"Nothing is as bad as that," he said. "Suicide is never the answer." He paused briefly. "Kerry, you will make it through this. If Dr. Parker and I didn't believe that you were still capable of redemption, we would not have given our word to Brother Clarke to take you in charge, and talk him into allowing you to finish out this semester."

"I know, President," I said gratefully. "I want to change, but I don't know if I can!"

"You must leave that to me and to your psychiatrist," he said. I exhaled a deep breath. I was beginning to have a panic attack. My heart was palpitating so hard that I thought it might burst from my chest. "We have a plan to rehabilitate you and to bring you to full repentance," Wilkinson continued. "If you show progress in your rehabilitation, we can even get you reinstated as a student at BYU, perhaps even as soon as next fall. I think that you should consider continuing to live off-campus. Even though you are no longer a registered student, you could take home study course to keep up, while you follow through on whatever the civil and church courts decide as just punishment. That way Dr. Parker and I can continue to meet with you weekly. This would make the scandal less visible to your friends here and for your folks back home. And if you continue with your Rehabilitation Program, Dr. Parker and I will go with you to your church tribunal on the 5th and to your civil trial on the 7th."

"Thank you, President," I replied gratefully. "I appreciate the support that you and Dr. Parker have shown me. It gives me hope."

"As it should, young man," he replied gently. I burst into tears.

Wilkinson walked over to me and put his arm around my shoulder. "All sin can be healed with the Lord's forgiveness, Kerry."

"I want to believe that, President Wilkinson," I replied.

"Brother Kerry, I think you have had quite enough excitement for one day. I'll drive you home."

Once he dropped me off at my apartment, I tore off all of my clothes and got under the covers of my bed. What would I tell my parents when I went home for Thanksgiving?

In fact, I lied to my parents when I returned home, telling them that a professor had made unwanted sexual advances toward me in a campus restroom, that I had refused his advances, but that the Standards Office, since they did not know which one of us to believe, had expelled us both. My parents were shocked by the news, but agreed that I should stay in Provo and take home study courses, to hide the scandal.

When I returned to Provo after Thanksgiving, Harlan dumped Jennifer. Angel was devastated, as was Bridget, and I was surprised.

On December 1st, Harlan and I went shopping for a Christmas tree. We found a beautiful seven-footer and set it up in his living room. Our BYU family decorated the tree that night for Family Home Evening. After the party, Harlan and I knelt by the two beds in his bedroom and said our evening prayers. After our prayers were said, I undressed in the dark, as I always did when staying over at Harlan's place. After plopping into bed, I suddenly worked up the nerve to ask what had been weighing on my mind. "Harlan can I ask you something?"

"Sure," he replied. "Of course you can."

"Why did you break up with Jennifer?"

Harlan cleared his throat. "Do you want a bullshit answer or the truth?"

"The truth," I admitted.

"Like you always said, she was a Molly Mormon. I was never in love with her. I only dated her so I could go out with you and Bridget. And besides, she wouldn't put out."

I was still slow on the uptake in such matters. "Put out?" I asked.

"Come off it, Babe. I always knew she was a good Mormon girl and that she would never go all the way. Still, I wanted her to take care of at least some of my manly needs, you know, to at least do things with her mouth. But she never would, so I dumped her."

"Wow!" I replied. "Thanks for telling me the truth."

"You're welcome, Babe," he said. "Now let's get to sleep."

The wind howled ferociously outside the window that night. As often happened when I slept over at Harlan's place, I couldn't sleep. I tossed and turned, thinking about what Harlan had said. If Harlan had asked me—as he had asked Jennifer—to take care of his manly needs, I knew I would have dropped to my knees in sheer gratitude and joy. No doubt, I was wicked to the core. Closing my eyes, I saw Harlan naked in my fantasies, an idol of love that I knelt before and worshipped. I was tempted to play with myself—to defile my latest vows of chastity made anew with God—but I resisted. As the wind slapped branches against the windowpane, I imagined that Lucifer was prancing in the snow outside like a wicked elf, shrieking with lustful gales of laughter.

When I finally fell asleep, I dreamt of sweeter things.

Wilkinson counseled me as we drove to my church tribunal on December 5th. "Brother Kerry," the Branch President cautioned, "if your repentance is real, you will never masturbate again, and you will never again commit any act of sexual indecency." He paused and took a deep breath, as if to drive home his point. "Catholics are lucky; they can sin all week, confess on Sunday, and sin again on Monday, but in the Mormon faith, true repentance requires that you repent and never commit the sin again."

Once we arrived at the LDS Stake Center, Dr. Parker greeted us in the foyer, and then we walked into the conference room. The President and High Councilmen sat on one side of the table facing us, and the three of us sat on the other side facing them.

Elder Monson, the Stake President and Head of the church tribunal, sat back in his chair, conferring with the other judges of the tribunal—each looking quite corporate in their polyester-knit business suits. "How do you explain your actions?" Monson asked.

"Lucifer led me astray," I replied, telling him exactly what I believed at that time.

"And then you were found weeks later in a restroom on campus, passing notes about fellatio, under the toilet stall to an undercover Officer of the BYU Security Police Force?"

"Yes, Sir," I answered, feeling my face burn with shame.

"And for this, you were arrested by the BYU Security Police?" Elder Monson asked.

"Yes, Sir," I muttered.

Had I not believed my homosexual leanings to be every bit as wicked as I had been conditioned to believe from a lifetime of Mormonism, I might have told them to stick the church up their butts and flown out of there with the freedom of a butterfly. As it was, I felt the fear, the absolute terror, any butterfly must feel when they know that it is time to emerge from the cocoon, but can't find their way out. So, when Stake President Monson asked if I was repentant, I cried and replied that I was.

Later, both Dr. Hugh Parker and President Cyrus W. Wilkinson assured the Elders that I was genuinely repentant. Eventually, Stake President Monson asked the three of us to step into the outer foyer while they deliberated my fate.

I spent all of my time in the lobby while the three of us awaited my fate, I prayed constantly that I would be sparked the humiliation of an excommunication from the Mormon Church.

When the tribunal reconvened, calling all three of us back into the main conference room, I stood before all of the church Elders and faced each of them as they pronounced their verdict.

Elder Monson spoke quietly but forcefully.

"Brother Kerry," he pronounced, "since we believe that you are sincere in your repentance, this tribunal has determined that you are to be disfellowshipped for the sins that you have committed, but that you will be spared excommunication from the church."

Offering up a secret prayer of thanks to my Heavenly Father, I addressed the men of the tribunal. "Thank you, Brethren, for giving me a second chance. I won't let you down."

Two days later on December 7, 1972, I stood before the judge in a Provo courtroom and pleaded guilty to a misdemeanor. Since both Dr. Parker and President Wilkinson testified on my behalf, the judge was more lenient in my case than he might have been otherwise.

"I am not sending you to jail, Mr. Ashton," the judge said quietly from the bench, looking down upon me ominously from above. "But I am putting you on probation, and assigning you a probation officer who you will meet with weekly. If you complete a year of probation without further incident, you can apply then to have your police report expunged." He brought the gavel down on the top of his desk, and called out, "Next case!"

Later that day, I met with my assigned probation officer, Mr. Harry Smithfield. An LDS straight arrow, Elder Smithfield apparently had no clue about gay men. "You like guys?" Smithfield asked, as he shook his head with disgust.

"I guess I do, Elder Smithfield," I replied, shamefacedly. "But I'm trying to change."

Smithfield required me to attend a weekly gathering of convicted murderers, thieves, and rapists held every Tuesday night at his probation office, where I confessed my sins.

Since Elder Smithfield likened my crime to theirs, he thought this would help me "go straight." Smithfield called this a support group, but it was essentially a weekly *Shame the Fag* session.

It wasn't that Brother Smithfield was unkind to me; he was simply ignorant, having never dealt with a gay man before. If anything, he saw me as just another one of the misguided criminals in need of his guidance, who attended his weekly support group.

Until semester's end, I prayed, repented, and read scriptures until I thought *The Book of Mormon* would sprout from each armpit. Meanwhile, I felt like a puppet on the end of a string being pulled by others. Following Dr. Parker's advice as precisely as I could, I tried to cultivate sexual feelings for Bridget. At the end of every date, I took Bridget to the Mormon lover's lane overlooking the Temple, and forced myself to make out with her. What was worse, Bridget yielded to my ever-increasing advances with giddy passion.

Once I was disfellowshipped, it was difficult attending church meetings at BYU, but I did it anyway. If I hadn't attended my meetings faithfully, President Wilkinson would report this failure to Brother Clarke. Whenever I entered the classroom where our church services were held on campus, I often heard whispered rumors circulating between gossipmongers and former friends, which quickly died down as soon as I entered the room. When the Holy Sacrament was passed among the congregation, I could not partake. Many stared at me as though I were a leper. Harlan noticed of course, and asked me about it later after church.

"I can't talk about it, Harlan," I replied. "Please don't ask me about it, okay?"

"Okay," he replied. "But if you ever want to talk, I'm here."

Of course, I kept my weekly meetings with Wilkinson and Parker and my probation officer's convicts, all very secret. I dreaded anyone finding out the truth.

Facing the combined forces of the Lord's University, the whole of LDS society, my Mormon parents, family and friends, as well as Utah's judicial system, I thought the war that I was fighting was with all of them. Now, as I look back on this *Holy War*, I realize that it was a war fought entirely within myself, waged between me and my inner child, and no one else. Wrongly, I chose to stand with all of the foes that my inner child was fighting against. Taking their side against my true self was a shameful mistake, and a deep betrayal.

Naturally, I didn't see it that way at the time. I thought I was honoring my authentic desire to repent. Not yet possessing the self-awareness, self-esteem, or the inner strength to do battle with all aspects of the Mormon culture that surrounded me then, I couldn't see that I was merely yielding to the thorough brainwashing imposed on me from the cradle up. I was simply doing then what I had always done, choosing to survive, to live another dreadful day, and every day after that, as a lie. I had, of course, already abandoned myself many times since that Sunday at the age of nine, when I had gone upstairs to the small chapel, stripped naked and desecrated the altar. "Don't forget me," my inner child had cried out that afternoon. "Though you must bury me now to survive your childhood, remember me. Come back and find me someday. Come back and save me."

But I had forgotten him. Time and again and without any conscious awareness of the fact, I had given him away—along with any authenticity I had ever hoped to possess—simply to please everyone but myself.

No matter how many times I would later profess a healthy self-love for my true self, my inner child knew better. He knew that I had betrayed him in the *Holy War*. Later in my adult life, he would make me pay again and again for that betrayal, depriving me of the success that my talent and work ethic could have otherwise secured.

In time, I would see the need—the imperative, in fact—to speak with my inner child, hoping to find forgiveness, but the process of self-forgiveness would not come easily or quickly in my life. Rather, it came in fits and starts, during a lifelong process of healing, usually settling on a temporary truce at best.

******

When I returned to New York City after Mom's funeral, I was inconsolable with grief. None of my friends knew what to say or do to help me. It was Steve Sondheim who comforted me most, by telling me what he would later say lyrically in his Broadway musical several years later, *Into the Woods*:

> *"Sometimes people leave you halfway through the wood,*
> *Do not let it grieve you. No one leaves for good.*
> *No one is alone."*

"Kerry," Steve told me over the phone, "at least you know that your mother loved you. Not everyone has that." Then he told me about his mom, a story I have since heard him share in a documentary interview. "When my mother was dying, she told me, 'Steve, the only regret I have is giving birth to you.' And that was how she really felt! When she died, I knew that she never loved me and never wanted me as her son!"

My relationship with Steve was complicated. I hoped he would open doors for me, the same doors that others like Rodgers and Hammerstein had opened for him, but Steve was understandably wary of being used. I didn't understand this then, but I do now. Still, I will always appreciate that Steve did his best, as a real friend would, to comfort me during my time of grief.

Those first few months after Mom's death were agonizingly painful. The sorrow was unrelenting. One early morning, as I stood on the southwest corner of 57th Street and Eighth Avenue, the sun in the east suddenly broke through the clouds, flooding my face with sunlight, just as I smelled my mother's perfume all around me. The stoplight changed but I made no move to cross Eighth Avenue, standing perfectly still at the curb, while pedestrians passed me by on both sides, as I felt the spirit of my mother take me in her arms and hold me close. It was as though I could hear her soul speaking to me, comforting me. Then the clouds blocked out the sun again, the scent of her perfume evaporated, as the sense of her presence gradually dissipated.

Afterward, my heart felt lighter. My eyes were full of tears, but they were tears of gratitude. It was yet another spiritual experience that I could not deny, no matter how anti-religious I felt later on.

Dad did not do well in the months after Mom's death, so I flew home to Pocatello during the summer of 1981 to spend more time with him, as we were now the only single men in the family now.

Once we were settled into his living room at his home on Elm Street, I asked Dad if he had thought of dating again.

"No," he replied. Even the thought of it brought consternation to his face. "I'm an old man now. I'm almost 60. Who'd want to date me?"

"Sixty isn't old, Dad. You're still in your prime. There must be tons of widows who'd love a little companionship."

My father looked at me with sad brown eyes. After 38 years of marriage, Dad was experiencing the pain of isolation and enforced bachelorhood. My married siblings couldn't understand the loneliness of single life, but I knew all about it, having been the only single member of my family for years.

"Dad," I said, "what you need are some friends that you can go out with and talk to."

"Oh, I don't know, Kerry, I'm too old for all that."

"Too old!" I replied. "You're never too old to have friends."

The next day, Dad decided to drive south to Logan, Utah, to visit his mom and sister Doris, and he asked me to join him.

Once we left for Logan in Dad's gold Dodge Monaco, driving south on Interstate 15, my thoughts centered on my father.

All I knew about Dad's childhood I had learned from Mom. In fact, Dad had never shared anything about his life prior to his marriage, keeping even his war memories to himself. All I knew about Dad's service during the war was gleaned from Mom or from sneak peeks at the black-and-white snapshots from the war that Dad had kept hidden in scrapbooks stored in our basement washroom.

Grandma Ashton's house, the tiny house she shared with her adult daughter Doris, was the same farmhouse that Dad grew up in. It had once stood on a farm in a desolate desert valley on the border of Idaho and Utah near the town of Malad, Idaho.

The original farmhouse had only two rooms, a small kitchen and a small living room; it had no refrigerator, just an icebox, and a cutout in the ground to store meats during Idaho's long winters. The house had no bathroom, only an outhouse. And it had no heat, just a wood stove. Keeping the fire stoked was a task given to Dad as a young boy. Both of Dad's parents and all of his four sisters slept on the main floor. Being the only boy, Dad was forced to sleep in a dirt cellar. Mom had told me that as a young boy, Dad was terrified by the spiders and other bugs that crawled over his body when he tried to fall asleep at night in the dirt cellar.

According to Mom, Dad's father beat him frequently; and that one day after a particularly bad beating, Dad had prayed that the Lord would strike his father dead.

When Dad's father had died a few days later from pneumonia, Dad had felt guilty and responsible.

When we arrived at Grandma Ashton's place, my father promptly fell asleep on the davenport in the living room, as was his practice whenever we visited his family. Later, I woke him up so that we all could eat the dinner together that his sister Doris and mother had prepared for us.

After dinner, and after Dad and I finished our visit with Grandma and Aunt Doris, we drove first to the Logan LDS Temple, where Mom and Dad were "sealed to each other, for time and all eternity," and then to the LDS Hospital across the street from the Temple, making note of the hospital room where I was born, realizing for the first that this may have been the reason why I had refused for days to leave my mother's womb. Clearly, it was an inhospitable environment for an unborn child who knew he would be gay.

"All you kids were born here at the LDS Hospital in Logan," Dad explained, "even after we moved to Pocatello, since your Mom wanted all of her babies delivered by the same doctor."

After sitting in Dad's Dodge Monaco for a while, taking in the view of the hospital and the lush and beautiful Temple grounds across the street and the majestic Wasatch Mountains to the east, we drove on to the home in Logan where Mom was living when Dad first returned from World War II. Mom and Dad had married during a military furlough in Logan, while she was still a junior in high school at Grace, Idaho. While Dad had fought the war with the Japanese in the Marshall Islands of the South Pacific, Mom had finished high school. After graduating, Mom had moved to Logan to work as a nurse's aid in the war effort, helping as many wounded soldiers as she could. She was still living and working in Logan when Dad returned from the war.

Mom had told me many times how Dad, in wanting to surprise her, had shown up at her tiny upstairs apartment in Logan, without notice, in uniform, with roses in hand. Apparently, when he entered the kitchen where she was cleaning the oven, her hair was still in curlers, and she was wearing a ratty bathrobe. She had hoped to make herself as pretty as possible when he first saw her again, but that hadn't kept her from breaking into sobs when he took her in his arms, as she thanked God that her young husband had returned from the Great War, alive and safe and whole.

I cried when Dad told me the story from his perspective for the first time: "I didn't care whether or not she had curlers in her hair and was wearing an old bathrobe or not! I've never seen any one in this entire world more beautiful than your mother was in that moment," he explained. "When I pulled her out of that greasy oven, and took her in my arms, and kissed her, I knew I had found Heaven itself!"

After Dad and I left Logan that afternoon, we drove north on Interstate 15, heading back to Idaho. As we crossed the state line, driving into the desolate high desert valley where Dad was born and raised, I queried my father carefully. "Dad, would you show me the farm where you grew up?"

"We did that as a family years ago, when all you kids were little."

"I know, but I was too young to remember all of it."

"Okay, Honey, we can do that," Dad replied softly.

He took the next exit off of Interstate 15, heading down into the forlorn village of Woodruff, driving a mile or more into nothing but sagebrush and isolation, before we crossed a narrow single-lane bridge crossing a small but deep creek. Dad stopped on the bridge and pointed at the water crossing under the bridge.

"That's where I was baptized. It was in early February, and there was five feet of snow on the ground at the time! I remember, they had to break the ice with axes just to get me into the water!"

Driving past the creek to the end of the road, he pulled over and stopped the car. "That's where our farm was," Dad said, pointing at the barren field of sagebrush on our left. When I asked about his childhood, for the first time Dad answered my questions in details that not even Mom knew.

Parked on the dirt road in front of his childhood farm, with only sagebrush around us, I sensed that a pivotal and important moment in my life had arrived. As ready as I would ever be, I spoke quietly.

"Dad," I said, "I have something to tell you."

"Okay," he said, turning off the car's engine. "Shoot!"

Taking a deep breath, I took off my mask. "Dad, I'm gay."

"Gay?" Dad asked, a vacant look on his face, as he let out a long, slow breath. He sat silent for a long time before adding, "I could see the signs when you were little, but I hoped you would outgrow it."

"You suspected?" I asked, barely able to hear what he was saying. After all I'd done to protect my parents from this truth, they had known all along!

"Your mother and I talked about it a few times," he replied softly. Apparently, I was the only one in the universe who hadn't known I was gay. "But that doesn't mean you have to give into it," he added. "It goes against the Lord's commandments. But it's my fault. I made so many mistakes with you."

"That's not true, Dad," I explained kindly. "It has nothing to do with how I was raised."

"It does, Kerry. It has everything to do with it! You were always your Mama's boy. She claimed you from the start. I let her turn you into some kind of ..." His voice halted.

"Sissy?" I interrupted. "Or were you going to say queer?"

"I didn't say that, Kerry!" he exclaimed. "But you are the way you are because I failed you," Dad added. "This is God's judgment upon me." He paused. "I failed you just like I failed your brother Dennis, and just like I failed your mother."

"What are you talking about?" I asked, pressing him.

"I am a man with more secrets than you," he replied, as he slowly unburdened his soul. "There was this woman that I'd been seeing for a while, at nights when your mother thought I was out selling insurance. And there were a few women before her."

I took a moment to digest what he had said. "Did Mom know?" I asked finally.

"She found out in 1978. But it wasn't at my choosing." He paused. "When the woman I'd been having an affair with, finally confessed to her Bishop, he called my Bishop, and then I was called in and forced me to confess. I had no choice but to come clean." He paused, his face hot with shame. "The Bishop forced me to tell your mother everything," he continued, as he began to weep, "which I did not want to do! It was the hardest thing I ever had to do. But your mother forgave me, Kerry. She forgave me!"

My father began to sob unrelentingly, as though a lifetime of tears were pouring out of him. I took my father in my arms and held him close, until his sobbing finally ceased.

"Your mother stood by me," Dad added quietly, pausing to wipe his eyes with his handkerchief. "Even when I was disfellowshipped, even when I was stripped of my Priesthood, she stood by me," he continued. "Even with all the shame I laid at your mother's feet, she stood by me to the end. That's why I know for a fact that Heavenly Father took her from me. It was because of my sins, and to punish me for all of my transgressions."

"I don't believe that," I replied. "God wants us all to be happy."

"No, son. He took your mother from me because of my sins."

******

I still felt like a marionette, dangling from Brother Clarke's strings, when I was expelled from BYU at the end of that semester, and as I prepared to return home for the Christmas holidays of 1972.

I kept all of this from Bridget and Harlan, of course, though Bridget had sensed that something was bothering me when we traveled north to Salt Lake City on our way home for the holidays, to see Streisand's sixth film *Up the Sandbox*, that had just opened.

I loved the film and I appreciated it artistically; it was the first time that as an actress she had ventured into drama, but it was her first failure at the box office. In fact, Bridget and I were shocked there were only a few people there for that afternoon's showing.

"So what did you think?" Bridget asked carefully, as we walked out of the movie house after seeing the film, knowing how much I worshipped Barbra. "It was a very different film role for her," I replied. "The film had so much to say about how hard it is for women to balance raising a family and being a good mother, with having a career."

"I agree," Bridget responded. "I really loved it. I thought it was wonderful." She took a deep breath, even as she took my hand in hers as we walked back to Oscar.

"Kerry, are you okay?" she asked, once we were inside the car. "You seem so distant lately."

"I'm fine," I lied. "I just have a lot on my mind."

"Is there something going on with you that I should know about?" she pressed, her woman's intuition clearly acute.

"No, nothing at all," I replied. To change the subject, I got out of the car to rummage through Oscar's huge trunk to find Bridget's Christmas present among those for my family that I had safely hidden there.

After she opened her present—an adorable teddy bear that I knew she would love—we exchanged holiday kisses while still parked in the movie parking lot. "Merry Christmas, Bridget!" I exclaimed, giving her a heartfelt kiss. "I love you, Sweetie."

"And I love you," she murmured softly, kissing me back tenderly. Then she added thoughtfully and with great excitement, "I have a Christmas present for you, too. It's something I made for you. But it's back at my house."

I drove east into the foothills of the Wasatch Mountains to drop Bridget off at her home overlooking the Salt Lake Valley. Once we were in her spacious living room, Bridget excused herself, and soon returned with a huge box in Christmas wrapping. "Here," she said, handing me the box. "I hope you like it. I've been working on it for months."

Ripping through the wrapping paper quickly, I opened the box to find a huge, hand-sewn pillow covered in a stunning blue fabric. "Wow!" I exclaimed. "It's big enough for both of us to cuddle on while we watch TV at my place!"

"That was the idea," Bridget smiled broadly. "Do you like it?"

"Oh, I love it!" I pulled the pillow out onto the living room carpet, and plopped down on it. "Come and join me, Bridg!" She came down to rest at my side, lying on the enormous pillow that nearly swallowed us both. "Merry Christmas, Sweetie!" she said.

"Merry Christmas, Sweetheart," I replied, giving her a kiss. "What a wonderful Christmas this has been already, and it's only December 23!"

I carried my huge blue pillow out to the car as Bridget walked with me. And then we said our last romantic goodbyes before I pulled out of the driveway, heading home for the holiday break.

Officially expelled from BYU, I felt so much shame during that drive home for the holidays.

As it happened, our family received a wonderful holiday gift that year on January 2, when Craig's wife Peggy gave birth to my nephew Marc, the first of their three children. They would later add my niece Alicia and my nephew Michael to their family.

Mom and Dad were, of course, thrilled to have yet another grandchild, and I felt blessed to be an uncle again. Though after Marc's birth, I became keenly aware of my newfound status as the only unmarried and childless member of our ever-expanding family.

I returned to Provo in January 1973, masquerading as a registered full-time BYU student. What I hoped Bridget and Harlan and none of my fellow students knew was that I was returning to Provo as a pariah, carrying enough home study courses to match the credits I could have earned that semester if I had remained a registered full-time student.

My roommate Doug and I were joined in our apartment that semester by two new roomies. Doug had been an easy roommate to live with, though we never became close, but I can't even remember the names of my new roommates that semester. The three RMs, Doug and the other two, all chose to room together in the sleeping alcove beyond the drawn curtain, while I continued to sleep in my single bed out in the main living room, as though they hoped not to catch my disease. I suspect that my roommates had been warned by the Office of University Standards to stay clear of me. But regardless of the reason, they were as modest and circumspect around me as I was around them. When my roommates were all away at school during the day, I did my home study courses in our apartment.

Having spent much of the Christmas holidays working on my new one-act play, I finished it in early January, and gave a copy to both Bridget and Harlan to get their opinions.

After Harlan and Bridget both finished reading the play, which I had titled *The Scrapbook*, the three of us met at Heaps Of Pizza. Raising his 7-Up, Harlan said, "Kerry, your new play is a cinch to win the Mormon Festival of the Arts!" And Bridget was just as complimentary. I melted like the cheese on our pizza.

I had high hopes, of course, when I submitted the play to Dr. Charles Whitman to be considered for the Mormon Festival of Arts. I was even more excited when I received a call from Dr. Whitman only a few days later, asking that I visit him in his office regarding my play, believing that he had great news to offer me.

Instead, once inside Whitman's office, he handed me two memos, one from the Drama Department Chairman, Dr. Harold I. Hansen, and one from the University's Standards Office.

"Here, Kerry," he said, "You need to read these."

I took the memo from Standards, and read it aloud:

> *"Given Brother Ashton's violation of University Standards, and because he was expelled at the end of last semester due to immoral activities, he should not be selected as a winner in this year's Festival of Arts competition. Regardless of his accomplishments, we cannot honor a student who has violated the high moral standards of this institution."*

Dismayed and embarrassed, I stared at Dr. Whitman. "Who received these memos?" I asked fearfully.

"Every member of the Drama Department faculty," he explained.

My face flushed with shame. The feelings of hurt and anger built inside me until I finally blurted out, "Why didn't they just me put a huge scarlet F on my chest?"

"An F?" he asked quizzically.

"A scarlet F for Faggot!" I replied hotly. "An F for Failure!"

I paused a moment to compose myself. "Here, I'm trying to repent of my sins, but all they can do is cast stones!"

"Perhaps I did wrong to show you these memos," Dr. Whitman explained. "But I didn't want you to think that your play wasn't good enough to win. As a matter of fact, I was going to recommend it for the festival next March, until I received these two memoranda."

"Thank you, Dr. Whitman. That means a lot to me," I replied quietly. The ache and shame in my heart expanded throughout my body, from the tips of my toes to the hair on my head.

"By the way, I read *The Scrapbook* all in one sitting the other evening. It's one of the best plays by a student playwright that I've read." He paused. "For what it's worth, I hope you will resubmit it next year, if they reinstate you as a student, that is, and you choose to stay on here at the Y."

I left Dr. Whitman's office terribly shaken.

A week later, I auditioned for the biggest show of the BYU season, the Broadway musical, *1776*, which would be produced in early March. Anyone could be cast in a BYU production, whether they were registered as an official student or not, so I thought it would be okay. And at first things went swimmingly. Dr. Charles Metten, who was directing the production, cast me in the leading role of Benjamin Franklin. All theater students checked the Drama Board daily, so virtually every student in the Drama Department saw the notice and knew that I was cast as a lead, so much so that I received calls of congratulations from all of my friends in the BYU theater world. I was over the moon! This was just what I needed to offset all of the shame that I was feeling at the time.

The next morning, however, the Drama Board showed a line drawn through my name, listing the actor's name that would replace me. So I went to Dr. Metten's office to confront him.

"Why was I blacklisted?" I asked pointedly.

"I received two new memos about you early this morning," Dr. Metten explained. "Both of these memos were far more detailed and explanatory than the two previous memos I received about you only last week. A memo came from the Standards Office explaining precisely and in graphic detail why you were expelled at the end of last semester. The second, from Chairman Harold I. Hansen, cautioned that you should not be cast in any production on campus while you are officially expelled for committing disgraceful acts of perversion! I posted the casting notice last night, and did not read these latest memos until this morning, so I had to replace you. As far as I am concerned, you brought this on yourself, as you have brought disgrace upon our University and the whole department!"

Once he completed his sermon, I said nothing other than to excuse myself, as I did not want to weep in front of him.

Soon after that, Dr. Preston Gledhill announced a casting call for his upcoming production of *The Diary of Anne Frank*, which would be produced both at BYU and at the Promised Valley Playhouse in Salt Lake City, where it would have a month's run. I went to visit Dr. Gledhill at his office.

"Hello, Dr. Gledhill," I said softly. "Thank you for seeing me."

"My pleasure," he replied pleasantly.

"Not many BYU professors would say that any more," I said. "I assume you got the memos about me from Dr. Hansen and the Standards Office."

"Yes, I did," he replied. "I was sorry to hear about your troubles."

"I am working hard to earn the forgiveness of my Heavenly Father and to return here as a student. But Dr. Metten replaced me in *1776*. Now everyone in the Drama Department knows about it."

"It is regrettable how that was handled," he said sadly.

"Will you consider me for *Anne Frank*? If you can't, I understand, and I won't bother to audition."

He looked into my eyes as I wept. Finally, Dr. Gledhill spoke. "Can you promise me that you will fully abide by all of the standards of the University and the LDS Church, during the entire time of the production's run?" he asked quietly.

"Yes, Professor, I can," I responded strongly.

"That's enough for me," he stated. "Audition, and we'll see."

I auditioned for Dr. Gledhill later that week. And, going way out on a limb, he cast me in the role of Mr. Van Daan, a small but powerful character part.

When the play opened to good reviews, I was singled out for my performance. I felt grateful, as I had worked hard to give a performance worthy of the trust that Dr. Gledhill had shown in me. More than that, I was humbled and grateful to be given an opportunity to accomplish something worthwhile at a time when I was overwhelmed by shame.

******

Dad and I both shared tears together that afternoon in the summer of 1981, as we sat parked in his Dodge Monaco, in front of the abandoned sagebrush covered site of Dad's childhood farm. "Come on, Honey," Dad said, finally starting up the car's ignition, "I want to show you something."

We turned around and drove back up the isolated road, heading toward the Interstate, until we came to an abandoned, worn-down, one-room schoolhouse. Dad pulled the car over and parked.

"This was where I went to school for the first eight years, and where I attended church meetings, too," Dad explained. "I always was a rotten kid. I started sinning here, even when I was a little boy. I even did nasty things with my female teacher here, many times." He paused, and wiped away the tears of shame from his eyes. "I always was a bad seed from the start!"

I was alarmed by his confession, but not for the reasons he assumed. "Dad," I said softly, putting my arm around his shoulder, "How old were you when these things happened?"

"I guess I was seven or eight."

"And how old was your teacher?"

"She was in her early 30s, I suppose," he said.

"Dad, you didn't do bad things to your teacher! She did bad things to you! She sexually abused you when you were a little boy."

"No," he said defiantly. "The whole thing was my fault."

"Dad, if a girl is molested by a grown man, whose fault is it?"

"The man's fault!" he exclaimed with certitude.

"That's how the law would see it, too," I said. "Whether the molested child is a little girl or a little boy, and whether the adult doing the molesting is a man or a woman, it's still sexual abuse. You were sexually abused as a child!"

He shook his head. "No, I was the bad one. I was the one who was always interested in doing awful sexual things. Heavenly Father took your mother from me, to punish me for my sins."

"I don't believe that, Dad," I interrupted. "God doesn't punish us in such cruel ways, no matter how badly we sin."

"No, Kerry, the Lord is punishing me, for failing your mother."

"Please don't say that, Dad," I implored him. "You're a good man. We all make mistakes, and hopefully we learn from them."

"No, Kerry," he argued, needing to hold on to his victimhood, "we must always obey our Heavenly Father's laws, or suffer the consequences."

My coming out talk with had revealed far more about my father than it had about myself. I simply couldn't take it all in; I felt as though I were about to explode. Yet, Dad kept talking, mercilessly chastising himself about every self-perceived mistake and failure of his entire life, as though everything he had held in for a lifetime was bursting out of him from the depths of his soul, all at once, until I felt like I might explode from all the new information.

Over the next few days, I went to Pocatello's Ross Park several times to an area hidden in the rock cliffs, where I knew closeted Mormon men went to find sex with other men, seeking an escape.

As I walked among the rock walls and caves that I had explored as a child, I felt overwhelmed by feelings of betrayal, realizing the hypocrisy I had grown up in: At the same time Dad was railing against moral transgressions in our home, he was out fornicating with other women behind Mother's back! Venting my anger, I picked up some rocks and pelted them against the cliff walls. "To hell with Latter-Day-Saints! To hell with Dad!"

A few days later, I gave Dad the self-help book, *Loving Someone Gay*. Dad locked it in his desk drawer, and promptly lost the key.

I came out a week later to my sister Denise and my brother Craig. When I told my sister, we were sitting along together on a blanket in Ross Park having a picnic, while Denise's children played on the swings. Although she was shocked by my announcement, she said she accepted me as I was. Feeling my sister's genuine love when I came out to her that day, given how steeped she was in Mormon dogma, meant more to me than I can say. That Denise and I have a close relationship to this very day—despite the religious and cultural differences between us that have only widened over time—has proven to be a steady and enduring salvation in my life.

Craig, on the other hand, insisted that I could choose to live according to LDS Church doctrine, if I wanted to.

"It's your choice," Craig proclaimed.

"I didn't have a choice. I was born gay."

"I don't believe that," he countered.

"I know you don't, because you don't want to," I replied. "If you accepted the fact that the Lord made me this way, you would have to rethink everything you believe."

For the rest of my visit home that summer, Dad and I got along, until the very last day before I was to fly home, when we had another religious argument. "We can't go on like this, Kerry Lynn," Dad had said firmly. "You must either return to the church and live the kind of life your mother wanted you to, or I have to find some way of accepting you as a Gentile."

We had stared at each other from opposite sides of the room, the LDS Church standing like the impenetrable wall of a Mormon Temple between us. It was the very same wall that had separated me from Mom. I wanted to scream with frustration and couldn't. "Will these conflicts never end?" I had asked myself.

"Never," was the inevitable reply. "The LDS Church is and always will be, a part of you just as your parents are part of you." The battle with my father would seemingly rage on forever.

The next day, a day in July 1981, I returned to Manhattan.

I was shocked, of course, when Dad called me in October to tell me that he was marrying again, after having met Sarah less than a month earlier. In her mid-30s and 25 years younger than Dad, Sarah had married twice before but both of her husbands had died, and she had three teenage children. Dad could not marry Sarah in the Temple, since Sarah was already sealed in a Temple marriage to her first husband, so the standard marriage vows of "till death do us part," had to suffice.

In an LDS Temple marriage, as opposed to a civil or church marriage, a man and wife are "sealed to each other for time and all eternity," to live together in the hereafter with all of their offspring, as an eternal family, perhaps on their own planet. Since Mormons believe that Heavenly Father lives on the Planet Kolob with a huge harem of women and with His offspring, and since a sacred principle in the Mormon Gospel states, "As man is, God once was; as God is, man might become," the goal of every devout Mormon man is to eventually rule his own planet with a harem of his own wives—just as God rules the Planet Kolob—and to populate his new planet with as many of his celestial offspring as possible.

Dad married again before Thanksgiving, and moved in with Sarah and her three teenagers in their home in the tiny LDS farming community of Shelley, Idaho.

Less than a year later, my half-brother Isaac was born.

******

On the first really sunny day of January 1973, the carillon bells rang out across the wide expanse of campus, announcing that it was time for the required Devotional Assembly. I was waiting for Bridget in front of the Brigham Young statue when she ran up the concrete steps, her face beaming. "Sorry I'm late," she gushed, gasping for air. "I got tied up with a story."

"It's just as well," I said. "In fact, let's skip the assembly, period!"

"We can't," Bridget explained. "It's required attendance. Ezra Taft Benson is speaking." Since I was no longer registered as a student, I was not required to attend, but I couldn't let Bridget know that, so we scurried up the steps toward the Marriott Center.

212

As it turned out, Elder Benson's sermon concerned itself with chastity. From where Bridget and I were sitting at the top of the huge indoor arena, Elder Benson looked as small as an ant, but he certainly didn't sound like one, his voice booming from the speakers in the arena's ceiling overhead. It was the voice of Elder Ezra Taft Benson, one of the Twelve Apostles of the LDS Church, the voice of Mormon power and priesthood authority, emanating from an almost unseen yet awesome source. It was the voice of the Biggest Brother of them all. The 26,000 students packing the arena nodded their heads in unison like LDS robots. Taking this in, I suddenly wondered to myself, "Beyond being a programmed LDS robot, who am I?"

Both President Wilkinson and Dr. Parker encouraged me to concentrate upon Bridget as a potential wife whom I would want to make love to once we were married. But President Wilkinson cautioned me about going too far. "You should never do anything with Bridget that breaks *The Law of Chastity*," he ordered. "You must remember that the natural man is an enemy to God."

"And the unnatural man?" I thought. "Is he God's friend?"

Forced to walk a tightrope between encouraging a natural sexual desire for women but not acting on it, I counted on Bridget to block all of my sexual advances. She never let me down until late that semester, when Bridget and I lay kissing each other in Oscar's backseat while parked at our favorite spot in the foothills overlooking the LDS Provo Temple, just down the street from my off-campus apartment.

I moved my hand to the top button of her purple blouse, but this time Bridget didn't stop me. Instead, she moaned and pressed her tongue even harder into my mouth. I undid the button, sliding my hand to the next one, thinking she would stop me, but she still didn't resist. Nervously, my fingers worked their way down to the third button, slipping it free from its hole, and then to the fourth button, and then to the fifth! And still, she didn't stop me.

"Oh, Bridget!" I thought. "Don't make me go any further!" The last button slipped free. Her blouse billowed open, exposing the fine taut flesh and the lacy white bra encasing her breasts. I kissed her passionately—as I knew a normal man should, as Harlan must have done countless times with Jennifer.

Bridget moaned loudly, throwing her long slender arms about my neck, as my tongue danced with hers inside her mouth. I panicked. What now? I moved my hand up her body. It was soft and yielding, a contrast to Harlan's hard, muscular frame. My hand reached the edge of her brassiere. Still, she didn't stop me.

Gasping with anxiety not passion, my hand cupped her right breast through the lacy material of her bra. The mound of flesh felt firm yet soft. An erect nipple poked through the lace and tickled my palm as my penis curled into a shrinking snake.

Angry at my impotence, I kissed Bridget frantically, hoping for rescue but there was none, as she moaned with submission, gasping with desire. I pinned her firmly to Oscar's back seat, making a wet tongue-trail down her neck to her cleavage when I pulled her bra free, licking on her erect nipples. But I felt no passion, only self-contempt, even as I ran my hands underneath her skirt, until her hands finally pushed me away.

"Kerry," she admonished, "We have to wait until we're married."

"Here," I said, handing her the blouse and bra, "cover up." Obviously embarrassed, Bridget put her things back on as quickly as she could. Oscar's windows were steamed up in the backseat, so I cracked a back window slightly, breathing in the frigid February air.

Bridget moved up next to me, her auburn hair tossed and matted on her head. "Please don't be mad at me, Kerry," she said sweetly. "I had to stop you. You have to help me be good until we're married."

I laughed, my laughter bitter, hard, and full of sarcasm. Had she known how little she had to fear from my advances, she would have laughed bitterly, too. "This was my fault, not yours," I said.

Jon Stainbrook, the producer and owner of a professional summer stock theater, Dirty Jack's Wild West Theater in Jackson, Wyoming, came to BYU in 1973 to audition for *Annie Get Your Gun*, the play he would present at his professional theater during the upcoming summer. When he cast me in the role of Charlie Davenport, I was terribly excited, as this would be my first job as a professional actor.

After obtaining permission from my probation officer, I drove home to spend a few days in Pocatello, Idaho before making the three hour trip to Jackson, Wyoming in late May.

Working in Jackson should have been a break from the personal hell I was going through at Provo, but it didn't turn out that way.

When I got to Jackson, I shared a ratty old house with the cast and crew of the show. Most of the cast of *Annie Get Your Gun*, professionals all, enjoyed smoking, drinking and partaking of recreational drugs, not to mention all of the sex that they could find. As I was the only Mormon among them, and because I was sincerely committed to my repentance at that time, I certainly could not smoke cigarettes, drink alcohol, coffee or tea, or use drugs, and I most certainly could not have sexual relations outside marriage. Consequently, the entire cast and crew saw me as a "goody-two-shoes" and they treated me as such. Ironically, I felt even more alone among the liberal and wild-living actors in the cast that summer than I had among all of the conservative LDS students at the Y.

Cast members of both professional theaters in Jackson appeared in a nightly shootout at the center of town where a stagecoach was held up, and the Old West came to life for the tourists in the town square. It was fun playing to the thousands of tourists who gathered at the square each evening.

I played a drunken judge, earning huge laughs and applause, as I grasped at my bottle of whiskey and kept falling down repeatedly. My fellow actors found it ironic that I could play a drunk so convincingly since I had never had a taste of alcohol in my young life, and they rarely stopped razzing me about the fact.

Looking back on it now, my performance as the drunken judge was far better than the performance I gave in *Annie Get Your Gun* each night, as I was so overwhelmed with internal conflicts that summer that my performance onstage suffered.

I spent my days that summer in exile and alone, driving the few miles from Jackson into Grand Teton National Park every day to find solace in the natural beauty and solitude.

Mom and Dad came up in their trailer for a weekend visit to see the show, and brought Bridget with them. Since I had a night off from the show, we took the family trailer into Yellowstone Park and went camping overnight. It was the one bright spot in an otherwise miserable summer.

Later in the season, and given the clear animosity that the rest of the cast obviously felt about me, Mr. Stainbrook offered me an out, and I took it. I was never so happy to return home to Pocatello for the last of summer.

That August, once I was back home in Pocatello, I received word from the Office of University Standards that I would be allowed to return to BYU as a full-time student in the fall, but only if I continued my Rehabilitation Program with Wilkinson and Parker, while Brother Gilbert Clark continued to oversee my progress.

Naturally, I was happy to hear the news. It meant a chance to redeem myself at BYU in more ways than one.

Once I began my junior year at BYU in the fall of 1973, it became instantly clear that I had reenlisted for a second tour of duty in Hell. Indeed, I soon discovered that I was still being kept under surveillance, an ongoing aspect of my life at BYU that would last for several more months just so that Brother Clarke could make certain of my commitment to my Rehabilitation Program.

When I stopped in to the local 7-Eleven one late evening to visit my friend Skip, a friend from the cast of *Fiddler*, who worked the night shift, Skip invited me to join him in the back for a half-hour while he did his chores, as there were no customers in the store.

A few days later, Skip and I were both ordered to report separately to BYU's Standards Office to answer questions about what we were doing together alone, in the back of the 7-Eleven Store a few nights earlier. Then, in the first of several Witch Hunts—what I came to think of as Homo Hunts—Detective Hall called me into BYU Security Headquarters, to ask me about Dr. Banes, the professor who had befriended me in the past.

"Who?" I responded, uncomfortable under the light glaring down on me in the dark room. "I don't think I know anyone by that name."

"Oh, I think you do," Hall said, pulling out surveillance photos taken of me with Banes standing on his front porch on the night we first met, when I went to his home. "Now, do you remember?"

"I didn't ... I mean, he never gave me his name."

"But you do remember going back to his home at midnight that night, after meeting him in the parking lot of the Harris Fine Arts Center on campus?" he pressed.

"Yes, Sir," I answered.

"We put Professor Banes under surveillance a long time back before we did the same with you. What exactly were you and Professor Banes doing together alone, at his home behind closed doors, until 2am that morning?"

I felt like a dead fish caught in a net. "I don't remember," I said.

"Is that your final answer?" he asked, "Because I can make your life a living hell if I choose to, starting with a call to your probation officer, followed by a call to the judge, and then to your parents."

"Uh ... I remember that we ... talked about stuff ..."

"Like what?" he pressed.

"I told him that I might be gay, and he counseled me."

"You expect me to buy that?" he said, staring into me from behind the bright light. "We already have a student who will testify against Brother Banes in court if Banes doesn't step down from his faculty position. But we need collaboration. You don't even have to say that you did anything with him. Just tell us that he admitted to you that he was homosexual."

"Yes, Sir, he told me that. But he was only counseling me."

Professor Banes resigned later that week, citing health reasons.

******

As my sexual prowling in New York increased, I frequented he leather bars and private sex clubs like *The Mineshaft* in the meatpacking district, where a great deal of meatpacking went on.

In the spring of 1982, I had two sexual experiences within a

217

few weeks of each other that caused me to pull back from anonymous sex altogether. The first of these happened at a private sex club called *The Glory Hole* on West Street in the West Village, situated on a seedy, nearly abandoned block between two gay leather bars. The place had nothing but square booths with glory holes on every wall.

I was sitting in a booth at the club one late evening, when a leather man came into the booth next to mine. Looking at him through the large hole in the wall between us, I sized him up quickly. He was dressed in leather from the cap on his head to the heavy black boots on his feet. He was even wearing leather gloves. Slowly and ceremoniously, he stroked the package within his leather jock, unsnapping it and pushing his erection toward my anxiously waiting lips. "Okay, slave, suck me off!" he ordered.

I obeyed him instantly, providing him with the best oral service I knew how to give. When he neared orgasm, he shouted, "I'm getting ready to shoot. When I cum, I want you to hold my load in your mouth! Don't swallow any of it until I tell you that you can!"

When he ejaculated, I did as he had told me to, holding his cum in my mouth, awaiting his order to swallow.

He knelt down and stuck his face through the hole.

He had a full beard and a very handsome and masculine face, made all the more attractive by a wicked smile. Putting his gloved hands through the glory hole and shoving poppers into my nostrils one at a time, he took hold of my nipples and squeezed each of them harshly with his fingers. "Okay, slave!" he commanded. "Swallow! Swallow all of it now!" Once I obeyed him, he looked in through the hole and gave me another evil smile. "Well, slave, aren't you going to thank me for my special gift?"

I was enraged and humiliated, but I had an erection as hard as steel. Noting this and giving my left nipple a hard twist, he added, "Obviously you loved it. You should thank me for my gift."

"Yes, Sir," I replied, "Thank you for your gift, Sir."

"That's a good boy!" he replied matter-of-factly, as he gave my face a light smack with his gloved hand.

Pulling his leather jock back into place, he walked out of his booth without thanking me or even looking back, letting the door slam shut behind him.

His utter indifference, if not downright disdain that he showed toward me, turned me on immensely. I remained on my knees, beating off until I came. Then I ran out of there as fast as I could.

As I rode home in a cab, I couldn't shake off the feeling that something about the sexual scenario I had just played out at the club, felt all too familiar. It was as though some man in my distant past had treated me this way, like an object to be used for his pleasure, like his own personal toy that he had then disposed of. But when had this happened to me? Who had done this to me? As hard as I wracked my brain, I could not remember. But the shame washing over me, as the cab rushed up Eighth Avenue, the shame that heated my face and numbed my thoughts, didn't feel new. Instead, it was a very old feeling, clearly a reenactment of something that had happened to me long ago. But when had it happened and with whom?

Later that spring, I found myself involved in another intense sexual experience. This time it happened in the men's room of the 55th Street Playhouse, a gay porn theatre in Manhattan, serving another self-appointed master. As men came into the restroom, this 'master' encouraged them to form a line so that I could service each of them orally.

"The pig slave loves swallowing cum, doesn't it, pig?" the master asked, twisting my tits and dragging me from one man to the next. There were ten guys crammed into the men's room, and I was the only naked one among them. Humiliated, I was furiously masturbating nonetheless. When the master saw that I was close to cumming, he asked two men to stand on either side of me to restrain me from touching myself, as another stepped in to hold my feet in place. Meanwhile, the rest of the men lined up to use my mouth as they pleased. Eventually someone said, "Maybe you should let the guy up!"

"Are you kidding?" he replied. "Look at its hard dick! it loves being used." Turning to me, he asked, "Isn't that right, slave?" He twisted my tits until I replied, "Yes, Master! it loves this!"

Once the men realized that my self-appointed master was only giving me the humiliation that I wanted and needed, they took great pleasure in assisting him in my utter degradation.

"I bet there isn't anything my little pig wouldn't do for me!" the master scoffed. Though restrained and unable to touch myself, I suddenly ejaculated, sending volleys of cum in all directions. Seeing this, the men released me quickly.

Feeling utterly degraded and thoroughly exposed, I got up and worked my way through the crowded men's room to the stall to get my clothes. As I pushed through the crowd, I heard someone chastise the master, saying, "You went way too far! You could damage someone psychologically acting that way!"

The 'master' replied in sneering fashion, still in his dominant role. "Are you kidding? I just showed it what it is! Someday it will thank me! I guarantee you, it'll never forget me!"

Still naked, I ran down the stairs clutching my clothes in my arms, and dressed in the lobby. Something about the experience felt like a reenactment of something I had experienced before. But when had it happened, and with whom? What was I trying to make myself remember?

Anxiety overwhelmed me as I ran to my apartment on West 54th Street, when I suddenly heard the voice of my angel, as though he were invisibly running beside me. "Kerry," the voice warned, "you are meant to explore these things and in time you will discover the answers to all of your questions, but for now you must back away from sexual experiences like this."

Because of this warning, I stopped having anonymous sex, and gradually became available for a more loving, fulfilling sex life.

******

Streisand's seventh film, *The Way We Were* opened in October 1973. Both the film and the theme song of the movie became the biggest hits of the year, and Barbra was nominated for her second Oscar as Best Actress. I took Bridget with me to see the film's premiere in Provo. We both loved the film, and during our make-out session afterward overlooking the Provo Temple, I kissed her the way Redford had kissed Streisand in the movie.

Halloween of 1973 came and went without fanfare. Since my roommates had planned an evening out, Bridget, Harlan, and I spent it in my living room. All three of us were lying on the huge blue pillow that Bridget had made for me the previous Christmas, as we watched old black-and-white horror movies on TV. Suddenly, I thought of Jack and Jennifer and Debbie, all missing.

"I was thinking of Jack just now," Bridget said quietly, as though she had listened in on my thoughts.

"I was too!" I responded softly.

"Why would he just drop out of school like that?" she asked. "So suddenly and without warning to any of us?"

"I have no clue," I replied.

Having taken Dr. Whitman's advice from the previous year, when I was officially expelled from the university, I decided to resubmit my one-act play, *The Scrapbook*, for the Mormon Festival of Arts.

Shortly after submitting the play, Dr. Whitman called me into his office to tell me the good news: My play was one of the four winning one-act plays that would be presented at the prestigious Mormon Festival of Arts that March.

Only a few days later, I confessed my fears to Bridget that the production of my play at the upcoming Festival might end up a failure. "My play's going to bomb, Sweetie, I just know it."

"The Festival honors the best in Mormon Art," Bridget reassured me, "and your play was chosen. That says something."

I grimaced, trying to describe what I was feeling. "They talk about Mormon Art at BYU as though it were the ultimate form of artistic expression," I stated carefully, "but to my way of thinking art is art."

Bridget looked stunned. "What are you saying?"

"I think Mormon artists should create art for art's sake, not for the Mormon Church."

What I had said may sound innocent enough to Gentile ears, but to most Mormon students and LDS faculty at the Lord's University, I had uttered heresy. Bridget looked at me as though I had slapped her in the face. As much as she wanted to play the role of a burgeoning liberal Mormon woman, she was still as morally conservative as the other students on campus. "I disagree," Bridget said emphatically. "Everything we do should serve the church and the Lord."

"Should it?" I asked, questioning both her and myself. "I want to create art, not dogma!"

Bridget was unnerved. "You know, Kerry, you're becoming quite the rebel. Even a month ago you wouldn't have talked that way."

"You must bring it out in me," I said with a wide grin, trying to get her to smile.

"Either that or Harlan does," she replied. "Sometimes I think that he's a bad influence on you."

"Harlan is the best friend I've ever had, Bridget!" I replied with fierce loyalty. "I won't have you or anybody else say bad things about him."

"I'm sorry," she offered. "I didn't mean anything. I love Harlan. You know that. It's just you're changing before my eyes."

"I am changing," I replied. "Sometimes it scares me."

"You're becoming radical," she observed, just as a respectable news reporter might.

Harlan, who sat hunched over his desk, was cramming for an upcoming test in his Philosophy class, when I visited him at his apartment in mid-November.

"How's it coming?" I asked, as I peered at him from my portable typewriter that I had brought with me that night.

"Awful," he replied, his voice weary and frustrated. "I hate this stuff. I'll never remember all of it." He yawned, stretching his arms. "Oh, wow, what I wouldn't give for a massage right about now."

Without thinking, I offered him one.

Harlan gratefully accepted, instantly stripping off his shirt and pulling his Temple garments down to his waist. "What are you doing?" I asked nervously.

"You can't give me a rubdown through my garments.

"I suppose not," I replied warily.

Harlan turned face down on the sofa.

"Come on, Babe!" he said. "Where's the massage you promised?"

"What do I do first?" My voice tightened with sexual tension. Seeing his muscular back and broad shoulders made me dizzy.

"First, put your hands on my neck," he instructed gently.

The contact of my trembling hands with his solid muscular flesh caused a passion that I believe pervaded us both. My breath stopped for a moment. "Now," he instructed, "apply some pressure with your hands and knead the muscles."

"Need?" I asked. I couldn't have heard him right.

"You know, like you were kneading bread."

"Oh! Okay, sure." I began working on his neck, as a swelling passion hardened in my loins. "Does that feel okay?" I asked, barely able to speak. He let out a moan that was both sensual and alarming. "It feels terrific!"

"I'm glad. I want to do it just the way you like it."

"Is something wrong, Kerry?" he asked gently.

"No. Why?" I replied, my voice shaking.

"Your hands are trembling," he noted.

I felt like crawling under the bed.

"I guess I'm afraid I might hurt you," I offered lamely.

"Don't worry! I'm tough enough to take a little back rub!"

"Okay!" I said, managing a fearful titter.

"Now, just rub your hands over my shoulders and back," he suggested. I massaged his shoulders as though I were absorbing his soul. "That's it, Babe," he moaned. "Rub 'em down good!" I gulped down my fear. "You might want to straddle me, so that you can get my whole back," he added.

"All right," I murmured.

Situating myself above his body on the sofa, my fingers raced to explore the breathtaking landscape of his back.

"Hey, slow down, Babe! Take your time," he instructed tenderly.

I slowed down, as he had instructed me to. "That's it, Babe," he whispered, moaning with pleasure.

"I hope this is helping you," I said sheepishly, wishing my erection would disappear.

"More than you know, Babe." He let out a deep sensual growl as the tension oozed from him. "You're a pro and you didn't know it."

"Thanks," I replied. For a moment I fantasized what it might be like to caress his back with my lips, but I quickly ended the fantasy.

In early December 1973, a year after my sentencing, the judge expunged my police record, and my association with my parole officer, Brother Smithfield, came to an end. It felt like a complete relief that I no longer had to attend the support group he ran every Tuesday night with convicts. I felt like a new man. But the feeling would not last.

Parked with Bridget on a winter's evening in December 1973 during finals week, on a secluded, snowy road overlooking the Provo Temple, the sparkling lights of all of Provo and Utah Valley stretched out beneath us. After kissing for a long while, I got Bridget's bra off, as Oscar's windows became steamy. I couldn't figure out how to get her pantyhose off though, so I finally ripped them off in frustration. I didn't know what to do next, even as she lay panting with desire.

"I love you, Bridget," I said suddenly. "But we have to stop."

Bridget pulled her skirt down and put her bra back on. She even got her hair back in place before I spoke again.

"Oh Bridget," I added, "I love you, but I can't be your boyfriend."

"What?" she asked half-laughing. "You're kidding, right?"

"Bridget, I'm serious. It's not going to work out between us."

"Why?" she asked loudly, fighting for the future life we had talked of sharing together. "Is it because of tonight?" She clutched at her blouse. Her voice was full of hurt and shame. "Did I disappoint you?" she asked. I said nothing in response. "You know," she continued, "when I'm laying back like that, my breasts don't look as big as they actually are."

"Your breasts are beautiful, Bridget. It's not you. It's me. I can't do it anymore."

"Do what?" she asked. "Is there someone else, Kerry?" Her voice cracked with emotion and I could feel her heart breaking. "Have you met a girl you like more than me?" she said, asking another question. Her hazel eyes were tearful, her face full of wounded vulnerability.

"It's not another girl. I'll never love a woman more than I do you."

"But you and I … we even talked about marriage. Don't you want to marry me now?" she asked with the heartache of a lover scorned. Pushing the front seat forward, she opened the car door, and ran down the snowy lane toward the illuminated Temple.

I chased after her. "Bridget!" I shouted. "Come back Bridget, please! I have to talk to you."

"Oh, Kerry," she screamed back, "Just leave me alone."

I caught up with her within 30 yards or so.

"Let me go, Kerry!" she shouted, as tears streamed down her face.

Wind whipped down from the mountains above us, twirling her hair into a mess. "I have to talk to you, Bridget," I said, holding her in place. "I can't just let you run off like this."

"Why not?" she yelled. "You don't love me anymore!"

"You don't understand. This is my fault, not yours."

"Why?" she asked. Mascara ran down her cheeks, as new snowflakes began to fall.

"I have a problem, Bridget," I explained.

Her eyes searched my face for an explanation. "What is it?"

I tried to speak, but the words wouldn't come out. How could I tell her? I wanted to pull her back to the car and start the evening over again, but it was too late now. "What is it?" she pressed. "Will you please just tell me?"

I let the words burst out of me: "I'm in love with Harlan."

Her eyes widened with shock. "Harlan?" she asked in horror, slowly absorbing what I had implied. "You're … homosexual?"

"I've been going for counseling for a long time now," I explained, "but nothing helps; I'm not attracted to women."

"What was all that back there in the car just now?" she asked.

225

"Me trying to be something I'm not," I replied gently.

"Maybe it's me. Maybe I'm not your type of woman."

"It's not you, Sweetie. You're beautiful, and I love you." I took a deep breath. "If I had to choose a wife, I would choose you."

"But you want Harlan!" she bit back. She took a deep breath. "Is he homosexual, too?"

"Hardly. You know Harlan! He's as straight and masculine as they come. He's a Marine, you know."

"Does he know how you feel about him? Have you told him?"

"I've never had the guts," I explained quietly. "I've tried everything to change how I feel, but I'm still in love with him."

She let out a sob of despair, matching the despair I felt within.

"I don't believe this!" she shouted. "I don't believe any of this!"

Bridget tore herself from me, and ran through the snow toward the illuminated Temple.

"Bridget!" I shouted. "I have to talk to you!"

I ran after her, catching her near the bottom of the snowy hill at the edge of the Temple's parking lot. She struggled with me, pounding her fists against my chest, trying to escape.

"Bridget, can't we just talk?"

"I thought you loved me," she wailed, pounding her hands against me. "And all this time you were in love with Harlan! How could you?" Bridget's right hand flew through the air, slapping me across the face. "I hate you!" she screamed, her body falling into the snow.

"I don't blame you for hating me, Bridget," I replied, kneeling beside her. "I wanted to tell you for so long; I just didn't know how."

As we knelt in the snow looking at the illuminated Temple, I told her the whole story. When I finished, Bridget seemed calmer as she wiped the mascara from her cheeks. "Who else knows about this?" she asked. "Who else have you told?"

"Just you and the Brethren on campus," I explained.

"How can you feel that way about another man?"

"I don't know," I replied, looking at the Temple with its golden spire a vivid phallic symbol of Mormon male dominance. "I'm still trying to figure that out," I added.

"It's revolting, Kerry. You're disgusting!" The tone in Bridget's voice sounded as bitter and cold as the winter night that surrounded us, and very much like the way I felt inside.

"Now can you understand why we can't stay boyfriend and girlfriend?" I asked finally. "I want you to find a husband who can love you the way you deserve to be loved."

"I understand," she replied, her intonation as chilly as the air.

She stood up, brushing the snow from her skirt and blouse. With her mascara-streaked face and windblown hair, she looked like a battered Raggedy Ann doll. I stood up and tried to hold her, but she pushed me away. "Don't touch me!" she warned, snapping at me. "I just want you to take me home."

We walked back up the hill to where Oscar was parked on the deserted snowy lane, saying not a word to each other.

On the drive back to her apartment, we both remained silent. Then, when I pulled up in front of her place, she jumped out of the car and ran to her door as fast as she could. "Bridget," I shouted, as I got out of the car, "can I see you tomorrow?"

She slammed her apartment door behind her in reply. Feeling like a lost and abandoned child, I found a note from Bridget in my mailbox the next day:

> *"Dear Kerry, I know it was hard for you to tell me the truth, but you did the right thing. I have completed my final exams, but I won't be coming back to BYU. I'm transferring to the University of Utah where I can live at home with my folks, and begin a new life without you. This is goodbye. If you love me as you say you do, let me find my life apart from you. I wish you only the best, Kerry. I love you, and I always will."*

******

Mom was not merely our family's matriarch. She was our rock. She was and always had been the glue that had held us all together as a family, even during horrible domestic violence. After her death, it became ever more evident that our family would split apart without Mom to hold us together as the family we once were. This only became more apparent once Dad began a new family of his own, complete with a new wife, a new baby, and her three teenage children. Now that Dad and all of my siblings each had families of their own, it became glaringly obvious that I was utterly alone. Clearly, if I wanted to be part of a family, I had to create my own. Mine had to be a family of choice,

When I called Dad in August 1982 from New York, our conversation quickly turned to the Mormon Church, as it always seemed to. With Dad pressing me to return to the LDS faith, our talk quickly became overheated. "Dad, I allow you to believe as you want," I shouted. "Can't you do the same for me?"

"I'm sorry. But I can't allow you to berate the church."

I sat on the ratty sofa in my studio apartment on 54th Street, with the phone pressed against my ear, and my gut aching with tension. "I'm not berating the church, Dad," I countered. "I just don't want to talk about the Mormon Church, period." How could I make him understand? "My beliefs and my values weren't handed to me by any religion," I explained. "I had to discover them for myself. And after I found them, I had to fight for them."

"But the church is true, Kerry Lynn," Dad responded.

"Don't preach LDS Doctrine to me. I've heard it all my life!"

"Why don't you start living it then?" he chastised.

I slammed my fist into the sofa with frustration, nearly throwing the phone across the room.

"There you go again with your damn expectations!" I said.

"All your mother wanted was for you to return to the faith!"

"Leave Mom out of this!" I snapped, gulping back emotion.

"Kerry, the Adversary's caught you by the tail!" Dad's words were harsh, yet spoken with a Saint's prayer on his lips. "If you continue to deny the truth, the Lord will have no choice but to cast you into Outer Darkness as a Son of Perdition!" I laughed more out of frustration than anything else. "Kerry Lynn," he retorted, "don't laugh at me! You are denying the true Gospel! What sin could be worse than that?"

"Oh, I have so many! I don't know where to begin."

Dad took a deep breath before exploding in rage. "I'm glad that I don't know what activities Lucifer has dragged you into!"

"Dad, I'm so tired of listening to your goddamn judgments!"

"Kerry, please don't take the Lord's name in vain ever again."

"That's funny coming from you, Dad. You're the one who taught me how to take the Lord's name in vain!"

Dad gasped at the other end of the phone line, as though I had just slapped him in the face. There was a pause in our conversation as we both breathed heavily. "I apologize for that, Father," I said quietly.

"I deserved that," he said. "I made so many mistakes as a father."

As an actor in Manhattan, agents, producers and the like, often told me that to make it in New York, "If you want to star in your own play, you need a name." Meanwhile, I worked as hard as I could to make a name for myself and for my play.

Occasionally, I worked with celebrities, mostly as an extra, appearing once with both Meryl Streep and Robert DeNiro in the same scene in the film, *Falling in Love*. I was always professional in such cases, but inside I questioned whether I was good enough to be in the same scene, even as an extra or as a bit player, with such famous and acclaimed actors. I had already proved onstage that I was just as talented and professional as the best of them, but inside I still felt inadequate. Since I didn't have the success that matched the famous actors I worked with, since I didn't have the name that they did, I did not feel equal to them. Working with celebrities only made me more aware of my shame.

In 1982, I was cast in the leading role of Nick in Richard Hall's new play, *Happy Birthday, Daddy,* which had a successful run at The Glines Theatre in New York City, and was later published. The play called for me to appear onstage nearly nude for the first time. Fearful that the audience would sneer and laugh at me when I walked out onstage in only the skimpiest of shorts, I was quite surprised when no one laughed, and that a few gay men actually murmured approvingly from their seats. But because of the shame still within me, I was full of self-doubt.

After *Happy Birthday, Daddy*, I opened *The Wilde Spirit* in an Off-Off-Broadway production with my longtime friend Lewis Kerman acting as my producer. Happily, the show received glowing reviews from the New York critics, and I was thrilled, since I had worked hard to perfect both my play and performance.

Though Steve Sondheim and I were no longer lovers, I invited him to attend. He declined, even though I was performing very near his east side townhouse. After that, I let my acquaintance with Sondheim fall by the way, telling myself that I had only been his boy toy. The shame I felt about my affair with Sondheim became so great that I never told a soul about it for decades afterward.

Because of the success of the Off-Off-Broadway production, I met Mitch Douglas, a literary agent with International Creative Management. The night that Mitch invited me to dinner, he brought his most famous client Tennessee Williams with him. The three of us sat down to dinner at Curtain-Up, a café on the corner of 43rd Street and 9th Avenue in Manhattan Plaza, a complex for professional actors and writers where I would later reside. Tennessee and I kept asking each other questions about the other's work. It did my heart good to have the fellowship of such a great playwright as Tennessee Williams, but I had inner doubts, still questioning whether I deserved to be in such company.

Mitch knew what he was doing when he invited Tennessee to join us for dinner, since Mitch and I agreed to work together that same night. Once Mitch became my literary agent, he encouraged me to write a fictional account of my experiences at BYU.

That fall, I took my one-man play on tour throughout the western United States. By that time, I had already performed my one-man play in every type of theatrical engagement and in every sort of venue in America. I performed the play on a makeshift platform in a community college cafeteria before an audience of less than ten people, and I presented the play to packed houses of more than 2,500. When touring, I always arrived with my makeup kit and all of the costumes and props. The university, arts center or regional theatre provided all of the furniture that was used onstage, as well as the lighting and sound equipment, and the staff to run cues and the front of the house.

Whether performing at a regional theatre or at a university, when I arrived at the venue, I would first get the furniture set in place on stage for an all-day technical rehearsal. Sometimes there would be a brief timeout for local TV and radio interviews. Regardless, I would always do a full dress rehearsal, then run backstage to get into my costumes and makeup, and *voila!* The curtain would open, and I would give the best performance that I could. Then afterward, I would collapse backstage.

******

After my breakup with Bridget in late December 1973, a special meeting was held in Brother Clarke's office where Clarke, Wilkinson, and Parker—what I had come to think of as the Holy Trilogy—met to decide my fate. "Brother Ashton," Brother Gilbert Clarke demanded to know why I had told Bridget about myself.

"Young man," Clarke said, "whatever made you feel you had to tell your girlfriend about your abnormal sexual inclinations?"

"She deserved to know the truth," I replied, knowing that I had done the right and honorable thing. "It was the right thing to do."

"The right thing?" Clarke asked, his face upset. Seated behind his immaculate desk, Clarke looked through my voluminous file. "Obviously, we need to take stiffer measures in your Rehab Program." He paused dramatically. "Dr. Hugh Parker has recommended that you need to begin to undergo electroshock therapy sessions, and I concur with his recommendation."

I felt the blood drain from me. "You mean shock treatments?"

"I wouldn't call it that," Dr. Parker interjected. "In Aversion Therapy, as many refer to it, we only use a mild electrical shock as part of the electroshock therapy to make distasteful what once seemed pleasurable." Dr. Parker let his words sink in. "It sounds scary, I know, but it has proven very effective in cases like yours."

"I don't want shock treatments!" I replied, my voice rising as I considered running from the office.

"Calm down, Brother Kerry," Clarke replied. "We aren't going to do anything without your permission, nor would we want to."

The tension I felt within me eased too soon.

"However," Clarke continued, "If you aren't willing to go forward with your Rehabilitation Program, I will be forced to expel you and inform your parents."

"You would inform my parents? About everything?"

"Yes, we would need to," Clarke replied. "But take the Christmas break to think it over." He paused to let all of this information sink in. "You can let us know what you decide when you return to campus in January."

Once I was back at my apartment, I threw my schoolbooks across the room. I felt lucky that my roommates had already left for the holidays and that I was alone.

Suddenly everything in the apartment suddenly became blurry, as my heart began palpitating furiously. I found a razor blade in the medicine cabinet. Tearing my clothes off, I filled the tub with water and then, slipping naked into the tub, I pressed the razor blade against the base of my penis, the root of all my problems. But then I thought of what Mom would say when she heard I had done it that way. No, I couldn't do it like that! I jumped out of the tub and put the razor blade on the vanity.

I didn't want to be naked when they found me, so I ran to my dresser in the main room to pull on some fresh undershorts.

Heading back to the bathroom, I stopped at the telephone sitting on the top of my desk. Knowing that Harlan hadn't left yet for Christmas break, I picked up the phone and dialed.

Hearing his voice when he answered made me cry.

"It's me, Harlan," I uttered, my voice shaky.

"Kerry? Is that you, Babe?" he asked. "What's wrong?"

I felt my knees wobble beneath me as my head whirled.

"Bridget and I broke up," I whispered. "She's left BYU and she's not coming back." Suddenly the sad images and music from *The Way We Were*—the film that Bridget and I had seen together only two months earlier, filled my thoughts and brought me to tears. My heart was racing and I felt dizzy.

"Harlan, I found a razor blade and I have to use it," I exclaimed. "They're forcing me to have shock treatments!"

"Where are you, Kerry? Are you at home?" he asked.

"Yes," I whispered. Though I had no idea of what was happening to me at the time, I now realize that I was in the early throes of a full-blown anxiety attack.

"Just hang on, Kerry," he said tenderly. "I'll be right there."

I dropped the phone, crumpling into a heap by my desk, as the room whirled around me. Panicked, dizzy, and overwhelmed by emotional pain and shame, all I could think about was bringing the bad feelings to an end. It wasn't that I wanted to die; I only wanted out of my suffocating LDS cocoon, to fly away as an escaping butterfly, like Harlan's dove. Remembered the razor blade that I had left on the vanity, I crawled into the bathroom and locked the door behind me, snaking my way through the red shag carpet to the vanity. Reaching up, I found the razor blade—what felt to me at the time like my only salvation—and took it in hand.

Lying down on the red shag carpet that would soon be far redder, I held the edge of the blade at my left wrist, pressing it unsteadily against the thin layer of skin separating life from death. It would take only one slice of the razor blade on each wrist, and I could lie back into the red carpet, as my life's blood slowly drained into it. Then, as though on cue, I heard the loving voice of my unseen spiritual guide who had joined me in the bathroom, whispering in my ear, saying, "Kerry, this is not the way." But I was beyond listening or caring.

Wave after wave of anxiety pounded me deeper and deeper into the red shag. I thought of Mom, and how she had once poured all of the contents of ten cake mix boxes into the middle of our kitchen floor. Now I felt as though I were pouring all of the contents of myself, every part of me that used to matter, into the middle of the deep red shag carpet of my bathroom. I was melting into red. And soon I would be gone. In the distance, I heard pounding on the bathroom door and Harlan's voice calling me back from whatever deep, dark hell I had fallen into. "Kerry, open the door!" he shouted desperately.

Lost in the middle of the blood-red carpet, clothed only in my white underwear, I was unable to find my way to the door. In a moment, I heard a key—apparently furnished by my landlady—turning in the lock.

Harlan rushed inside, coming to me. "Are you okay, Babe?" he asked, cradling me in his arms like a baby.

"Harlan?" I called out, "is it you?"

"Yes, Babe, it's me," he said gently. From far away I heard myself babbling like a nuthouse idiot. Suddenly Harlan was on the floor beside me, holding me tightly in his arms. I clung to him, sobbing, never wanting to let go. "Oh, Babe," he exclaimed, nearly in tears. "What's wrong?"

"They're trying to kill me, Harlan," I heard myself saying over and over again.

"Ssssh, Babe," he whispered, his strong arms holding me. "It's all right now. I'm here."

Harlan held me close to him on the bathroom floor, until I gradually calmed down and finally fell asleep in his arms.

I awoke an hour later still in Harlan's arms. Realizing for the first time that I was clad only in my underwear, I slowly moved away from him and managed to stand up, though I was still unsteady on my feet.

"You okay now, Babe?" he asked, as he rapidly stood up to keep me from falling.

"I think so," I replied, still somewhat dizzy.

"What's going on? You said someone was forcing you to have shock treatments."

"I can't tell you, Harlan," I said weakly, unable to look him in the eye. "I'm an abomination before God."

"That's nonsense!" he exclaimed.

"I only wish it were," I said, as I made my way into the living room. I found a blanket in my closet and covered myself in it, as I lay down on the sofa, turning to face the wall.

"All I know is that you're suicidal, and that you're shaking all over," he observed, as he followed me into the living room. "I can't help you if you won't tell me what's wrong." His hand stroked my shoulder with the touch only a very best friend can give. "Talk to me," he entreated.

If I didn't have to look at him, I thought, perhaps I could confess the shameful nature of my sins and of my very identity.

"Harlan, I'm … homosexual," I said, as tears burst from me.

Harlan quickly withdrew his hand from my shoulder.

At first, I thought Harlan was going to hit me. But he walked away from me to sit on the edge of my bed.

Still lying on the sofa and facing away from him, I broke down and told the whole story to the wall, as Harlan listened, leaving out the fact that I was desperately in love with him. When I finished talking, Harlan tried to make me look at him but I refused, ramming my face against the sofa. "Babe," he pleaded, "turn around. Believe it or not, I understand."

I could hardly believe my ears. "I thought you would hate me," I admitted, still facing away from him.

"I think you've been doing enough of that for the both of us," he said quietly, "as have too many of the LDS Brethren on campus." He stood up and ran to get a cold towel from the bathroom, returning to the sofa. "Turn around," he said softly. "Let me wipe your face off." My body stiffened. "Turn around, Babe," he prodded tenderly. Gently, he put his hand on my cheek and forced me to look at him. I'm sure my eyes were red and puffy, my face damp with tears which he quickly wiped away.

Finally I looked him in the eye. "I never thought I would confess all of this to you," I admitted.

"If this were four years ago, I would have reacted differently." He paused, before finally adding, "Babe, I have something to

235

confess, too." His voice, normally strong and deep, was weakened by feelings he obviously found difficult to express. "I knew, or at least I suspected, about your being ... the way you are ... from the first. It wasn't just that you looked like Danny, it was also that you acted like him, in that same way."

I sat up on the sofa, still wrapped in a blanket, trying to make sense of what Harlan had just told me. I still couldn't believe it: Harlan had known that I was gay before I did.

"When I was in high school, my best friend Hank and I did everything together," Harlan continued. "Then other buddies of mine caught Hank making out with another guy in a dark hallway at school. So I started calling Hank names like they did. One night after basketball practice, he confronted me. I was afraid he might try to kiss me or something queer like that, so I hit him, not once but a dozen times. I beat him up!" I let out a whimper and Harlan winced. "I left Hank bleeding in a hallway after school," he confessed. "I was so ashamed of myself."

I nodded slowly, taking in what he had just told me.

"After that," Harlan explained, "I tried to turn myself into a better man. I went on a mission. I put on more muscle and tightened up my body. I even put on a Marine's uniform and signed up for Vietnam, but nothing helped. I couldn't run away from myself! I had beat up my best friend! Where did all that rage inside me come from?"

His question hung in the air like a neon sign, impossible to miss.

"I should never have gone to Vietnam," he whispered, as his face clouded over with memories of the War. "I only went there to prove that I was a real man. I wasn't ready for what I saw there. I saw a whole village of Vietnamese women and children massacred, for God's sake." Harlan walked to my living room window, looking out on the beautiful view of Mount Timpanogos to the north. "Then Danny arrived," he continued haltingly. "He was the sweetest kid, fresh off the farm from Wisconsin. He wanted to be a filmmaker. He always talked about how he wanted to win an Oscar someday, just the way you do. One day, when snipers attacked our camp, I ended up saving his life. After that, we bonded."

"I can imagine," I said, wide-eyed from all that he was sharing with me.

"When Danny and I had our next leave in Saigon," Harlan explained, still staring out my living room window, not daring to even look at me, "we went to a whorehouse together. It was the first time for both of us, so we decided to hire the same girl, to give each other moral support, if that makes any sense." He paused. "But while he watched me screw her, he tried to kiss me!" His face turned red. "I told the whore to get out. That's when Danny confessed that he was in love with me. It was so disgusting!" He stared at me long and hard, before he spoke again. "I avoided Danny after that," he stated flatly. "He tried to apologize, but I wouldn't hear it. A few days later, when we got back to camp, Danny died in a trench at my side. After that, I swore I would make amends. Does that make sense?"

"I'm not sure," I replied, trying to take it all in.

"He died before I told him that I still cared about him, even though he was gay." Harlan cleared his throat. "After that, I prayed that God would give me a chance to make up for how I treated both Hank and Danny." He cleared his throat yet again and looked deeply into my eyes. "Then that first day when I saw you sitting in church, I hoped to make amends by treating you better than I treated them."

"So it was out of pity?" I asked, feeling terribly hurt.

"No, Babe!" he replied. "Once I got to know you, I knew I needed you much more than you needed me. I look strong on the outside, but you're so much stronger than I am on the inside." He put his hand in mine, and added, "Gay or not, between the two of us, you're the stronger man, though you may not know it yet."

Later that night, I told Harlan that the school wanted me to undergo shock treatments. "I don't know as I have any choice but to go through with it," I explained.

"Yes, you do," Harlan countered. "You can drop out, transfer as many credits as you can, and finish college somewhere else!"

"No, Harlan, I can't! They threatened me. If I don't go along with them, they'll tell my parents. And besides, I still want to change; I want to be normal." Even as I said the words, I felt my stomach tighten in knots, unaware that my inner child had just decided that he despised me for my betrayal.

"Normal or abnormal, gay or straight, I'll always be your friend," Harlan promised. Then he hugged me, giving me the embrace I needed, an embrace that I could not yet give myself.

Harlan saved my life that night. It was the greatest gift that any man can give another.

******

I took a break from my tour during the fall of 1982, stopping in San Francisco to stay a few nights with Stacey Taylor in the beautiful Victorian home where she was housesitting.

On the weekend, Stacey's sister Katie and her friend Rex came from Sacramento to visit. I was still sleeping in the third-floor guest room, when I heard voices from the patio behind the house.

Going to the window, I looked down and saw Rex Landis, a young man with beautiful blonde hair and a dark tan, laughing gregariously at something the Taylor sisters had just said. In that same instant, I heard an unseen voice whispering in my ear, saying, "Kerry, this is the man you are meant to fall in love with."

Throwing on a pair of shorts and a T-shirt, I dashed down the stairs as fast as I could.

When I went out onto the patio to say hello, Rex greeted me with a warm hug. "Wow!" he replied happily, "I've heard so much about you, I came all the way from Sacramento just to meet you!"

Rex Landis was a handsome young man, two years younger and several inches shorter than me, and he was a Mormon who was currently going through inner conflicts about his gay identity just as I had done at BYU. He reminded me of myself when I was but a few years younger, and he possessed an infectious laugh, a wicked charm, and an ingratiating sense of humor that attracted me to him immediately. Stacey and Katie were talking about this and that, but I could only focus on Rex.

After breakfast, we went for a ride to Sausalito in Katie's

cream-colored Volkswagen bug, with Stacey driving and me sitting in the front seat, as Rex and Katie chatted in the backseat.

I was already falling in love with Rex as we sped across the Golden Gate Bridge. Turning in my seat, and looking directly into Rex's sparkling blue eyes, I startled everyone when I said, "Rex, I know this is an odd request, but would you mind very much if I touched your hair? It's the most beautiful blonde hair I've ever seen. I just have to touch your hair, or I think I'll die."

"Well," he said shyly, "I guess that would be okay."

I can only imagine how difficult that moment was for Stacey, who still had feelings for me, when I brushed my hand through Rex's golden hair, as I'm sure it was for Stacey's sister Katie.

On the other side of the bridge, we pulled over to take in the view of the city across the bay. I stood close to Rex and he to me, as we took in the view with the Taylor sisters. It was all I could do to keep from taking him in my arms and kissing him full on the lips then and there in public and in full daylight, but somehow I controlled myself.

We drove on to find a lovely restaurant nestled in the hills above Sausalito, where we sat and had lunch. Later we strolled down to the piers, walking in and out of galleries and shops.

Once it got dark, we drove back to the lookout by the Golden Gate. As it was now dark, the lights of San Francisco shimmered across the bay, and the full Harvest Moon—like a huge orange balloon—seemed larger on the horizon than any I had seen before. Silhouetted behind the city's skyscrapers, casting its reflection across the bay to where we stood, it was the most romantic sight I had ever seen. Whether inspired by the view or simply overwhelmed by feelings of love, I suddenly took Rex in my arms and kissed him passionately on the lips, right in front of the Taylor sisters and everyone else. Rex was taken aback, but his lips quickly melted into mine, even as I felt the boy that he still was suddenly melt into the man I had just become. Our kiss went on for a while, even as the Taylor sisters stewed.

The next day, I showed Rex all of the gay haunts he yearned to visit but hadn't dared to, taking him to all of the gay bars in the Castro District. Later I took him to Fisherman's Wharf, treating him to an elegant meal. After dinner, we strolled along the dock of the bay, kissing as we went.

When Rex and I returned to Stacey's place extremely late that night, the Taylor sisters were already in bed.

"Come upstairs with me," I whispered gently, taking Rex's hand in mine as I pulled him up the stairs to my bedroom. Knowing that Rex was sexually inexperienced, and aware of how nervous he was, I undressed slowly and undressed him even more gradually, as we kissed. Once we were both naked, I eased him down onto my bed and gently caressed his entire body with my lips and mouth, until he was awash with passion. Moaning with desire, he murmured softly, "Please, Kerry, I want you … to …" and then he hesitated, blushing bright red. He looked so damn sexy in the moonlight, red-faced and naked, with that gorgeous blonde hair of his.

"Yes, my boy, what is it that you want me to do?" I prodded, as I felt a delicious smile spread across my face.

"I want you to … go inside me," he said cautiously, shy and yet seductive. "I've seen it done in gay porn, and I've always dreamed about having it done to me," he added, "but I'm afraid it will hurt."

I felt my erection throbbing with desire for him. I had to take him and make him mine. "Trust me, I'll be gentle," I reassured him. "And I'll stop if you want me to." I took him into the bathroom with me and prepared him properly, getting him cleaned out and washed, then lovingly drying him off with a towel.

Giving him a gentle but passionate kiss, I took him by the hand and brought him back to the bed, putting lubrication in all the right places. Then I lay him on his side, and slowly pressed inside him. He moaned as I kissed his neck and stuck my tongue into his ears, driving him wild. "Oh, oh yes!" he exclaimed. "It doesn't hurt any more. All I feel is pleasure! Put more of it in me, please!"

Despite his enthusiastic encouragement, I proceeded with caution until I found myself completely encased inside him, even as my tongue encircled his in a magical and passionate dance. Gradually I built momentum as I thrust in and out of him, taking my cues from him, already very much in love. And our lovemaking lasted for hours, until the sun came up.

I left Rex in Sacramento a few days later, ending my tour in my hometown of Pocatello at Idaho State University's Frazier Hall, on the same stage where I had given my first public performance years earlier at age 14 in *The Imaginary Invalid*. Dad and his new wife Sarah, as well as Denise and Lee and their daughter Tara were all present to see the show, as was my high school drama teacher Mrs. Joan Kisling, and nearly every person in my hometown whom I had grown up with. Among all of these special people, there was one woman, Connie, who had worked with my mom as a fellow teacher at the same elementary school. And what a special evening it was!

As any performer will tell you, some nights go better than others, depending upon how each audience reacts. Great live performances happen when the flow of energy goes back and forth between the audience and the performer in an almost mystical way. Those are the nights that both performers and audiences live for, when magic strikes. This was the type of magic that happened during my performance that night.

After I took my bows, both Connie and Mrs. Kisling ran onto the stage and threw their arms around me. "Kerry!" Mrs. Kisling said, "Your mom would have been so proud of you tonight!"

It was less than two years since Mom's death, and their comment made in unison caused me to burst into tears. Somehow I managed to reply, "I only wish she could have been here to see it."

"Well, maybe she was, Kerry," Connie replied.

Once I was out of costume and makeup, I ran into my sister and her family in the hall, and they smothered me with kisses and congratulations, while Dad and Sarah stood in the background looking more than a little uncomfortable. Though Dad was proud of me, I also knew how strongly he disapproved of the subject matter of my play. He and Sarah barely said a word, other than when Dad shook my hand, adding, "Good job, Son."

That night, I missed Mom more than ever.

The next day, I flew back to Sacramento to spend more time with Rex. It was then that I got to know Rex and his family better.

Rex's mom Owassa, who was part Cherokee and a convert to the LDS Church, took a liking to me right away, and I to her. I started calling her my California Mom, a nickname she loved. I also became close with Rex's father John and with his brother Mark. Mark was also gay, which was tough on Owassa, as she had raised both of her sons to be diligent in the Mormon Church and to honor their Priesthood, but it was not meant to turn out that way.

As I came to understand, Rex and I had much in common. We were both raised to be Saints and expected to go on missions, and follow the straight and narrow Mormon path. Like Harlan, Rex had served his mission in France. And Rex had suffered at BYU as I had, where in trying to come out he had attempted suicide.

After spending two weeks with Rex in Sacramento, I returned to my life and work in New York City. But I couldn't get him out of my mind. Eventually, I returned to Sacramento to live with Rex in his downtown apartment for four months, arriving just in time for Christmas. Rexy and I both loved Christmas, and together we made the holidays of 1982 both magical and joyous.

******

Christmas of 1973 was difficult for me, since I was heartbroken about my breakup with Bridget. Mom sensed my heartbreak and broached the subject carefully. "You must miss Bridget terribly," she observed cautiously. "She was such a lovely girl. I had high hopes the two of you were going to marry."

"Me, too, Mom," I replied. "But it wasn't meant to be."

Seeing the tears in my eyes, Mom joined me on the sofa next to our Christmas tree, and gave me a hug. "No matter what," she said lovingly, "you and your Dad and I are still going to have the best Christmas ever."

After returning to BYU in January 1974, I grew much closer to Stacey, who slowly began to fill the void Bridget had left in my life.

It was very early in the new semester when I met with my psychiatrist, Dr. Parker, who took me to the lab in BYU's Health Center where the electroshock therapy sessions would take place. He showed me the chair where I would be strapped into place, and explained how the voltage would be administered through electrodes attached to my legs and arms.

He showed me a slide projector, and the screen on the wall in front of a chair. "This projector is attached to a special aversive shock generator," he explained. "The edge of the shock slides, the slides of attractive men, are marked with ink. The neutral slides, those showing attractive young ladies, do not have marked edges. The slides are automatically advanced. When a shock slide is shown, a phototransistor reads the mark and triggers the shock. The patient is automatically conditioned by the visual stimulus paired with the aversive shock. I can, of course, adjust the level of shock, if and when I need to, to make the therapy more effective."

There was a motion picture screen on the wall in front of the chair. "I also add the use of sound," he explained, through earphones, adding pleasant music when you see photographs of women, and highly negative and disturbing noises when a shock slide of men is presented. I also add unpleasant flashes of light when the patient views a shock slide, adding to the aversion that all patients will want to avoid." It sounded terrifying.

"What happens if I can't be modified?" I asked.

"Any behavior can be modified," he said. "I'll start you at 150 volts, then increase the voltage to 200 volts, but only if necessary."

Nothing Dr. Parker told me that day made me any less wary of submitting to what I considered electric shock treatments.

In an effort to spare me electric shock treatments, President Wilkinson scheduled an appointment for me to meet with Spencer W. Kimball, one of the Twelve Apostles and in line to become the next President and Prophet of the Mormon Church. It was a great honor to be granted a private meeting with Apostle Kimball, similar to when a Catholic is given a private audience with the Pope. But beyond the prestige of such a meeting, Wilkinson hoped that Kimball would intervene on my behalf and save me from the aversion therapy sessions that I was being forced into.

Picking me up at my off-campus apartment in Provo in the early evening, Branch President Wilkinson and I drove north together on Interstate 15 heading to meet with Apostle Kimball at his home in Salt Lake City. Once we arrived at the Apostle's home, we exchanged pleasantries before President Wilkinson and I explained my predicament. Unfortunately, Apostle Spencer W. Kimball thought that the conversion therapy and electroshock treatments that had been proposed for me were good ideas, and chose not to intervene.

Instead, the next Prophet, Seer, and Revelator of The Church of Jesus Christ of Latter-Day-Saints gave me this stellar advice: "Never touch your penis again; when you have to clean your genitals, make certain that you keep a washcloth between your hand and your privates; when you urinate, be careful to not touch your penis as you fish it out of you fly, and then afterward let it drip dry before tucking it away without touching yourself; find a nice Mormon girl; get married as soon as possible and start making babies; oh, and pray constantly for your redemption."

Apparently, this was the best advice the next Prophet of the Mormon Church—whose words would be considered gospel by untold millions—could offer me. A new thought, one I had never entertained before, suddenly flashed in my brain like a neon sign: **"MAYBE THE CHURCH NEEDS TO CHANGE, NOT ME!"**

My first electroshock therapy session was scheduled for Monday morning at the BYU Health Center, on January 14, 1974 at 9am. The session was expected to last two hours. When I drove into the campus Health Center parking lot that morning, I was full of fear and apprehension. I wanted to turn around and drive in the opposite direction. Fighting back my fear, I parked and went inside, meeting Dr. Parker as arranged at his lab.

In a jovial mood, Dr. Parker chirped, "Good morning, Kerry," before leaving me alone for a moment, apparently to contemplate my fate. Soon a nurse with raven-black hair entered the room. "Now, just take a seat in the chair, Kerry," she said. I sat down in the chair facing the screen. She quickly began attaching suction-like conductors to both my arms and legs, plugging the wires into the control panel of the nearby aversive shock generator sitting on top of Dr. Parker's desk. "This is a similar process to getting you set up for an EKG," she explained, "except rather than reading your electrical responses, we'll be conducting a small electrical shock to various parts of your body." I gulped. "Now, just relax," she continued. "This won't take long." She placed the electrical conductors on my extremities and attached a monitor to my thumb apparently to take my pulse, explaining, "This way Dr. Parker can keep an eye on your vital signs during the session."

After I was prepared, Dr. Parker reentered the room. "Kerry, just sit in the chair and try to relax," he said softly, "and we'll begin shortly." Then the nurse began strapping me into the chair, wrapping my arms tightly on the armrests. "What are the straps for?" I asked.

"They're for your safety," Dr. Parker reassured me. "And it will make the electrical shocks easier to bear." Dr. Parker must have seen the panic in my face because he tried to calm me down. "There's no need to be frightened, Kerry," he said kindly, "I'll go slow and gauge your reactions."

The nurse took my pulse and blood pressure, and made some notations on a chart, as Dr. Parker approached me from the front with a pair of headphones. "This is for the music to go with the slideshow," he said. "I think you'll find the songs to your liking." Before putting the headphones over my ears, he patted my knee, adding, "Don't worry, Kerry, I'll be right here if you need me."

Once the headphones were in place, covering my ears, the overhead lights were turned off, and I sat strapped in the chair, plugged in like an appliance, waiting to be turned straight.

Then suddenly, Dr. Parker projected several slides of beautiful women on the screen in front of me, as the music of Streisand's "People" filled my ears, having done his homework as far as his musical selections were concerned. The women in the photographs were posed seductively in swimsuits, but I didn't find myself the least bit sexually aroused. The screen went black and Barbra's voice faded.

Then new photographs appeared, but these were of attractive young men in swimsuits, all taken at a beach. Suddenly electric current shot through my body, jerking me about in the chair that held me fast. My ears were lambasted with noise, and stark flashing lights bombarded my eyes. Then the screen went black as the voltage and noise ceased, leaving me shaking. Dizziness and nausea engulfed me; I wanted to flee but the straps held me fast.

There were soon more photographs of beautiful women, this time with Barbra singing "The Way We Were." Then there was blackness—a foreshadowing of the electrical shocks and the pain to come. As the image of other semi-nude male appeared in front of me, my ears were blasted again with noise as electric current surged through me, shaking me into senseless horror as more flashing lights bombarded my eyes. The torturous assault seemed to never end.

Finally there was blackness again, followed by soothing music and more photographs of women. Then came the darkness and male photographs accompanied by merciless electric shocks, as this so-called therapy seemed to go on forever. Several times I pleaded with Dr. Parker to stop. Each time, he reminded me that Aversion Therapy was for my own good.

When the session ended, Dr. Parker seemed pleased.

"I'm sure this first session wasn't easy for you," he commented. "But you have to remember that these ongoing treatments will make your transformation from homosexual to heterosexual not only possible but probable."

As far as I was concerned, transformation couldn't come too soon. It took ten minutes after the session ended before I could stand without feeling like I was going to pass out, and another ten minutes before I could make it to my car.

Harlan was waiting for me at my apartment when I returned home. Seeing the semi-hysterical state that I was in, Harlan took me in his arms and carried me to my bed. Clutching to him, I shook violently and wept. When I told Harlan about the whole awful experience, he exploded in rage, swearing more than he ever had before. "I hate them for doing this to you!" he exclaimed.

"They're just trying to help me," I admonished.

"Help you!" he snapped at me. "The Viet Cong were more compassionate than the Mormon Elders at this shitty school!"

It took me a few days after my first session of shock therapy before I finally understood and accepted the implication that the Mormon Brethren wanted me changed or they wanted me dead. Sadly, this was just the first of many shock treatments that I would endure over the course of the next year-and-a-half.

After several sessions, my hands began to shake uncontrollably— a result of the electrical current sent through my body once a week. It is a physical and medical condition that has persisted ever since, and one that I assume will be with me until I die.

******

During the four months that I lived with Rex in Sacramento, I wrote most of the fictional version of this book, titling it *A Stranger Among Saints*.

In early February 1983, I took a break from my writing so that Rex and I could visit my family in Idaho, as I wanted them to finally meet Rex, and for them to meet them.

When Rexy and I arrived at Dad and Sarah's place in the little town of Shelley, they did not know how to deal with Rex or with us as a gay couple. Though they had a vacant guest room in the basement, they put us up in the trailer, parked in the driveway beside the side door leading to the kitchen. During our first night sleeping in the trailer, I told Rex that since we were relegated to the trailer that we should make it rock and roll all night long.

When Rex and I showed up for breakfast in the kitchen the next morning, Dad and Sarah seemed embarrassed. Apparently, they had heard our trailer rocking during the night.

The eight of us—Dad, Sarah, baby Isaac, Sarah's three teenagers, Rexy and me—sat down to breakfast, and I reached for the scrambled eggs on the table. "Can't you at least wait until we've said the blessing?" Dad scolded. My face turned red. Dad still had the capacity to shame me to the core.

"Of course, I'll wait," I said, putting the offending eggs back on the table so that Dad could pray over the food.

After breakfast, Sarah and the children went to an event being held at their ward chapel.

Rex excused himself and returned to the trailer, while Dad and I sat in the living room in La-Z-Boy recliners facing each other.

"So what's the latest family news?" I asked.

"Your brother Dennis got himself in trouble again," Dad offered sheepishly, seemingly ashamed at the mere mention of the latest incident. "There was more domestic violence and Kathy had to call the police. Once the cops got there, he attacked one of the police officers and they took him off to jail. After that, Kathy was so scared of him that she took the kids and went into hiding."

"I'm sorry to hear that, Dad," I replied sullenly. "At this point, there isn't any news you could tell me about Dennis that would surprise me."

The path I had taken in life had diverged from that of my oldest brother, yet both Dennis and I had each in our own way rebelled against our Mormon upbringing. Where Dennis had swerved far right, becoming the ultimate redneck, I had moved to the far left, ever more liberal in thought and deed.

As Dad told me more about the latest incident, it became clear that my father had bailed out his oldest son yet again, no doubt because of the guilt Dad still felt over the mistakes he knew he had made in raising Dennis.

"Dad," I asked, "When are you going to let Dennis face the music for his own actions?"

"I had to step in, Kerry," Dad muttered. "I made your brother the way he is." He paused, before adding, "Now, he's searching for Kathy and little Marty." A two-year-old, Marty was the child that Kathy and Dennis had had together. "And Dennis has hired a lawyer to sue for custody of Marty."

"That's laughable," I retorted. "No court in the land would give Dennis custody of anyone, nor should they." I paused to gather my thoughts. "Dad, can't you see that Dennis knows you feel guilty and uses that to play you like a violin whenever he needs something from you? Can't you see how he manipulates you?"

Dad didn't respond to my questions. Instead, he stewed in his thoughts for a few minutes before changing the subject. "So, how's your career coming along, Kerry?"

"Good!" I said, excited about my news. "I got signed by Tennessee Williams's agent. I even got to meet and have dinner with Tennessee!"

"That's nice. He's a fine singer," Dad replied.

"I think you're thinking of Tennessee Ernie Ford," I explained gently, my grin fading. Mom was the only one in my family, other than myself, who even knew of—or cared about—the great Tennessee Williams or any of his plays. Realizing this, only made me miss my mother all the more.

"Well," Dad replied, "we're sure proud of you, gettin' on with your plays and all."

"Thanks, Dad." Now it was my turn to change the subject. "So, Dad, how do you like being married again?"

He eyed me with careful, sensitive eyes.

"It's an adjustment," he replied gently. "I love Sarah very much, but I miss your mom."

The next morning Rex and I drove back to Sacramento.

When it came time for me to perform *The Wilde Spirit* at the Charleston Heights Arts Center in Las Vegas in February, Rex traveled with me from Sacramento to see me perform for the first time. He seemed impressed by my opening night performance.

Dad drove from Shelley, Idaho by himself to see my Las Vegas debut. Although he never approved of the subject matter of my play, Dad made the effort to show me that in his own way, he was rooting for my success. He even captured one of my Vegas performances on video, and I believe he was genuinely proud of the standing ovation I received at curtain call. In fact, when I saw him afterward, he had tears in his eyes.

"You were very good, Honey," he said. "Everyone thought so."

A few months after my Vegas performances, Rex moved to Manhattan and moved in with me, beginning our new life together, living as a couple in my studio apartment on West 54th Street, turning it quickly into our home and love nest.

Since Rex was a sexual novice, I enjoyed teaching him everything I had learned about lovemaking. Eventually he found the courage to ask me if I would allow him to anally penetrate me. I was not opposed to the idea, particularly since I knew he had never experienced this, and I wanted to accommodate him. But I failed in my first attempt with him, as I had with every other partner who had ever tried anal penetration.

I can't begin to describe the amount of terror that came over me when I felt the head of Rex's erection pushing past my tightened sphincter muscle. As best as I can remember, it felt as though I were about to be raped, that I was about to lose control of my body and my mind, that I was suddenly a small and helpless child, about to be hurt in a shaming manner far beyond what my soul or my heart could bear. I literally trembled with fear, and I began to cry. "Oh, Rex," I screamed in pain, "please, please, take it out! I can't do it! I just can't! Please don't ask me to!"

"It's okay, Kerry," Rex replied gently. "Of course I'll take it out." Withdrawing as quickly and gently as he could, he added softly, "It's not that big a deal to me, one way or the other."

Sobbing, I collapsed into his arms, still trembling, fearful and unaware of where these irrational feelings were coming from. Why had I had this reaction? Why had I always had this same response whenever anyone had tried to enter me in the past? Why did I fear that I was about to be brutalized again, as though I had once been horribly raped, causing damage to my body and to my psyche?

Now I have the conscious memories that I once repressed. Now I know that I was brutally raped as a young man, and that the experience damaged me in ways that I am still dealing with to this day. But at the time, I had no inkling of this. A stranger to myself at the time, I felt I had let Rex down.

Rex and I tried again on several occasions, but I could never get past what seemed to be my irrational fear of losing control. Whenever Rex came close to entering me, no matter how I tried to relax, my entire body and my sphincter in particular, would tighten down, leaving me in despair. Rex had to be disappointed by all of these failed attempts, but he was always acted very understanding about the situation. "You're just not a bottom," Rex would say. "That's okay. I love being your bottom. I like it that way." Then we would kiss and hug, and I would find other ways to please him.

Eventually Rex and I opened up our sexual relationship to include a third man on occasion, so that Rex could experience what I could not provide him sexually. But once we began hearing rumors about a new and mysterious gay cancer, we abruptly ended our sexual trysts with others.

Soon young gay men were dying all around us, and we were introduced to a new disease called AIDS. As AIDS tore its way through the gay community, I watched the world's most sexually liberated city become one of the most sexually repressed, while panic spread through the city. I held gay men, dear friends of mine from the theater world, as they took their last breaths in my arms, not knowing why they were dying in their youth. "Had the Mormon Church been right after all?" I wondered. "Was this God's curse? Were gay men abominations as I was taught?"

Living through the height of the AIDS crisis in New York, Rex and I were blessed to be in a monogamous relationship. So the inner voice that I heard when I ran home from the 55th Street Playhouse the previous spring, led me out of harm's way—where I might have contracted AIDS—to safety and to love in Rex's arms.

Rex and I shared many wonderful times together. Since we

both loved all things Disney, we deeply enjoyed our summer vacation at Disney World, and since we both were passionate Streisand fans, we loved attending the New York premiere of her film *Yentl* in 1983.

Few couples play together as joyously as Rex and I could. But our relationship also had its abusive aspects. Since Rex never thought he was attractive enough, he felt there had to be something wrong with me. Once, seeing a handsome gay couple walking down the street, Rex asked, and in a deeply cruel way, "You see those two hot guys over there?"

"Yes," I replied, not yet onto his ways.

"We could never look like that!" he exclaimed, explaining that I was carrying too much weight in the wrong places, and that if I would just be willing to get a liposuction, then he might eventually find me attractive.

Still wrestling with my own low self-esteem, the more Rex shamed me, the more I felt like I was still playing out a game with myself that I had already lost too many times. Ironically, when I look at photos taken of me during those years when I lived with Rex, I can see now that I was quite a looker, though I never saw myself that way at the time.

I loved Rex flaws and all, but Rex never loved me unconditionally. He just never loved himself that way.

******

Aside from Harlan, I told no one about my electroshock treatments, other than Dom—my closeted gay friend at BYU—who was full of questions. "Do you think electroshock therapy is working?" Dom asked. "Do you think I should try it, too?

"I'm not sure if it's working or not," I replied unsteadily, "but my hands shake now, uncontrollably, all the time."

As unpleasant as my weekly shock treatments were, I needed to believe that they might be working, helping me transform from a horrible and sinful homosexual into a normal heterosexual male. I

252

had, after all, managed to give up masturbation since my last sincere promise to God, and I had even had some success in keeping my sexual fantasies about men in check.

Of course, gays can't be turned straight, any more than straights can be turned gay. Anyone who believes otherwise is uninformed.

The Mormon Festival of Arts arrived on campus in March. The largest gala at BYU and throughout Mormonism, it was a formal affair held in the lobby of the Harris Fine Arts Center. It included a formal dance with a full orchestra, and the presentation of the winning works of Mormon Art, including the four winning plays.

Harlan and I were handsomely attired in rented tuxedos, and our dates looked radiant. I had asked Stacey to go as my date, and, as was often the case, Harlan had asked out another beautiful and petite blonde, who had readily accepted his invitation. Stacey wore a lovely green formal gown, which made her red hair look even brighter and silkier than usual. Harlan's date wore a dress made of yellow chiffon, and she looked stunning.

As we walked up the rolled-out red carpet laid out on the steps of the Fine Arts Center, I imagined we were attending the Oscars. "What a night!" I exclaimed, as we walked through the entrance at the top of the stairs, all of us gasping at the sight of the inner atrium of the Arts Center, magically transformed into a huge ballroom. As a 70-piece orchestra played Strauss, thousands of handsome couples in formal attire waltzed around the floor. When the moment arrived, my group made our way to the theater where my winning play, *The Scrapbook*, would be presented on stage. My friends and I chose to sit at the back of the theater.

At curtain call, the audience stood and applauded, and I was called forward to center stage to take a bow.

When I returned to my seat at the back of the auditorium, my friends greeted me joyously. "They loved it," Harlan said, as he embraced me in a long hug. "It was truly magnificent, Babe!"

"It was wonderful, Kerry," Stacey gasped, as we prepared to leave the theater. "You are so talented!"

253

In the spring of 1974, before the end of my junior year at BYU, I received another summons, ordering me to report to Clarke's office for yet another Homo Hunt.

I felt instantly uncomfortable once I was seated in Brother Clarke's office, facing him as he sat in a chair slightly above me behind his desk. "We must identify any homosexuals on campus, and expel or rehabilitate them," Clarke said. "Since you have reformed, I thought you could help us by informing on male students who may have shown prurient interest in you."

"Inform?" I asked. "On their prurient interest?"

"You must know other men in drama who have interest in other men," he stated. "Everybody knows the theater is full of gays."

"I hadn't heard that," I said baldly, taking a deep breath to calm myself down. "Do I have to answer these questions?"

He walked to the files behind his office desk and pulled out the papers I hoped someday to see burned, laying them out on the desk in front of me. "Remember these, Kerry," he reminded. "This is your sworn statement when you were arrested. If you want, we can send your parents a copy."

"I don't want that," I said, panic flowing through my veins.

"Might not settle too well with your folks, right?"

"I'll answer your questions," I replied with quick resignation.

"Good. I knew you'd see it my way." I felt like a puppy being thrown a bad tasting bone. "We're looking for names of anyone who might be homosexual," he pushed.

I couldn't provide Clarke with names that afternoon, but someone did, since many male students in the drama department, my friend Dom among them, were soon called in to answer similar questions.

After Dom's equally harrowing experience with Standards, Dom and I made plans to move in together at semester's end. We found a basement apartment beneath a chocolate shop on University Avenue, just a few blocks from Harlan's place, and we moved in together.

The apartment had a living room, two bedrooms, an eat-in kitchen, and a nice bathroom. Being in the basement, the apartment was dark except in the kitchen where light streamed in through a large window. But the scent of chocolate occasionally wafting in from the shop upstairs was intoxicating.

I worked two jobs that summer of 1974, one as a janitor on campus and one as a professional actor, performing as Uncle Max in *The Sound of Music* at the new summer stock theater, Pioneer Playhouse near Park City, Utah. Luckily, my second professional acting job proved to be a much happier experience than the one I had in Jackson, Wyoming the previous summer.

That summer I also began writing a new play that I titled *Children of the World*. Unlike *The Scrapbook*, which I had written in two months or so, this new play seemed to require endless rewrites and an enormous amount of work.

I also made a decision that summer to stop taking education courses and give up my pursuit of a teaching certificate. Since I wanted a career as a professional actor and writer, I reasoned that I would not need or want to teach. If anything, I saw obtaining a teacher's certificate as surrendering to my father and giving up on my dreams before I even gave them a chance. Later, I would regret the decision, since it affected my ability to make a living at something I enjoyed and found meaningful, requiring me to work at all sorts of demeaning and meaningless jobs while pursuing what few professional acting and writing jobs that came along.

But making this decision was hardly the most startling change I made that summer. Having coped with stress by overeating, I had gradually grown from 195 to 245 pounds, and my self-esteem had suffered. To finally address the problem, I went on a strict diet and began an exercise regimen that summer. In all, I lost 75 pounds, before beginning my senior year in the fall.

Having trimmed my waistline from 48 to 32 inches, while becoming strong and lean, I even gave Harlan a run for his money. No one was more supportive of these positive changes than Harlan, since I had often confided in him that I hated myself for gaining weight. More than anyone, he told me how proud he was of me and how fantastic I looked as my appearance improved.

When I ran into Jennifer Wells one day on campus in early

September, shortly after our senior year began, she didn't recognize me at first, given the radical change in my physical appearance. "Kerry," she asked. "Is that really you?"

"Yes, it's me!"

"You've lost so much weight! You look fantastic!"

"Thanks," I said, finding it hard to accept such compliments.

Since Nixon had been forced to resign as president only a few weeks earlier, our talk quickly turned to the Watergate scandal. "As it turns out, Kerry, you were right about Nixon from the beginning," she admitted sadly. "He really was a liar."

"In this case, Jennifer, I'm sad about being right. I'm sad for our country."

But when the subject of Harlan came up, Jennifer broke down in tears. "I loved Harlan so much. I still do," she said. "But now I know that Harlan never loved me the way I loved him."

I didn't know what to say to comfort her, so I simply took her in my arms and gave her a huge hug. "You're still an Angel, Jennifer, and you always will be."

"Thanks, Kerry," Jennifer said quietly. "You are a wonderful man, even if you are a Democrat."

We both laughed, and gave each other another hug.

Once my physical appearance improved, a change in my physical relationship with Harlan became possible, not because Harlan found me more physically attractive, though I'm sure that's true, but because I finally saw myself as worthy of love.

It was on Halloween night of our senior year that Harlan invited me to sleep over at his apartment, and I accepted.

That night we watched old horror movies on his tiny black-and-white portable TV in his living room. But the real Halloween nightmares began after we went to bed, when I dreamed I was tied to a platform, naked, bound and gagged, with Harlan standing over me with a whip, lashing my back into bloody ribbons.

"You dare to think such thoughts!" he shouted as I felt the whip come down hard on my back. "How can you live with yourself?" he asked. "Queers like you deserve to be hurt! I'm just giving you what you deserve!" The whip fell again and again, tearing at my flesh.

"No, Harlan!" I screamed. "Don't hurt me, Harlan! Please!"

Harlan turned on the lamp and tried to wake me. "It's okay, Babe," he said softly, stroking my hair. "You're having a nightmare!"

I still wasn't conscious; I only knew that the monster was trying to kill me. I fought back, grabbing at Harlan's Temple garments and tearing them savagely. "Kerry!" Harlan shouted. "Kerry, wake up!"

Harlan moved away from me, as we both stared with wide-eyed horror at the rips I had made in the holy cloth.

"I ... I didn't know what I was doing. I'm so sorry," I tried to explain. "The Devil's got ahold of my soul, I guess."

"Sssssh, Babe, don't talk like that!" Harlan touched my arm gently. "You were having a nightmare. It was an accident."

Harlan's physical closeness caused shivers of passion in me as my manhood stiffened in my undershorts. Terrified that he would notice, I pushed him away and turned toward the wall.

"Come on, Kerry," he asked, stroking my shoulders as I quivered with desire for him. "What's wrong, Babe?"

"Nothing," I replied abruptly.

The silence between us was deafening. I felt his breath against my neck, as he whispered again, "What's the matter?"

"Nothing," I repeated, clutching the blankets to my neck like protective armor as tremors of both fright and desire shook me violently. Deep within me I was saying a silent prayer.

"Please, God," I prayed fervently. "Please, help me change."

Harlan turned me around to face him. His handsome face was close to mine. My hand came down to rest on his, our fingers caressing gently.

"You have to know how I feel about you, Harlan," I said, pausing and taking a deep breath. "I'm in love with you," I added in a whisper. "I've been in love with you since the first day I met you." The dam of self-contempt burst within me, causing a flood of tears. "Please don't hate me for how I feel about you."

As my lips inched toward his, Harlan's soulful brown eyes bored into mine. "Kerry," he gasped, "we can't."

"Harlan, I'm going to kiss you," I challenged. "If you want to stop me, then stop me. But I'm going to kiss you or die trying."

******

In 1983, I completed the novel that I titled *A Stranger Among Saints*, and my agent Mitch Douglas got me a contract for the book with a gay publisher. But I wanted my book published by a mainstream publisher, so I foolishly turned the offer down.

"Are you a masochist?" Mitch hollered.

"Probably, since I was raised LDS," I replied. "But I want my book to reach everyone, not just gay people; I wrote this book for everybody."

"You're nuts! We have an offer to publish. If you turn this down, we're through."

In the end, I lost an agent who only had my best interests at heart. But the book I wrote then was not the story I wanted to tell; it's the story I am telling now.

Sadly, the dark side of my relationship with Rex—based on our codependence and shame—eventually got the better of us. And by June 1985, our relationship was on the rocks. When Rex flew out to visit his family in Sacramento, leaving all of his things with me in New York, he bought a one-way ticket and never came back.

Finally I flew out to Sacramento to confront him face-to-face.

When forced, Rex confessed that he was no longer in love with me, and we ended our relationship. Making love for the last time that night in the guest room of his parent's home in Sacramento, in a bittersweet sexual farewell, our lovemaking was tender and as passionate as ever but with our eyes flooded with tears and conflicting emotions swirling inside us both.

I left Rex, saying goodbye early the next morning. Owassa, my California Mom, told her baby boy that he was making the biggest mistake of his life, and I couldn't have agreed with her more.

After I returned to Manhattan, I got a call from Manhattan

Plaza—a building that offered subsidized housing to theater professionals—asking me if I wanted to see a one-bedroom apartment that had just become available. The apartment was on the 42nd Floor at 43rd Street and 9th Avenue, with views to the north and east as far as the eye could see.

I lived in that apartment for the next 17 years, from 1985 until 2002, never tiring of the view, never failing to feel grateful that I lived in such a beautiful space in the most exciting city in the world. The view of Manhattan from my apartment was always breathtaking, but especially at night when the lights shimmered in the towering buildings, and the few dotted lights of Central Park flickered in the distance. Whenever I looked at the view, I knew how my Mormon ancestors must have felt when they found their Promised Land in Salt Lake, for it was in New York, not among the Mormons in Zion, that I had found a place to belong.

In the fall of 1985, I met a handsome Jewish fellow by the name of Elliot at a dance held at the Gay and Lesbian Community Center in Greenwich Village. He was a sweetheart of a man and very fun to be with, and soon we were dating seriously.

During the summer of 1986, Dad, Sarah, and my half-brother Isaac came to visit me in New York City.

Being a wonderful cook and a fabulous host, my partner Elliot made several marvelous dinners for my family during their visit. After a week spent in New York City, Dad and Sarah drove to Canton, Ohio, where Denise and Lee were living at the time, and I flew out to join them, since we planned to all drive together in two cars, first from Canton to Niagara Falls, then to see the Hill Cumorah Pageant in upstate New York, and lastly back to New York City to take in more of the city's sights with my sister and her family.

As we all sat chatting in Denise and Lee's spacious living room in their Canton home, Dad asked me a disturbing question. "So, Kerry," he asked, "have you been dating any nice girls lately?"

I was flabbergasted by his question. I had come out as a gay man to my Dad six years earlier, and Dad had not only met my first partner Rex in 1982, he had just met my second partner Elliot, who had cooked Dad and his family several lovely dinners in New York.

"Come on, Dad!" I exclaimed, grabbing him by the arm and pulling him out the door. "We need to talk!"

As my father and I walked past dozens of matching suburban Ohio homes, I confronted my father. "Dad," I exclaimed, "I am a gay man! Remember? My sexual preference is for men, not women. I have a partner Elliot that you just met when we were in Manhattan. I respect your relationship with Sarah, so please, please respect the relationship I have with Elliot."

Dad was visibly shaken by my confrontation and, to his credit he never again asked me if I was dating any women.

My family and I left Canton, Ohio early the next morning in two cars, heading to Niagara Falls.

Staying in a motel that night outside Buffalo, we all went to breakfast together at a diner the next morning, when a waitress came over to our table, and asked, "Coffee, anyone?"

Since drinking coffee is taboo for Mormons, my entire LDS family shouted "No!" in such loud and violent unison that the poor waitress nearly came out of her sneakers.

That was when I spoke up. "Yes, I'll have coffee, please," I said, to gasps from almost all of the members of my LDS family. Worse, when Mormon ladies are offended, they sometimes make their righteous disapproval known either by making a clucking sound with their tongues or by gnashing their teeth, and Denise and Sarah seemed to do both when I ordered coffee.

Once we returned to New York City, my entire family took up residence in my Manhattan apartment. Wanting to make their first visit to the city as memorable as possible, I took Denise and Sarah and my niece Tara to see *A Chorus Line* on Broadway our first night back in the city, thinking it would be a safe choice. But when the actress sang "Tits and Ass," Tara and I were treated to the same tongue clucking and teeth gnashing that had greeted my coffee drinking in Buffalo. Turning to Tara, then 14, I whispered in her ear, "Honey, your Uncle Kerry is so busted!" But Tara Lee loved the show even more than I had hoped she would.

I was never able to make the commitment to Elliot that he both wanted and deserved. But Elliot and I had marvelous fun over the two years we dated each other. One of the best times that Elliot and I spent together as a couple was at our 1987 summer vacation rental in Sag Harbor in the Hamptons. Since the house had a swimming pool and I was an avid swimmer, I enjoyed getting up each morning and going for a long swim while Elliot prepared a delicious breakfast for us. We both loved the pool and the private grounds surrounding it. In fact, the last time we made love was in the swimming pool. Not only was our lovemaking remarkably erotic that afternoon, it was also tender and emotionally stirring.

Sadly, when Elliot forced me to fully commit to him at the end of that idyllic summer, I walked away. Looking back on it now, it was simply a case of bad timing, as I had not yet gotten over my breakup with Rex.

In 1987, not long after splitting with Elliot and only two years after ending my relationship with Rex, I agreed to meet Rex for a drink during his planned return visit to New York.

After that, Rex and I established a new basis for a lifelong friendship. Rex, in turn, stayed in Sacramento, first becoming a successful hairdresser and then a successful salon owner, eventually owning seven locations in Sacramento.

Building his business into a million dollar operation with hundreds of employees, Rex bought himself a beautiful home and a fancy car. And he got himself the kind of spouse that he had always said that he wanted, a guy with a physique that Rex could show off and feel proud of. The guy's name was Craig, and although I never thought he was all that hot, Rex licked his lips whenever Craig was around. Craig was a ne'er do well, as is usually the case in situations like this, but Rex made him the manager of his business anyway.

After Elliot and I broke up in 1987, I met Tony, a successful dentist who lived on Central Park South, and eventually he became my third spouse. An Italian-American, Tony was the classic example of a tall, dark, and handsome man, and he was very sweet and good to me. Still, I was unhappy in the relationship, but I didn't fully understand why.

During a visit that I made alone to visit my family in Idaho in the late spring of 1988, Dad and I went camping in the Grand Tetons.

As we sat quietly by our campfire, taking in one of the most beautiful sights in America—a view overlooking the Snake River with the sun setting behind the majestic Tetons—Dad commented, "It's beauteous, isn't it, son?"

In that moment, I felt that Dad and I were not only connecting authentically with the natural beauty around us, but with each other. "Yes, Dad, it's beauteous!" I replied quietly.

We sat for a long while in silence, taking in the surroundings as the sky darkened, before I told Dad the whole story of all that had happened to me at BYU, though even then I chose not to go into the true nature of my relationship with Harlan.

"I wish you would've told your mother and me sooner," Dad said sadly. "We might have been able to get you to another doctor, the right doctor, to help you." I stared at him blankly. "Another doctor?" I asked. "The last thing I needed at BYU was another doctor! I had too many doctors as it was."

When I told him about the electric shock treatments that I was subjected to, Dad's mouth gaped open. "I was never the same after those treatments," I explained. "My hands still shake; I guess they always will. That's what I let them do to me."

"You went through all of that so that your mother and I wouldn't have to know the truth?" he asked.

I nodded my head slowly in the affirmative.

"You shouldn't have let them do that to you," he replied gently. "But you can't judge the church by its people. They didn't mean to harm you. They were only trying to help."

"How was reinforcing the worst feelings I had about myself supposed to help me?" I asked. "Harlan was the only person at BYU who accepted me as gay!"

"Even now, if you saw a specialist," he said, "it still might help."

"Dad, now that I've learned to accept myself as I am, I love being

262

gay. I wouldn't change it now, even if I could."

"I feel so sorry for you," Dad said. "You will never know the joy of being a father or of having a woman who loves you."

******

Harlan didn't say anything, nor did he move away from me, as we each held our breath. I prayed that he wouldn't hurt me for what I was about to do. Tenderly, I pressed my lips to his. To my joy, Harlan didn't pull away, nor did he push me away or try to stop me. He even returned the kiss hesitantly, as though tentatively exploring his own feelings, before I finally ended the kiss, thinking to see what might happen next. "Kerry," he murmured, "we shouldn't let ourselves. This isn't right."

Rather than pay heed to his warnings, I let my fingers roam sensually through his hair, as I pressed my lips to his again, but this time with more urgency.

"Babe!" he warned, losing self-control, "We should stop while we're ahead. Oh, God ... Babe!"

"Harlan," I whispered, "I'm so deeply in love with you! I can't help myself." Our lips met again in our first truly romantic kiss, the single most important and beautiful moment of my young life. A fire seemed to explode inside Harlan, as he thrust his tongue deep into my mouth and throat, quickly churning my insides to butter.

For one perfect moment, I felt no guilt or shame. Harlan and I were simply one with each other, perfect and one with God. It was spiritual communion; it was love as chaste and beautiful as any that exists. We were both free and flying like his dove. I fantasized that he would pick me up and carry me to his bed, discard his Temple garments once and for all, and take me with him to the only Celestial Kingdom I ever wanted to know or care about.

But the moment ended, as Harlan pushed me away. "I can't do this, Kerry!" he said, almost spitting at me. "I ... I don't know why I let you do that to me, or why I kissed you back. That isn't how I feel about you!" I was battling with my own shame, refusing to let it defeat me again, even as he added a dire warning: "Kerry, you can never tell anyone about what we just did together. Promise!"

"I promise," I said, quietly weeping.

"And we can't confess this to our Branch Presidents!"

"I won't tell, don't worry," I whispered solemnly. I saw clearly then and really for the first time, that it was not Clarke, the Standards Office, the Security Police, the University, or even the Mormon Church that was my enemy, but internalized shame that was my enemy, just as it was Harlan's enemy, too.

Harlan walked to his bedroom window, looking out as the full Halloween moon cast a bluish glow across his backyard. "You may never understand this, Kerry," Harlan explained, "but I'll never do anything more with you than what we just did." He turned out the lamp, as though he needed darkness to tell me the full truth. As he walked back to sit on his bed, I thought I could see evidence of his desire beneath his garments, even as my own erection propped up my blankets. But even in the moonlight, I could see the resurrected horror of Vietnam in his eyes. "When I told you about Danny," Harlan explained, "I didn't tell you the whole story."

Harlan sat silent on the edge of his bed for the longest time before he continued speaking. "Danny and I snuck off into the jungle one night," he finally confessed, with his head lowered, "and I let him blow me." He paused again, as though he were taking in my reaction. "After that," he continued, "we did it whenever we could. I hated myself every time I let him get me off, but I let him do it anyway. I used him to forget the War and all the Hell that surrounded us."

I averted my eyes. I couldn't stand the thought of him with another man. "You loved him?" I asked, like a dying plant needing water. "Like you love me?"

Harlan began to weep. "I've never loved anyone like I love you, Kerry," he admitted. "But I've hurt you, just like I hurt Danny."

"Harlan, you can't blame yourself for Danny's death. Soldiers die in wars. It wasn't your fault he died over there."

"It was my fault!" he erupted violently.

Slapping his fists hard against his stomach, he added, "If it hadn't

264

been for me, he would still be back in Wisconsin milking cows!"

"I still say it wasn't your fault!" I retorted.

"You don't understand, Kerry," Harlan replied. "I killed him!"

I shrank back against the headboard of my bed, unable to take in what he had just said.

"It was late at night," he continued, his voice faltering at times as he tried to explain what had happened. "The only ones not in bed sleeping were me and Danny and the night guards. Danny and I were in a trench together. Danny was on his knees in the trench, giving me what he knew I wanted what I had asked for. Suddenly there was an explosion and Cong guerillas came running into camp, moving fast. That's how they attacked, in and out fast, in the dark when you least expected it. Guys were at their posts in ten seconds flat, but Danny and I were trapped in that trench, out in the open with Cong all around us. It all happened so fast. I didn't have time to pull up my pants. Danny was on his knees with my cock still in his mouth, when a grenade came flying into our trench. Danny threw himself on top of it to save my life. And then he just blew apart: His blood and bones and guts were all over me, on my cock, my shorts, my uniform, all over the trench. He fell on a grenade to save my life!"

"If he hadn't, you both would have died," I reminded him.

"We wouldn't have been in that trench in the first place if I hadn't told him I needed him to suck me off! When I crawled out of that trench with his blood and brains all over me, I knew that the Lord had punished us both for our sins. That night I promised God that I would never defile myself again with a man, and that I would find some way to make amends." His voice cracked with emotion as more tears streamed down his face. Seeing him like that on the sofa, I threw off my covers and ran to him. "No, Kerry!" he shouted. "Don't touch me! Don't come near me!"

I stood in the middle of the room—naked except for my white undies—not daring to move. "Harlan, please, I just want to hold you," I whimpered.

"Get back under your covers where I don't have to see you like that! Or better yet, put some clothes on!" He shoved me back toward my bed. "Get back in bed before I kill you, too!"

His powerful deep voice echoed like thunder in the room. I crawled back into bed and hid beneath my sheets, as he wept the worst kind of tears, those that one will not share with another.

"The first time I saw you, that first day in church," he confessed, "you looked and acted so much like Danny, I couldn't take my eyes off you. I knew I should stay away from you, but I couldn't. You gave me back my life, Kerry. If not for you, I would have blown my head off long ago." Harlan's voice was dull like a lifeless thing. "But look at what I've done to you now," he continued. "I've hurt you just like I hurt Danny!"

I sat in bed huddled under my sheets, silent for a long time. "Danny gave his life to save yours," I whispered. "Just like you saved his life earlier in the War. Just like you and I saved each other at BYU. You know what I think? I think you love me just as much or more than I love you."

Harlan stood like a statue in the middle of his bedroom. I wanted to fight him until either one or both of us were dead from the struggle. When he spoke again, his voice was as sharp and unyielding as a blade. "Even if we are in love, so fucking what! You want to act like you're my wife or something? I won't let you do it! I care about you too much!"

There was another deafening silence between us. I took a deep breath and gathered my thoughts.

"I'm not asking you to be my lover," I explained, "just be my friend. Please."

"That I can do," Harlan replied gently. "I am your friend, forever and always."

Though I was still unaware of the inner child buried within me, I realize now that the true self within me was cheering for the choices I had made that Halloween night to be true to myself. For the first time in decades, my inner child saw that I was standing up for him and taking his side. I was born again as a gay man that Halloween night.

Though the Holy Trinity of Wilkinson, Parker, and Clarke—as I now thought of them—would not find out about it until I graduated, my Rehabilitation Program was over. From then on, I wanted to learn how to love and accept myself as I was. If I jerked off, it was nobody's business but my own; if I chose to have sex, I would never again get caught in the act.

From that day forward until the day I graduated, I made the restrooms on Interstate 15 the places where I could find at least some measure of honesty while serving the Mormon men of the community as best I could, bringing joy to their otherwise shame-filled lives.

******

As with Elliot, I had two good years with Tony. While we were together, Tony bought a home for us to share as a gay couple in the northern Poconos of Northeast Pennsylvania. Situated on a lake, the house had a breathtaking view and served as a serene getaway from our hectic lives in Manhattan. When my sister and her family visited us in New York again during the summer of 1989, we invited them to our lake house, where I spent a good deal of my time in the rowboat with my nieces and nephew. As usual, Tara loved the time spent with her Uncle Kerry, and it seemed she enjoyed being around her Uncle Tony, too.

As it happened, I ended my romantic relationship with Tony during the summer of 1989, declaring my independence on the 4th of July. I certainly didn't blame Tony for our breakup. If anything, I felt gratitude that I had met him, since it was in taking his advice in the early June of 1988, that I had began therapy, choosing to work with Jim Enders, a licensed CSW. Ironically, it was as a result of my year's work in therapy that I was able to leave Tony the following year without needing to build a case against him or to make him wrong. This alone showed the progress I had made in therapy in only one year, finally overcoming at least some of my internalized shame.

The work in therapy that I began in June 1987 would last 12 years and became an inner journey of self-discovery and healing.

Through therapy, I came to understand and accept how my

parents' expectations of saintly perfection had damaged all of their children: It turned the strong and defiant spirit of my brother Dennis into one who hurt anyone who dared try to love him; it forced my naturally kind and sweet sister Denise to carry an unnatural weight of guilt and shame throughout her life; it pushed my brother Craig into the role of family hero, forcing him to deny and remove himself from the realities of our childhood; and I, the youngest, spent years in therapy getting out from under all of the shame I had internalized.

Jim proved to be an incredibly supportive guide on my inner journey. A true advocate, Jim's affirmation, love and non-judgmental support helped me find my own voice. With Jim, I was finally able to tell the truth of what happened to me in my childhood and to finally be heard. He became a witness to my pain and an advocate for the inner child that I had buried inside me as if frozen in ice, who was still waiting for me to find him again and set him free.

Year after year, I chipped away at the false mask that I had cultivated since early childhood—a mask meant to please everyone but myself—until I eventually found the authentic Kerry, and released him from his prison. When this magical inner child first emerged from his lifelong prison, he understandably raged at me like an infant with cause. Nor did he trust me.

During a particularly powerful therapy session in 1990, Jim helped me realize that I had subconsciously blamed myself for my mother's death. "You have to understand this, Kerry," Jim explained tenderly. "It was as though you and your mom went for a walk into the woods in mid-winter, when suddenly you were caught in a terrible blizzard. She was too weak to go on, so you protected her from the storm as best you could, leaving her under the shelter of a tree. You went on alone to get help, but when you returned, you found that she had died."

The lyrics written by my ex-lover Steve for his Broadway musical *Into The Woods*, resonated in my heart and soul:

"Sometimes people leave you halfway through the wood,
Do not let it grieve you; No one leaves for good;
No one is alone."

"But a question remains," he said. "Can you forgive yourself?"

My heart broke as I fell to my knees weeping. Jim came down to his knees to hold me in his arms, as the tears flowed from me.

"I'll try to forgive myself," I said between sobs. "I'll try."

As I gradually came to terms with myself and with my LDS family and the society that shaped me, I began to find answers to questions that I never knew I had. I even found new truth in many of the scriptures that I was taught as a child. I had often heard, "Know the truth and the truth shall set you free," both from the pulpit and on my mother's knee. But it was only in therapy that I found its meaning. Giving up denial and facing shattering realizations about myself and about the LDS home I grew up in, I found the truth.

As I traveled deeper on the soul journey that therapy became for me, I found many teachers who guided me along my path, miraculously appearing when I was ready to learn from them. First, I discovered the writings of Louise Hay, which led me to Alice Miller—whose writings about abusive childrearing practices broke new ground. After Alice Miller, I found John Bradshaw—whose books and PBS televised lectures on dysfunctional family systems helped me a great deal. Bradshaw, in turn, led me to Joseph Campbell, whose books and TV interviews with Bill Moyers encouraged me to explore the hero's journey that I was taking within me. And on and on it went, as I discovered many other teachers to light my way.

Deeper spiritual and emotional healing came in time, mostly from understanding and forgiving my parents and accepting them for the human beings they were, not as the Saints that they pretended to be. In time, I learned to love them for their mistakes and for their human frailty. But to get to forgiveness, I first had to accept that the shame I had experienced at the hands of LDS Saints was nothing less than an attempt to murder my soul—regardless of their good intent.

I find it sad that millions of people search for answers everywhere but within themselves. We live in a world where for centuries children had no rights; where children were born to be the victims of victims; where the pernicious yet unconscious attempt by otherwise well-meaning parents to murder the souls of their children—usually through the rigid enforcement of religious dogma—is the root cause of most of the violence and addiction that we see in our world today.

Though I was surrounded and smothered by religion for the first 23 years of my life, I began to realize that I was never once allowed or encouraged during all of those years to explore my own soul. If anything, my religious upbringing stifled and stamped out any honest search for a soulful connection or a true spiritual path. It was therapy—not organized religion—that encouraged me to look within, to meditate, and to seek a spiritual connection. But my first steps toward recognizing a need for spirituality in my life were awkward and uncomfortable at best.

From the time I left BYU and all of Mormon Zion behind me and moved to Los Angeles, until I began my work with my New York therapist in the summer of 1988, I wanted nothing to do with any form of organized religion. Though I had already experienced several profound spiritual experiences throughout my life, if anyone at that time talked to me about spirituality or religion in my presence, I would change the subject or excuse myself. At that time, I thought of all religion as a crock and a deadly nightmare that had plagued my childhood, one I felt grateful to have escaped. And I thought of those with religious beliefs as unhinged zealots of the extreme right. Religion was shoved down my throat for the first 23 years of my life, and I wanted no more of it. Period. So when my therapist first talked about a need to heal spiritually, I balked.

As my therapy process continued through the 1990s, it became obvious that I needed to heal from all of the shame that I had internalized during my Mormon upbringing. Since I couldn't afford both individual and group therapy, Jim encouraged me to find a support group where I could share my experiences from childhood, suggesting that I attend a 12-step program like ACOA.

"ACOA?" I asked. "What's that?"

"Adult Children of Alcoholics," he replied.

"But I didn't grow up with alcoholic parents."

"That's true," he replied gently. "But if you think about it, your parents were drunk on religion the same way alcoholics are hooked on booze. And more than that, ACOA may give you a place to grow spiritually and find deeper healing."

I was not convinced, since I had heard enough about 12-Step programs to know that a religious component was involved.

I nearly walked out of my first ACOA meeting, as soon as they started talking about turning over control to a Higher Power. There it was again: More crap about God! Whether they called Him a Higher Power or called him God, to me he was the same mean Son-of-a-Bitch who the Mormons referred to as their Heavenly Father. I wanted nothing to do with Him. The thought nearly made me vomit. But something or someone—perhaps my angel—told me to stay, to sit it out, and to simply listen.

I sat and listened in silence, contributing only my first name, but as I heard the stories of the courageous men and women who spoke, my heart began to open more and more to their sharing of pain and hurt and shame.

One gay man spoke of his dislike of the concept of God, but how he was able to work the program once he realized that he could define his Higher Power in whatever way that worked for him. It didn't have to be God. It didn't have to be an omnipotent and mean-spirited Heavenly Father. It could simply be a loving energy that surrounded us all, giving life to all living things.

What followed were many years spent both in therapy and in 12-Step programs. In ACOA meetings, when others introduced themselves as "an adult child of an alcoholic," I would introduce myself as "an adult child of a Mormon family," which was greeted with understanding and compassionate laughter. As I shared my stories within the safety of these rooms, I continued working on the necessary and ongoing healing process between me and my inner child, and began to earn his trust little by little if not his forgiveness, even as I continued to heal the toxic shame that had tormented me for most of my life, while finding a form of spirituality that I could finally embrace.

******

Despite Harlan's promise to remain my friend forever, our friendship changed as soon as I confessed that I was in love with him on that Halloween night of 1974. In fact, it was only two days after Halloween when Harlan started dating Leigh Edwards, a beautiful girl in her early 20s that he had met on campus. For the next two weeks, he spent most of his time with her.

When Harlan introduced me to Leigh two weeks later, it became clear that he was already far more serious about her than about any girl he had dated previously. A beautiful 5'6" blonde with a perfect figure, Leigh looked very much like Jennifer but Leigh was far more flirtatious and less modest in her demeanor than was Angel.

When Harlan confided in me that Leigh was taking care of what he called his manly needs, I was still mystified by the term.

"Manly needs?" I asked. "What do you mean exactly?"

"She blows me whenever I tell her I need it and I ask her to," he explained, his face reddening. "I think she even likes doing it."

"Ah!" was all I could muster, flummoxed by his honesty.

Harlan spent more and more of his time with Leigh in December, so when I had the time to socialize I spent more time with Dom or Stacey. When Harlan and I got together for our Christmas celebration before heading for home, Leigh joined us, making me feel like a third wheel for the first time with Harlan.

Auditioning in December for *The Music Man*, the biggest show on campus that would open in early February, I hoped to be cast as the leading man. I had, after all, transformed from an overweight character actor to a fit and handsome young man. But Dr. Ivan Crosland, who was directing the show, cast me in the juicy character role of Mayor Shinn. Despite my disappointment in not being cast in the leading role, I took on the role of Mayor with gusto, enjoying the rehearsal process throughout the rest of that semester.

When Harlan asked me in early January 1975 if I would like to go with him to do something alone together, I was thrilled.

Picking him up at his place that night, Harlan was already waiting for me in front of his place, shivering in his jacket, standing in snow and ice on his porch.

"Get in," I said, "before you turn to an icicle!" He jumped in Oscar and quickly closed the door behind him. "Brrrr!" he said, "As much as I love skiing, I can't handle Utah winters anymore."

"So what do you want to do tonight?" I asked.

"I feel like being wicked. Let's drive to Salt Lake to see porn!"

"I'm game if you are," I said, even as fear rose inside me. What if BYU Security Police still had me under surveillance? So as I drove, I kept an eye out to see if we were being followed.

"But it has to be straight porn, Babe," he said. "No gay stuff."

"Oh, I know the score where you're concerned," I replied.

His smile suddenly turned to a scowl. "That's why I had to see you tonight, Babe. I have no one else I can talk to."

Driving through snow to Interstate-15, I asked, "So what's up?"

"It's Leigh," he said. "The fucking bitch!"

"What? I thought you guys were doing great."

"We were. But then she told me something I can't forget."

"What? What was it?" I pressed.

"She told me that she used to take care of her ex-boyfriend the same way she takes care of me … with her mouth."

"Oh, I see!" I was surprised to hear it and equally surprised that he could discuss such things with me now without embarrassment.

"Now whenever she blows me, all I can think about is her doing the same thing to him. Sometimes I get so upset with her, I just want to take her by the throat and strangle her to death."

"I don't know what to say," I mumbled quietly.

As we drove past the rest areas on I-15 near Pleasant Grove, he pointed to the south side rest area and asked, "Is that where that leather guy taught you how to give a half-decent blowjob?" I was surprised but not ashamed when he asked me the question.

"Yup," I admitted freely. "I was so lousy at it. But by morning, I knew what I was doing. I've had a lot of practice since then. When I met him I didn't know how to do it. Now I'm a world-class cocksucker."

"Really?" he asked. Harlan seemed intrigued and then ashamed, and I noticed that he was beginning to get an erection. "I guess we should talk about something else," he concluded, his face reddening again.

"Sure," I replied, "Like what?"

"Actually there's something I have to tell you," he continued, pausing briefly. "Leigh told me tonight ... that she's ... pregnant." I nearly drove Oscar into the ditch, but managed to keep us on the icy freeway. "I've been fucking her for months now, ever since we started dating," he admitted. Apparently, he had knocked her up only a few weeks after I came out to him on Halloween night. "We were using precautions but she got pregnant anyway," he explained, interrupting my thoughts. "I don't know what to do. I'm too fucked up to marry anyone."

"You'll make a great husband and father," I replied, "if you're in love with her, that is."

"I'm not even sure what being in love feels like," he retorted, taking a long time before he spoke again. "I don't know if I told you," he said, "but I've stopped painting."

"What?" I asked, stunned by his revelation.

"And I threw away all of the art supplies you bought me."

"Why would you do that? You love painting!" I exclaimed.

"I wanted all of it gone before I brought Leigh to my place for the first time. I didn't want her to know anything about it."

"Why? Were you ashamed of her knowing the real you?"

"Yes, actually," he admitted. "I knew you wouldn't understand. That's why I didn't tell you sooner."

"But I do understand," I replied. "I understand too well."

We drove on to Salt Lake City in silence.

When we made our way inside the darkened porn theater in downtown Salt Lake City, the place seemed eerily familiar. In fact, it was the same porn theater where I had met my rapist three years earlier. But since I had blocked any memory of the rape, I could not explain why the place felt familiar to me.

As we took our seats on the aisle, I could hear men jerking off all round us as they watched the straight porn. As my eyes adjusted, I could see the substantial bulge in Harlan's pants. What would Harlan do, I wondered, if I suddenly slipped to my knees? Would he push me away or allow me to unzip his fly, release his erection, and service him properly with my mouth, the way Danny once had in Vietnam and the way Leigh was apparently doing now whenever he asked her to? I could only dream as the porn unreeled, and soon a guy on screen was getting a blowjob from a pretty young blonde. Then suddenly and without any warning, Harlan jumped up and ran up the aisle, saying, "I think I'm going to throw up!"

I ran after him, following him into the restroom. After he bent down and vomited in the toilet, he began washing his face. "I couldn't stand seeing that blonde sucking off that guy," he explained. "It made me think of Leigh with her last boyfriend. It's like she's used goods."

After Harlan washed his face, I handed him some paper towel.

"Thanks, Babe," he replied. "I know we just got here, Kerry, but I want to leave, if that's okay with you."

"Sure," I said. "Let's take a drive."

We drove to the seediest part of downtown Salt Lake, until I found the Sun Tavern—the gay bar I was told about. Though I had never been to a gay bar, I needed more than anything at that moment to explore this new and forbidden world.

"I don't expect you to come in, Harlan," I said as I parked out front. "I just have to see what it's like."

"It's okay, Babe," he said quietly. "I'll come in. It's cool."

Not only was this my first gay bar, this was the first bar of any kind that I had ever entered. It was surprisingly nice and clean inside, with colored lights decorating the walls, and there were booths where men sat eating, and a dance floor where gay men were dancing together, some of them slow dancing in each other's arms. Men were drinking and smoking, but the place wasn't sleazy at all. If anything, the gay men in the bar seemed respectable, clean, and polite. Once Harlan and I were seated at the bar, the bartender approached us, asking, "What can I get you hot men?"

"Two Cokes," Harlan replied. Drinking Coke was another thing we both enjoyed that set us apart from most Mormons, who saw it as sinful.

"Coming right up, you sexy thing!" the bartender replied, showing an intense interest in both of us but particularly in Harlan, an interest that I felt jealous of.

Once the bartender brought us our Cokes, we drank them slowly as I purveyed the room, watching two men dance closely together and kiss each other on the lips, as music blasted from the sound system. "I've never seen two men dancing together before," I admitted, "much less seen two men kissing each other like that!"

"Me either," Harlan replied. "It makes me want to puke."

After taking another sip of his Coke, Harlan added, "Sorry, Babe, but I have to get out of here."

******

After a few years of therapy in New York, my approach to sexual encounters evolved. Only then did I realize how I had always kept my soul cut off from the sexual experiences I had previously experienced. For me, sex had been a soulless adventure up to that point in my life. As I gradually allowed soul and sex to be in the same room at the same time, I began to experience sexual experiences in a fuller, much healthier, and far more enjoyable way than I ever had before. Pleasure is, after all, more enjoyable when one is fully integrated and present for the experience. And, as deeper trust was established with my therapist, I was able to overcome my embarrassment and tell Jim about some of the sexual fantasies and scenarios that I had explored in my past, but always with enormous shame and guilt.

276

Jim, of course, was unfazed by what I had shared with him and sat quietly in his chair, as nonjudgmental as a person can be. "Everyone has sexual fantasies," he replied softly. "And many people act on them. There's nothing wrong with that."

I sat smoldering in shame on his sofa, quite flabbergasted by his statement. "I can't believe that you aren't repulsed," I uttered.

"Why should I be?" he replied. "Having sexual fantasies can actually be quite healthy. If your inner child needs to get into the mud and play dirty, why not let him? But go with him, make sure he doesn't get hurt, and that he doesn't hurt anyone else. And above all, stop judging him."

"Do you really think it would be healthy for me to explore these fantasies? You know, to actually act them out?"

"Yes," he replied. "Who knows? You may find that your inner child has some important things to tell you about yourself."

As I came to learn, a soul's demand for growth and healing never relents, and it always wins. Trying to repress a soul's desires is futile and it can be damaging. Denying or repressing a soul's desires can only end in a heartless and brutal existence not worth living. Everyone, if they are to be happy, particularly in sexual relationships, needs to find a way to heal from sexual shame.

To heal the vast reservoirs of sexual shame that I had internalized, I first had to find out what my soul needed to experience sexually to find healing. To do that, I had to be willing to listen. Most of us rarely listen to what our souls are saying to us, and many of us deny the existence of a soul. For me, I had to get myself to a quiet spot, where I felt as comfortable and peaceful as possible. Then I simply had to stop my mind from racing to and fro, from thinking about anything, and focus on my breath. As I learned over time, if I simply focused on my breath for a few minutes, as it went in and out, I could enter into a meditative state.

I soon discovered that my soul dwelled within me, patiently waiting to talk to me whenever I was ready and willing to listen.

It is interesting that the root of the word *spiritual* simply means "the breath." Virtually all of the great spiritual teachers throughout the ages have talked about focusing on the breath while in deep meditation to find a higher spiritual consciousness. Anyone can develop this soul connection, whenever they choose. It might take a while before that soul connection is made, as it did with me. But that's okay. Any relationship of worth requires time and effort.

Of course, once I was willing and able to ask my inner child questions, I needed to learn how to wait for the answers, and how to listen without judgment when the answers finally came. As I would later come to accept, my soul needed to reenact what I had experienced sexually when I was young, either in the dominant or the submissive role, so that I could heal at least some of the internalized shame I had inherited from my LDS upbringing. But defining what my soul needed to experience was only the beginning. I had to be ready and willing to say yes to my soul's sexual yearnings. This was not easy for me at first. I was, after all, raised to be a people pleaser: My parents and those of the LDS community in which I was raised, were my ventriloquists, and I was their Mormon Muppet, saying whatever they required me to say in the way they wanted me to say it.

Once I began to accept and understand my soul's needs and desires, I discovered how to forsake *shameful* sex *(literally sex full of shame)* for *shameless* sex *(literally sex with less shame)*. As I integrated my mind, body and soul, as God had always intended, I began *unshaming* all of the sexual acts and relationships I pursued, following in the footsteps of my pioneering, nonconformist LDS ancestors, not the conservative Mormons of today. After all, Brigham Young had 27 wives!

In following Brother Brigham's lead, I became a new kind of Mormon pioneer, a sexual trailblazer like Brother Young, abandoning *the shameful path* that my LDS upbringing had demanded, to follow a healthier and more loving and *shameless path*—eventually healing much of my internalized sexual shame. Like the Mormon pioneers, who found their handcarts weighted down with things they no longer needed, I had to dump a hell of a lot of stuff over the side, or I never would have made it; the mountains were too high, the trail too dangerous.

My first foray into a healthier and a far more soul-connected form of sexual role-play began when I met George, an ex-Mormon like myself. Born and raised in Salt Lake City by an LDS family who could not accept him as gay, George had moved to New York City to start a new life. Short but very handsome, George eventually found love with a man who was soon diagnosed with full-blown AIDS and died. When I met George he had already contracted AIDS, so our sexual relating had to be extremely safe, and there could be no exchange of bodily fluids, so that I would not be exposed to the virus.

If anything, our relationship was more spiritual and emotional than it was ever physical. My sexual relationship with George came at a time when I was working through many issues in therapy. It was a gift for both of us. Since both George and I were raised Mormon, he understood why I yearned so deeply to please, if only to reenact my original family trauma. George and I loved each other as friends who were both dealing with the same Mormon shame. And over the course of our six-month affair, George and I helped each other heal some of the deepest shame inside each of us.

Eventually George became so ill that he was forced to return to Salt Lake City to live with his LDS family. I called George often. Usually he was sad when we talked, and often he said that his Mormon family still couldn't accept him. "They say that God is punishing me for breaking His laws," George explained one night.

"That's a crock," I replied. "You know that, right?"

"I know, but the little boy inside me," he admitted sheepishly, "who still needs and wants their approval, still believes them."

"George, you are a good and loving man; you didn't do anything wrong." I took a meaningful pause. "You and your partner were unlucky, that's all! You were exposed to a virus, not to God's judgment. God made us gay. He wants us to be happy."

"Thank you for saying that, Kerry," he whispered back to me, taking a deep and difficult breath. "I needed to hear that."

"Yes, Sir," I replied jokingly, reminding him of our play.

He laughed, which made him cough, spewing up some gunk from deep in his lungs. "I wish I could still be playing with you," he said. "I got so much good out of it."

George died two weeks after that phone call. I sent his LDS parents a sympathy note, but I never heard back from them.

After George's death, I found others to serve sexually, year after year connecting my need for these experiences to the sexual shame I had internalized and was still acting out, while in the process of spiritual healing. Gradually. I gravitated toward the dominant role, dressing myself in leather from the tip of my leather cap to the leather boots on my feet.

Over time, I developed a reputation as a leather master who could provide sexually submissive gay men with the experiences they needed to find healing. It was behind this leather mask that I hid for nearly two decades, while exploring my soul's yearnings, and gaining enormous spiritual, mental, and emotional growth. I had spent many years as a shamed Saint; it would take many more years to become a fully *unshamed* one.

******

I called Harlan a few days after our trip to Salt Lake City in early January of 1975 to let him know that I had finished my new play and wanted him to read it. Happily, he came right over.

As Harlan sat on my living room sofa, slowly reading what I had titled *Children of the World*, I bit my fingernails to nubs. After he turned the last page, I anxiously awaited his verdict.

"It's even better than your last play," he said, smiling broadly.

Hopeful that I might win the Festival of Arts competition for a second year, I immediately submitted it to Dr. Whitman for his consideration.

A day or two after that visit, Harlan came by my apartment again to tell me that he had decided to marry Leigh.

"You're getting married?" I ventured cautiously.

"She doesn't want an abortion." His eyes looked everywhere about my living room but at me. "We've already set the date," he explained. "We're getting married in the Temple, two weeks from Saturday."

"You're planning a Temple marriage?" I blurted out, quite in shock. This meant that both he and Leigh had told a great many lies to their church authorities, since they had both been breaking *The Law of Chastity* for several months. "So, how are you pulling that off?" I asked. "Since she's pregnant?"

Harlan was quite rightly embarrassed. "Leigh's parents are strict LDS," he tried to explain. "If we don't get married in the Temple, they'll lose their minds. She isn't showing yet, so if we get married right away, no one will be the wiser."

"Except Heavenly Father," I sputtered. "He'll know."

He was red-faced, yet Harlan stared at me defiantly. "Leigh's always dreamed of a Temple marriage, so what else can I do?" he replied, pausing before he gave me a sheepish grin. "We're going to have a wedding reception after the Temple ceremony in her parents' ward building, and I want you to act as my Best Man." He paused again. "So what do you say: Will you be my Best Man at our wedding reception?"

"Of course, I will," I replied hesitantly. I felt proud that he had asked me to be his Best Man, but I was also hurt and angered by his hypocrisy. Since I was not worthy to enter the Temple, and could never receive such a Temple Recommend as long as I told the truth about my sins, how could Harlan or Leigh?

"I'm hoping that Leigh and I will be a good match," Harlan added. "Though I'm not sure it will ever be like what ..."

"Like what we have?" I asked pointedly, interrupting him. "Like what we still could have?" The desire that I saw in Harlan's eyes confirmed what I had just said. "Harlan, I tried with Bridget, too. I had big plans of marrying her," I confessed. "But every time I kissed her, I dreamed I was kissing you. I couldn't keep living a lie. Finally I had to tell her the truth. That's why we broke up."

He was listening to me intently as I moved nearer to him,

caressing his name as I whispered, "Harlan, I love you."

He backed away from me. "We can't let it happen again! I'm getting married soon! I'm not going to let you ruin that!"

"Oh, Harlan, please let me love you," I pleaded as I came toward him, attempting to kiss him again.

Enraged with inner shame, Harlan threw me across the room, as I crashed against the wall, breaking the framed portrait of myself that Harlan had given me for our first Christmas celebration together. "Fuck it!" he shouted. "I can't see you any more, Kerry. I don't want you as my Best Man! I don't want you at my wedding reception! I don't want to see you again! Ever!"

Harlan stormed out, slamming the door in my face behind him as he ran up the steps from my basement apartment two at a time.

I ran after him, calling his name as I reached the front yard, "Harlan! Harlan, please come back!"

But he was already screeching away in his red Volkswagen as fast as he could. Devastated, I knelt on the snow-covered front lawn and bawled my eyes out.

I was still lying there in the snow, sobbing, when Dom returned and helped me back into our apartment.

"I just want to die," I said. "How can I live without him?"

"You'll have to," Dom said. "You need to let him go."

I ran to my bedroom and closed the door, shutting out the world behind me. Crawling into bed, I sobbed myself to sleep.

In late January 1975, I lay on the couch in Dr. Parker's office trying not to cry.

"You still haven't told me what you feel about Harlan getting married?" he asked. I pressed my forehead into my hands. "Nothing," I replied stoically. Dr. Parker probed gently. "You say that you've been in love with Harlan for years. How did you feel when he told you he was going to marry the girl? Did it anger you? Did it hurt?" he pressed. I said nothing, pressing harder with my hands against my cheekbones. "Come on, Kerry, don't shut me out. Tell me how you felt."

"I felt like hell!" I exploded, swearing for the first time on campus. "I felt abandoned. How else would I feel?"

Dr. Parker was clearly taken back by my outburst. "That's some anger you have inside you," he said.

"You asked for it, and I gave it to you."

"I see," he said quietly, taking notes at his desk.

"I'm not angry with you," I said. "I'm angry with myself."

When *The Music Man* opened in early February, I managed to stop the show nightly, mostly in my comic reactions to the actress playing my wife. During some of the performances, audiences laughed and applauded so hard at our antics, that it took a minute or two before the show could go on. In fact, the Drama Department nominated my portrayal of Mayor Shinn as one of the very best of the year, even as graduation drew near.

As soon as *The Music Man* opened, Dr. Gledhill cast me in the last major production that I would appear in at BYU, giving me the title role of JB in Archibald MacLeish's play *JB*, a modern retelling of the biblical tale of Job, which would open in early March. We went into rehearsals immediately.

By mid-February, I heard through the grapevine that Harlan and Leigh had married in the Provo Temple and were now living as man and wife in Harlan's apartment, turning his place into their new home, living out the Mormon dream. I felt lonely and abandoned.

During that last semester at BYU, I spent many late evenings at my two sacred temples, the rest areas going north and south on Interstate-15. Dom knew of my sexual exploits at the rest areas, and I knew about his. He had gone there on many an occasion, until he met and started dating Maria, a lovely young student from Bolivia where he had served his mission.

Around the same time, I received a wedding invitation from Bridget who had fallen in love with Grant Collins, a Catholic guy in Salt Lake City. Bridget had written, "Please come," in her own handwriting on the invitation.

In the end, I attended her wedding, and I am so glad that I did, as this rekindled our friendship, one that has never waned since.

I got a call from Leigh in mid-February 1975, asking if I could meet her at a café on Main Street in downtown Provo, and I agreed to meet her there for lunch.

After giving Leigh a hug and sitting down at her table, I asked her about their wedding held recently in the Provo Temple.

"It was beautiful," she admitted. "It's such a blessing that Harlan and I were able to marry in the Temple and be sealed to each other for time and all eternity."

I tried not to visibly wince as she said the words.

"So how is Harlan doing?" I asked, changing the subject.

"He misses you, Kerry," Leigh said, after I sat down at her table.

"He never says so in so many words, but I know he does," Leigh continued. "I don't know what happened between you two. I just know, you two would be happier if you made up."

"I'd be happy to do that, Leigh," I said. "But Harlan doesn't want to see me. Trust me, he has his reasons."

"I know he misses you," she replied. "He seems unsure about so many things right now."

"What do you mean?" I queried.

"He wants us to move to L.A. after he graduates. He'll have to get a regular job to support us, until he gets his acting career going, but his confidence seems shattered." She paused. "But what about you?"

"I'm heading to California, too," I said. "I'm trying to get an audition in Los Angeles and also with ACT in San Francisco."

"Good luck, Kerry," she said sweetly. "I've never seen you on stage, but Harlan tells me that you're the best actor at BYU."

"Thank him for saying that," I said. "And give him my best."

"I wish you would come to dinner sometime soon and tell him yourself." I shook my head no. "It's such a shame that you two are at odds," she continued. "Since we're all moving to California after graduation, we could all live in a big house, you and me and Harlan, and share the rent!"

"There's only one problem. Harlan can't stand to look at me."

"We're newly married, but Harlan seems unhappy," Leigh explained quietly. "I know something is wrong, but he shuts me out. He won't talk about Vietnam, or you. And he's still angry with me about mistakes I made with the man I dated before him. Harlan's my husband, but sometimes I feel like I don't know him at all."

I took her small, delicate hand in mine and patted it gently. "I know that Harlan loves you deeply," I said. "Be patient with him."

"Kerry," she said, pausing for the longest time, before she admitted sheepishly, "I know Harlan told you … about … the baby we're expecting."

Taken aback, I replied, "I'm glad he told you that I knew."

"I kind of expected he would tell you, given how close you two were. I know you guys used to tell each other everything."

"I hope that doesn't upset you," I responded. "I'm very good at keeping secrets. And it's nobody's business anyway, except yours and Harlan's."

"Thank you," she replied, as tears began to form in her sparkling blue eyes. "I appreciate your discretion. It would kill my parents if they found out. I'm not proud of some of the choices I've made, but I am happy about our baby, to have a life growing inside me that Harlan and I created together."

"That's beautiful, Leigh," I said. Suddenly I found myself wondering what it would feel like if I were carrying Harlan's baby as an embryo of our love, growing inside me as it was inside her.

I ran into Harlan a couple of times after that, in quick succession in February. It wasn't surprising that this would happen, as we frequented the same spots and we only lived a few blocks from each other. The first time, with snow on the ground, he was walking hand-in-hand with Leigh on University Avenue. We all stood frozen like oxen stuck in snow. "Hi, Kerry," Leigh whispered weakly.

"Hi, Leigh," I said, not looking at her but directly at Harlan, as I devoured him with lover's eyes. Harlan, on the other hand, would not look at me.

"Come on, Leigh," Harlan said, grabbing her arm. "Let's go!"

"But, Harlan," she prodded, trying to force a reconciliation.

"Come on," he said, pulling her back toward their apartment.

"We'll see you later, Kerry," she called after me, as I stood frozen on my front lawn like a snowman.

"No, we won't," I heard Harlan mutter under his breath, as they dragged Leigh up the sidewalk and turned the corner.

When I ran into Harlan a second time at Hawkins Drive-In, he grabbed his cheeseburger and ran out at top speed.

"It's such a shame what's happened between you two," Ma Hawkins said. "If either one of you had a lick of sense, you'd shake hands and make up."

"That wouldn't help," I explained. "Harlan doesn't want to see me. And I can't really blame him."

I received word from Dr. Whitman in mid-February that my play, *Children of the World*, was chosen as one of four winners to be presented at the Festival of Arts in March, making me a winning recipient two years in a row.

While *The Music Man* was still in production, I heard from the American Conservatory Theatre in San Francisco that I could audition for their company on April 16, 1975. This meant a drive to California between when final exams would be completed and BYU's Commencement Exercise to be held on Friday, April 18th.

After *The Music Man* closed, *JB* opened on March 5. Both shows earned me some of the best reviews of my college years.

******

Acting as producer, I took my one-man play to Provincetown, Massachusetts in May 1990, where it became the longest running theatrical production in Cape Cod history, running until November 1992—only closing during the winter months. Once my show became a hit in P'Town, it seemed that I could not go anywhere in town without strangers wanting my autograph or simply wanting to shake my hand. To a small degree, I finally got a taste of the fame that I had always yearned for, yet I felt uncomfortable with my newfound celebrity status.

I remember sitting on the beach at Herring Cove, when a handsome man came over to me and started flirting. You're Kerry Ashton, aren't you?" he asked. I nodded affirmatively. "Wow! You're famous in town!" he said, flashing me a bright and handsome smile. "You want to go into the bushes and fuck me?" he asked. "I've never been fucked by a star before!"

Turned off, I told him as politely as I could to go away.

There were several incidents like this during my three years in Provincetown, and I became increasingly unnerved by these attempts at fame fucking. Only then could I see how Sondheim must have felt when I looked to him for help in my career.

When my friend and booking agent Mark Stephenson came to see the show that first summer of 1990 in Provincetown, he brought with him the acclaimed actress Julie Harris.

After the play, Mark and Julie and I went out for dinner. I was thrilled to meet Miss Harris, and the three of us had a marvelous meal together. I had long admired her work and I told her how much watching her brilliant performance in the film *East of Eden,* in my high school English class, had inspired me to become an actor. Julie laughed in response. "And seeing you tonight on stage inspired me, too!" It was the nicest compliment she could have given me. If anyone knew about performing in a solo show, it was Julie Harris, who had won a Tony Award for her performance on Broadway in *The Belle of Amherst.*

We spoke about the difficult challenges of performing in a one-person show. "I find it exhilarating but exhausting," she explained.

"Me, too," I concurred. "I leave everything on stage. By the time I get back to my dressing room, all that's left of me is a rag and a hank of hair." It was one of my original expressions, and she laughed when she heard it. "You have a way with words," Julie replied, laughing, "both on stage and off!"

Happily, a good part of me felt that I had finally earned my place at the table with a luminary actress like Julie Harris. But, side from this, we could barely eat our dinner because people kept coming over to our table to ask for our autographs.

"Once you're in the public eye, Kerry," Julie explained, "the public feels like they own you. It's the price we pay for fame."

"I'm sure you're right, but I don't think I like it much."

"I don't know many actors who do," Julie said. "Most of us are quite shy."

"It's funny you say that," I replied. "Most of my friends think I am extroverted, but I'm quite shy until I get to know people."

In Provincetown, I came to understand how everyone wants and needs to know that they are loved, not because they are famous but for themselves alone.

After my first season in Provincetown, I returned to New York, only to lose three close friends to AIDS. The first to die was Tony Kish, a longtime friend who had made the trip to see my performance in P'Town, only to pay the ultimate price; the second was my stage manager Michael Prevulsky; and the third was my booking agent Mark Stephenson.

As Mark's young body withered away, his parents moved to Manhattan to live with him and care for him. Mark and his mom were extremely close, and neither of them wanted to let go of the other. When his parents asked me to spell them to see a Broadway matinee, I was happy to stay with Mark. After his parents left, Mark's breathing became labored.

Coming to Mark's side, I took his hand in mine and brushed his hair off his forehead. "Mark," I said gently, "your parents will understand if you're ready to go. It's okay to go if you need and want to." He opened his eyes and then he simply let go, breathing his last breath, as I took him in my arms, giving him a kiss on his cheek as I felt his soul depart his body.

My niece Tara married a sailor who was stationed at Pearl Harbor. At her invitation, I went to visit her in Hawaii while her married sailor was out at sea, in August 1993.

Like me, Tara had left the Mormon Church, so I felt safe in opening up to her about many aspects of my life that I had never shared with others in my family. We shared our secrets as we shared Hawaii. After telling Tara more about my gay adult life than I had ever told anyone, Tara asked me to take her out to a gay bar. "I want to find out what your life is like," Tara explained. At the young age of 21, Tara Lee had offered me a gift that I never thought I would receive from any member of my Mormon family. As I melted into tears as Tara took me into her arms and reassured me how much she loved her Uncle.

When we walked into a gay bar in Honolulu that night, looking to all like a married couple that had wandered into the wrong place, the gay men at the bar all sat silent as the grave. Sidling up to the bar and turning to face all of the gay men present, I explained, "Everyone, this is a special night for me and for my niece Tara. We were both raised Mormon, but she loves and accepts me for who I am. In fact, she asked me to take her out tonight to a gay bar, so she could experience gay life. I hope you can help me show her a good time!"

Suddenly the bar lit up with life. The bartender found fresh Hawaiian leis from behind the bar, and gave one to each gay patron, who each lined up to present Tara with a lei and with a huge hug and kiss on each cheek. In the end, every last gay man in the place, including the bartender, took a turn dancing with her. Tara, who has always loved to dance, was laden with leis and love that night, and never had a better night out in her entire life.

Later during that visit, Tara and I spent my 40th Birthday on a helicopter ride over Kauai. When we flew into the Mount Wai'ale'ale crater at the top of the island, surrounded by waterfalls and rainbows in every direction, the pilot announced through our earphones that it was my 40th Birthday, and asked everyone to sing me the "Happy Birthday" song.

From then on, Tara and I became Ohana, the Hawaiian word for family. Tara later divorced and had two children by a second husband, before resettling in Pocatello and divorcing for a second time, but she and her children and I remain Ohana to this day.

Sadly, it was only a few days after I returned from Hawaii in September 1993, that Dad was diagnosed with colon cancer.

A year later, in early September 1994, Dad called to give me the latest update. His doctors had confirmed our worst fears during their most recent testing: Dad's cancer had spread throughout his body.

The doctors gave him only a few weeks to live.

"But don't worry about coming out," Dad said simply. "You're busy now. There's nothing you can do to help me now."

I had already decided that I was going to Idaho to stay with Dad until his death, but I said nothing about my plans, as I wanted to surprise him.

As the plane passed over Illinois the next day, I thought of my Mormon ancestors who were forced out of their Nauvoo homes by mobs a century-and-a-half earlier. It was on a winter's night when temperatures were at 12 degrees below zero that they crossed the icy Mississippi River in mass exodus, only to look back from the Ohio shore, to see their town of Nauvoo burning like a fiery ember on the snowy landscape. I thought of the Mormon Saints who had followed Brigham Young west in search of their Promised Land, and of those who had died along the way, buried in shallow graves as the Saints trekked west, and how those who had marched on, pulling handcarts behind them, and how they sang:

> *"Come, Come Ye Saints, no toil nor labor fear,*
> *But with Joy, wend your way.*
> *We'll find the place, which God for us prepared,*
> *Far away in the west,*
> *Where none shall come to hurt or make afraid;*
> *There the Saints will be blessed.*
> *And should we die before our Journey's through,*
> *Happy Day! All is well!*
> *We then are free from toil and sorrow, too;*
> *With the just we shall dwell!*
> *But if our lives are spared again*
> *To see the Saints their rest obtain,*
> *0, how we'll make this chorus swell:*
> *All is well! All is well!"*

I had heard the Mormon Tabernacle Choir sing that song many times. Just thinking about the song moved me again to tears.

After renting a car at the Salt Lake airport, I got on I-15 driving toward the Wasatch Mountains that loomed ahead of me like the hand of God. It was over those peaks that my Great-Great Grandparents, led by Brigham Young, had pulled their handcart of belongings, and where, on July 24, 1847, a hot day—a day celebrated in the west ever since as Mormon Pioneer Day—that the Prophet Brigham Young had looked down on the Salt Lake Valley below, and declared, "This is the place!"

Those same mountains had often reminded me that I was expected to live in as saintly a fashion as my Mormon ancestors. As though Mom were inside the car with me, I could hear her saying, "It is your heritage, Kerry Lynn. Like it or not, you are, and always will be, a son of Mormon pioneers."

Driving north on State Street past Temple Square, the Mormon Temple stood on the left. It was where the Mormon Prophet talked face-to-face with God. With masonic-like carvings etched on smooth gray granite walls and massive spirals reaching up like outstretched fingers for God, it was an impressive sight. On the opposite side of the street, beyond a paved pavilion, stood the modern 28-story Church Office Building.

I found a parking spot and walked onto the serene grounds of Temple Square. The dome-shaped Tabernacle was lovely, as always, but the temple was the most inspirational sight. In a separate peace, I sat on the same bench where Mom and Dad and I had sat that last day before her exploratory surgery. That was the last day that she had looked the way I liked to remember her. We had stopped to sit and smell the peonies, listening to the Mormon Tabernacle Choir rehearsing, their voices carrying beyond the walls of the Tabernacle. "The music is beautiful, isn't it, Mom?" I had asked.

"Yes, I love the Choir." She had said, smiling. "You know, Kerry, I still expect to see you married in the Temple someday."

"You still hold out hope, eh?" I had asked. "But you know I'm married to the theater!"

She had kissed me on the cheek and held me close. "I love you so much, Sweetheart."

The bittersweet memory faded as I sat on the bench alone, feeling the loss of Mom as always.

******

On Thursday morning, March 6, 1975, the morning after *JB* opened, I received a surprising call at 9am. "Kerry?" the familiar deep voice said sheepishly. "This is Harlan."

Tears came into my eyes and streamed down my cheeks.

"Hi," I said. "I never thought I'd ever hear your voice again."

"I know." There was a long pause on his end of the line. "I need to talk with you alone and in person if that's okay," he added. "Is now a good time or is Dom still there?"

"Dom left for class, but I have to leave for class." I was holding my breath, trying to remain calm. "Could we meet this afternoon?"

"Okay," he said. "What about 3pm?"

"Sounds good." I paused. "I'll see you then."

"Great," he responded, quietly hanging up the phone.

When I opened the door of my basement apartment at 3pm that afternoon, Harlan was standing at the door, holding 24 long-stem red roses in his hand, done in a magnificent bouquet.

"Here," he said, handing me the flowers. "These are for you."

I burst into tears, taking the roses from him and smelling the promise they offered. "Oh, Harlan, they're beautiful! Thank you."

Harlan came inside the living room and got comfortable, sitting in the overstuffed sofa, while I went into the kitchen and put the roses in a vase with water. I came back into the living room, putting the roses down on the coffee table and sat on the chair opposite him. Then, he began speaking quietly, "I want to apologize for how I behaved. You're my best friend, and I treated you like crap. For that I'm sorry. I hope you can accept my apology."

"Of course I can," I said sincerely. "All is forgiven. I hope that you can forgive me, too, for all that I did to offend you."

"Kerry," he said, "you have nothing to apologize for." He paused, as though searching for the right words. "I overreacted, when you … when … when we …"

"I know," I interrupted. "That's water under the bridge now."

"Good," he said. "I just want you and I to be friends again."

"We always were friends. As far as I'm concerned, we always will be friends."

"Thanks," he said. "I can't tell you how much that means to me." He let out a deep breath. "I've missed you … terribly."

"I've missed you, too, Harlan," I replied.

"I'm sorry I didn't invite you to the wedding reception," he said. "That was wrong of me."

"I understood why," I explained. "It's all in the past now."

"I went to see your opening night in *JB* last night," he confessed. "I thought you were incredible. It was the best performance you've given at BYU hands down."

"Thank you," I replied. "Coming from you, that means a lot."

"Leigh tells me you're trying to get an audition with ACT."

"Actually it's all set! It's scheduled in San Francisco between finals and graduation," I explained. "In fact, I was working on my audition when you called earlier this morning."

"I'm proud of you, Babe!" he said smiling. And his smile sent shudders all through me.

"Thanks," I said. There was an awkward silence between us.

"About what happened," he said finally. "It was my fault. You didn't do anything wrong. I just … panicked." He paused. "I felt so scared of what might happen … next. I hope you understand."

"I understand," I said. "And I understood it at the time. Any straight man would have done the same thing or worse. I was way out of line, forcing myself on you like that. I know you don't have feelings for me like I have for you. I'm just glad that we can still be friends."

"Me, too," he replied. "Leigh tells me that you may move to L.A. when we do. If it turns out that way, we'll all see each other a lot more."

"That would be wonderful," I responded. "If you get a gig on a soap, you and Leigh and the baby will be set for life."

"I hope so. I'm not sure I'm cut out to be a family man."

After Harlan's visit, I felt happy for the first time in ages. Maybe, I thought, Harlan and Leigh and the baby and I would all end up in Los Angeles. It could be a new beginning, away from Mormon Zion, in a new Promised Land. It could be wonderful.

On the night of the 1975 Mormon Festival of Arts in mid-March, I wore a rented tuxedo and picked up Stacey at her apartment. I took out the corsage I'd bought her, and pinned it on her elegant white formal. "Stacey! You look stunning!" I exclaimed.

When we arrived at the Arts Center, we met Harlan and Leigh at the front entrance. Harlan looked ravishing in his tuxedo, naturally, and Leigh looked breathtaking in a beautiful floor-length pink gown.

As it happened, the evening was a highlight of our senior year, and happily my play was well received.

When I drove Stacey back to her apartment after the event that night, she snuggled close to me in Oscar's front seat. "I am so proud of you, Kerry. The play was so good. And the audience loved it!"

When I began making plans later that month for my audition at American Conservatory Theatre to be held in San Francisco in April 1975, Stacey suggested that we drive together and stay at her home in Sacramento the first night, and then with her sister just outside San Francisco the next night.

As we made our travel plans, sitting in two white rocking chairs on the front porch of Stacey's off-campus home, Stacey finally confessed what she had been keeping to herself for too long.

With her beautiful freckled face turning bright red, she spoke slowly. "Kerry, I ... I need ... to say something." With great difficulty, she finally admitted, "I'm in love with you, Kerry," as tears formed in her hazel eyes.

"Oh, Stacey," I replied as gently as I could, "I was afraid you were going to say that."

"Well, I thought you should know," she added cautiously.

I tried to think of a way to let her down softly. "Stacey," I said truthfully, "I love you as a friend, but I can't give you what you want and deserve, as much as I might want to try."

"I see," she said, disappointment etched on her face.

"But it isn't that you're not attractive. You're beautiful, Stacey."

"If not that, then what?" she pressed.

"I'm gay, Stacey," I admitted, breathing out my anxiety as I said it. "I've tried everything to change. I've even undergone shock treatments. But nothing has helped. I … I …" I tried to stammer out a more profound explanation, but Stacey boldly cut me off.

"You're in love with Harlan, aren't you?" she asked.

She had cut to the chase, so I wasn't skipping around her question. "Yes," I admitted. It felt so good to finally admit it.

"That's why he didn't want you at his wedding?" she asked.

"Yes," I replied.

"And that's why you two stopped being friends for awhile?"

"Yes. He still doesn't understand why I'm gay anymore than I do, but at least he's willing to try to accept the fact, for the sake of our friendship." There were tears in Stacey's eyes and a wounded look on her face. I went to her and took her in my arms. "I hope that you and I can still be friends, too," I continued. "The church doesn't approve of homosexuality, but I'm trying hard to accept myself as I am. I know you believe in the church, but I hope one day you can come to accept me the way I am."

"I'll try my best, Kerry," she said softly, as she broke down in tears and buried her face in my shoulder. "I'll try. I really will, because I love you, Kerry Ashton. I really do love you."

Once I told President Wilkinson about Stacey's declaration of love, he was enthusiastic. "I think that's wonderful!" he exclaimed. "You should ask her out and see if you can't cultivate some normal feelings for Stacey."

"If and when the Lord forgives me, if and when I change, then what?" I asked, exhausted from the effort. "I graduate, I get engaged to Stacey, I go on a mission, and then I marry Stacey in the Temple. Is that the plan?"

"That would be an ideal plan, yes," Wilkinson admitted.

"You have my life planned out so carefully," I replied.

"Your attitude of late has left a bit to be desired."

"How should I feel, President?" I asked. "Or haven't you planned that out, too?"

"What is it, Kerry?" he asked. "Why are you so angry today?"

"I apologize, President," I replied. "The last person I should be angry with is you. I just feel discouraged; the harder I try to change my gay feelings, the stronger they become."

"Don't worry. We'll get you on the right track soon enough."

Meanwhile, Clarke called another private conference in his office. The Holy Trinity—Clarke, Wilkinson, and Parker—sat around Clarke's office discussing me as usual, while I sat in the middle of the room, staring out the window at the Arts Center parking lot. Seeing Oscar parked there, I wished I could drive away into the mountains and never come back. It was a pleasant day outside, too nice a day to think about rehabilitation.

They jabbered on and on, making plans and offering suggestions, until I could take no more. "What about me?" I shouted. "Can I say something?" Suddenly, the three men stared at me, as though they had never seen the real me before. "What if I can't change?"

They all looked at me as though I had two heads.

******

On my drive to the tiny farming community of Shelley, Idaho to see Dad and Sarah, I stopped in Pocatello and spent some time at the family cemetery plot where Mom and Grandma and Grandpa were buried, placing flowers on each of their graves.

Dad's body, I knew, would soon be interred in the space next to Mom's remains, but where would his spirit go?

Later, as I drove past the house on Elm Street, the last house where Mom and Dad had lived together before her death, the house that Dad had sold, I felt very much alone. When I drove past my childhood home on Poplar Street, I was shocked to see the house so utterly dilapidated. The backyard fence that I had built with Dad was in need of repair. Pocatello would always be my hometown, but there was no place there to call my home. I no longer belonged there. Even Dad had moved to Shelley, 50 minutes north.

Depressed, I drove past the 15th Ward building on Jefferson Avenue, where I had attended church meetings for most of my childhood. It was a Friday afternoon but since cars were parked in the lot, I assumed the chapel must be open. On a whim I pulled in and parked. The large brick building and the huge lawn surrounding it looked just as I remembered it. The smell of freshly-cut grass was in the air. It smelled like home.

I got out of the yellow Datsun and walked up the wide sidewalk to the double doors. I let my hand grip the doorknob, briefly remembering that the last time I had stepped inside a Mormon Church had been 14 years before, at my mother's funeral in 1980.

The tile floor in the foyer was sparkling clean. I found the door to the chapel unlocked, and walked inside. It was exactly as I remembered it. The rows of wooden pews were as hard as ever. The platform at the front of the chapel had the same podium, the same choir seats, the same piano and organ, and the same portrait of Jesus hanging center stage, His brown eyes as loving as ever.

I remembered how as a small child, I had tugged on Mom's dress and whispered in her ear, "Jesus's eyes are brown like mine!"

"I see," she had whispered. "Now fold your arms and be quiet."

It was on the platform, I remembered, where I was ordained into the Aaronic Priesthood—first as a Deacon, then as a Teacher and finally as a Priest. And it was at the sacrament table where as a Priest, I had knelt hundreds of times and prayed over the Lord's Holy Sacrament. I had felt safe in this ward chapel. Here I had found a place to belong. As a six-year-old, I had sat with other six-year-old Sunbeams in Mormon Primary, each of us wearing yellow paper sunbeams around our heads, as we sang:

"Jesus wants me for a sunbeam, to shine for Him each day.
In every way try to please Him: At home, at school, at play.

A sunbeam, a sunbeam, Jesus wants me for a sunbeam.
A sunbeam, a sunbeam, I'll be a sunbeam for Him."

As a child of six I had stood on a stepladder behind that pulpit and with Mom standing behind me to prompt, gave my first public address. On the same platform, I was promoted to the class of Top Pilots in Primary. The song we sang that day was the same song I had learned at Mama's knee. The lyrics were carved into my heart:

"I am a child of God, and He has sent me here,
Has given me an earthly home with parents kind and dear.
Teach me, guide me, walk beside me, help me find the way.
Teach me all that I must know to live with Him someday."

I stared at the portrait of Jesus Christ for several minutes. Finally, I spoke out loud: "Jesus, you loved me when I was a Sunbeam, but do you love me now? Am I still a child of God?" Jesus wasn't talking, not that I expected Him to. I stared defiantly at the portrait. "So, until you can love me as I am, this is one sunbeam who'll never shine for you again!"

Less than an hour later, I was on Main Street in the tiny farming town of Shelley, Idaho. Making a right turn at one of the few stoplights in town, I crossed the railroad tracks onto Locust Avenue, lined with pine trees on both sides of the road, and pulled in front of Dad and Sarah's tiny white house, and parked in their driveway. Turning off the engine, I sat for a moment inside the car, gathering my thoughts.

When I rang the bell on the front porch, Sarah opened the door.

"Kerry!" she squealed. "We had no idea you were coming!"

"You weren't supposed to! It's a surprise!" I announced, giving her a quick hug.

Dad sat in his La-Z-Boy recliner, wrapped in a blanket, looking thin and gaunt. "Hello, Dad," I said, smiling, as I threw my arms around him and kissed him.

Dad was unable to hide his emotions and burst into tears.

"Kerry!" he exclaimed weakly, but with pride and excitement, "I told you not to come home!"

"I know," I said, "but that didn't mean I had to listen."

I sat beside him and took his hand in mine, patting his arm gently.

"Dad, I've come home, and I'm going to be here with you until the end." Once I saw the tears in Dad's eyes, I knew that I had made the right decision to come home, and to be with my father until the time came for him to go.

We chatted for a while, catching up on family news, before Dad admitted, "I've missed you, son. I'm glad you came home."

When Dad's pain suddenly increased. I called the home nurse in from the kitchen, and she gave Dad another shot of morphine.

Over the next few days, I told Dad about my true relationship with Harlan. I found myself crying like a baby in Dad's arms as he wept with me. Dad would always be Mormon and on occasion I still felt shamed by the Saints, but a channel of communication had finally opened between us. In sharing sorrow and healing shame, we found intimacy. And as the weeks passed, they put Dad on a morphine drip for the pain.

One day as I sat on the edge of his hospital bed holding Dad's hand, his eyes opened wide as he stared at the foot of the bed. "Your mother's standing right there at the foot of the bed, Kerry Lynn," Dad said weakly. "It's Millie Jane. She's come to take me to the other side. She's here." I looked to the spot where he pointed, and saw nothing but air. But quite suddenly I smelled Mother's perfume wafting through the room. "I know she's here, Dad," I said reassuringly, patting his hand. "I can't see her the way you can, but I can feel her presence. I even smell her perfume!"

Dad smiled peacefully, knowing that I believed him.

The last day that Dad uttered anything coherent, I was alone with him, sitting on the edge of his hospital bed in the family room. Squeezing my hand as his eyes slowly opened, I could tell he was trying to say something, so I placed my ear near his lips.

"Kerry," he said, "I'm so proud … that you were my son." Tears filled his eyes and he squeezed my hand in his, as if for emphasis.

Tears flowed from my eyes, too. I squeezed his hand in return, and I whispered in his ear, "I love you, Dad. I'm so grateful and proud that you were my father." The peace that came over Dad's face at that moment was a priceless and final gift. I had finally made room for Daddy, and he had finally made room for his only gay son. Dad gave me an unmistakable smile, the last smile he offered anyone. Then he whispered the last words that he would speak to anyone on earth. "I love you, Kerry Lynn."

As Dad and I held each other, and with Mother's fragrance still pervading the room, I knew that her spirit was in the room with us, sharing the blessed and magical moment when Dad and I breached the last chasm between us. In that moment, we became a Holy Trilogy of Father, Son and Holy Ghost.

As Dad drifted off into a coma-like state for the rest of the day, it became obvious that his demise was near. We sent out word to all of the family, and everyone except Dennis—who was out driving truck at the time—gathered around Dad that night to say our goodbyes. After Craig led our family in prayer, I took Dad's hand and told him that we would understand and be ready, if and when he needed to move on. I felt his hand squeeze mine in acknowledgement.

Dad's breathing became uneven and infrequent but still he lived on, even as we all found places to rest throughout the house. Then at 5am—Dad's usual time to rise, when he was always careful not to disturb the rest of us—his soul departed his body.

Denise and Tara and I went out onto the front porch to watch the coroner take Dad's body away, as sunrise came. That Idaho sunrise in early October 1994 was the most serene sunrise I have ever seen. There was a sacred hush over everything, a hush of the birds, a hush upon my heart and in my spirit. I needed to believe that Dad and Mom were together again, if not in the Celestial Kingdom, then in some other beautiful and magical place.

A veteran of World War II, Dad was buried with full military honors. When a uniformed soldier played "Taps" on his bugle over Dad's coffin while another uniformed soldier removed the flag covering his casket, folded it, and handed it to Sarah, I was overwhelmed both with pride and grief.

As we walked from the grave, I watched Sarah take 11-year-old Isaac's hand in hers, as I overheard her say, "Well, Kid, it's just you and me now."

******

It was Wednesday night, March 19, 1975, when Harlan showed up at my door. As it happened, Dom was on a date with Maria, so Harlan and I were alone. "Harlan!" I exclaimed. "What a surprise!"

"Kerry," he said quietly, as he walked into my living room and took his seat in the big overstuffed chair, "I have something I have to tell you." He paused, taking notice of the lamp sitting on the end table next to him. It was the only light I had turned on in the apartment. "Is it okay if I turn out the light?" he muttered anxiously.

"Sure, if you need to." Caught off guard, I sat breathlessly on the sofa as Harlan turned off the lamp.

"Can I join you on the sofa?" he asked sheepishly.

"Yes, of course," I replied, not knowing what to expect.

He took a seat on the sofa next to me, choosing to sit much closer than I had thought he would. "I ... uh ... I've been thinking a lot about you," he explained, as though he were searching for his words in the dark. "About us ... I mean."

His next words came out of his mouth in fits and starts, as though he were battling with himself, simply to say what he needed to say. "And I ... I think ... that I might be ... in love with you, Kerry."

Without waiting for a response, Harlan suddenly took me in his arms and crushed his lips to mine. Soon he was violently ramming his tongue into my mouth with a pent-up passion he must have been holding in for years. Taken utterly by surprise, I nonetheless yielded to his advances completely, even as I surrendered to all my yearnings, dreams and fantasies. We kissed each other passionately as he ran his hands down my body to my burgeoning erection, even as I noticed that his own obvious erection was trying to burst out of his fly. Sweeping me up into his arms, he carried me into my

301

bedroom where we ripped each other's clothes off. Clad only in my underwear and with Harlan only in his Temple undergarments, we lay down on my bed. Rolling on top of me, his strength pressed me against the mattress, even as his erection thrust against my stomach again and again.

Overcome with passion, I reached up and began to remove his holy garments. As though this gesture reminded him of his Temple covenants—the sacred covenants he had made with God in the Temple—he pulled his garments back in place and got off the bed. Standing with his erection tenting out the holy garment, he shouted, "What am I doing here? I can't believe what I'm doing here now!" Confused in a way I had never seen him before, he tried to talk through his feelings. "Now that I'm actually here with you, Kerry, the way I've longed dreamed of, I feel so happy, until I remember that at the same time I'm cheating on my wife and unborn baby!"

Getting off the bed, my erection pointed at him accusingly. "I can't take this anymore, Harlan!" I shouted. "You're hot for me. Then you're not! You're in love with me. Then you're not! You hate me. Then you bring me flowers and stick your tongue down my throat! Which Harlan will show up next? Or do you even know yourself?"

Harlan and I stood in the darkness of my bedroom and stared each other down, both of our erections acting as fervent reminders of the issue at hand. "Kerry, I'm stuck!" Harlan retorted. He paused and took a deep breath. "Babe, please, all I can think about is making love to you, the way I've dreamed about doing for four years now, so I guess that makes me ... gay!" He paused, as a dramatic silence overwhelmed the room. "There, I said it! Okay? I'm gay! Like you! Like Danny! Like Hank! I'm gay!" He paused again, swallowing all of his masculine pride. "But right now," he continued, "my pregnant wife is at our home a few blocks away from here, making me dinner."

"Harlan, we need each other. I'm in love with you."

"God forgive me, but I'm in love with you, too!" he admitted. As I heard him say those words, I began to cry. Taking me in his

302

arms yet again, we kissed once more. When he finally ended the kiss, and released me from his embrace, he spoke haltingly. "I don't know what I'm going to do about you, Kerry," he admitted. "I don't know what I'm going to do about you and me, or about Leigh and the baby." I tried to kiss the guilt from him, but he would have none of it. "We should get dressed," he said.

"Fine!" I said, pushing my erection down inside my shorts.

"I'm sorry about tonight. I thought I was ready for this, but I guess I'm not."

"Okay, but don't put me through this again," I replied tenderly but as firmly as I could. "I am in love with you, Harlan. So if and when you are ready to make love to me, I am more than ready to do that, and to make love to you without shame. But at this point, that will have to be your call and your move, not mine."

A few days later, Harlan and I lay in each other's arms on the couch in my basement apartment living room, having a hot make-out session. Even as we kissed and cuddled, my fears about losing him came gurgling to the surface.

"I feel like I'm playing the role of the other woman or something," I admitted. "I mean, how long are we going to keep this up, anyway? Leigh is going to have to know sooner or later. What's going to happen to us then?"

We stared at each other blankly. Neither of us had an answer.

Another late afternoon found us again in my living room, but this time we were in a serious discussion. "Babe," he queried, "what do you think I should do to support my new family after I graduate in a few weeks? I can't rely on acting, that's for sure."

"I don't know," I offered, "but I still think it was a mistake that you gave up painting. You love painting. It's nothing to be ashamed of."

"Sketching flowers can't pay the bills," he snorted dismissively, his comment aimed within and not at me, as his anxiety seemed to fill the entire room.

"I might be able to start auditioning for soaps and other acting gigs once I get to L.A., but I can't count on that. I'm going to need a real income. I have to think of Leigh and the baby, and what's going to be best for them. Maybe somewhere down the road, I can think about acting and even about painting again, but not right now. It's not sensible."

"You could if you believed in yourself enough," I challenged. "If you really believed you could make a living as an artist, you could do it!"

"Spoken like the true idealist that you are, Babe," he responded.

"Well, I bet you could, Harlan. Just look at me. I probably should be majoring in something sensible, too, but I'm sticking with theatre because I believe I'll be successful."

"And you will be, Kerry. I really believe that. You may have a lot of years of struggle ahead of you, but you'll make it, where I wouldn't. And you know why?" I shook my head no, dumbfounded by his words. "Because you're more of a fighter than I am," he continued. "You're more courageous. Just look at the way you take on Clarke and Wilkinson and all of those other jerks at school. But I do whatever the church and every Mormon expects me to, just so I can get them off my back. They wanted me married, so I got married. They wanted Leigh pregnant, so I got her pregnant, just to prove that I was normal. I play it by their rules, but you don't do that. That's the difference between us, Kerry." He paused. "You've got more spunk inside you than anybody I know. You're much stronger than I am."

"I don't have your muscles," I replied, wrapping my hands around his biceps, unable to keep my hands off him as I attempted to pull him close to me. But Harlan quickly pushed me away.

"Babe, I can't do this yet. I can't. I'm not ready yet."

"I understand, Harlan," I whispered. "I can wait. As long as it takes for you to feel comfortable, I can wait."

******

After Dad's funeral in October 1994, I returned to New York and began raising money for an Off-Broadway production of *The*

Wilde Spirit. And during the next two years I presented 25 backer's auditions to potential investors on a small stage that I set up in my living room, raising enough money to produce my show Off-Broadway.

In the late fall of 1994, after having had a shrimp dinner at my friend Mina's place on West 13th Street, the palms of my hands grew incredibly hot and itchy. As I started up the ignition of my blue Toyota Corolla station wagon parked out front, I saw my fingers swell to enormous proportions as my hands and arms began to swell in turn. I could not get my breath as my throat closed down; I was losing my eyesight. In panic, I drove to the corner and made a right, going down 5th Avenue, turning right on West 10th Street, driving as fast as I could to the hospital.

Somehow I got the car parked, and made my way into Emergency where a nurse was sitting behind a glass partition at a desk talking on the phone. I knocked on the glass wall.

"I'll be with you a minute!" she said, irritated that I had intruded on her phone call, not even bothering to look at me. My arm was now as big and as wide as my thigh, and it felt as heavy as concrete. I swung my arm again. This time it nearly broke the glass and caused the nurse to jump out of her seat.

"Oh my God!" she screamed when she actually looked at me. "I'm so sorry. I had no idea!"

Once she got me into the ER, my heart stopped and I dropped to the floor. Clinically, I had just died from anaphylactic shock.

Suddenly I found myself floating in the air high above the emergency room, and looking down on my dead body, but I felt nothing but peace. I watched dispassionately from above as the nurses and doctors scurried about doing what they could to revive me, until I noticed a beautiful white light above me. It seemed to be calling me home. Effortlessly, I moved upward into the tunnel of intense white light, and the more I went into the light, the more serene I felt. I began to see people standing in the light. I knew that Mom and Dad and Grandma and Grandpa Hamp were somewhere there, waiting within the light to welcome me home. I simply couldn't wait to see their smiling faces again. And then I heard the same loving and gentle voice of my unseen angel, the same voice that I had known since childhood, saying, "Kerry, it is not your time yet. You still have so much to do. You must go back."

I didn't want to go back, and I started to protest. But before I could say a word, I felt my soul whoosh back down through the tunnel of light and back into my body.

Taking my first breath, I felt physical pain again.

I was released from the hospital the next day. But I was never the same after that near-death experience. The reality of the spiritual lessons I learned from the experience made me a true believer in life after death. I was a child of God after all, and now I knew that He loved me.

In 1995, I took my one-man play to Key West where I played a successful season at the Waterfront Playhouse, a lovely venue for my show. Having given thousands of performances of my one-man play on hundreds of college campuses and in regional theaters all across America since 1977, my play had evolved as I had matured as actor, director, and author, until my play and my performance were honed to a fine gem.

When mounting the Off-Broadway production in 1996, I was advised by both my General Manager and Press Agent to hire a famous director to position the show properly. In the end, I hired a director who made many positive contributions. But as a neophyte Off-Broadway producer, I also allowed him to make decisions that undercut my play and performance. My first mistake was in allowing the director to remove most of my original music, replacing it with new background music. The play already had an original score that I was extremely proud of, with the orchestrations and arrangements done by my friend Ken Moore, who was then Head of the Musical Instruments Department at the Metropolitan Museum of Art. On top of that, it was a musical score that both Ken and I had spent years perfecting. And I had spent tens of thousands of dollars recording my original music.

Most of all, it was a score that worked superbly and that audiences loved. More than that, I knew from experience over the last two decades that my music helped me hold an audience enthralled for two hours. The changes undercut my performance.

Secondly, I let the director remove all of the furniture and hand props from the stage, while adding expensive smoke and mirrors, was a huge mistake and a costly one.

Third, my director kept insisting that I tone down my performance and shamefully I acquiesced. Worst of all, by the time I recognized my mistakes it was too late to change anything. Looking back on it now, I should have fought for what I knew was best for both my play and my performance. But having been deeply shamed throughout my childhood, I chose to please my director, rather than trust in myself and in my work.

The mistakes I made were not merely artistically wrong but calamitous financially, devouring the advertising budget. By opening night we were utterly reliant on a rave review from *The New York Times* just to stay open. But Ben Brantley's review was mixed. Essentially, he loved the spectacle of the show but thought that my portrayal was too toned down!

As it was, a proven *Can't Miss*—as we call it in show biz— closed sooner than it should have. And I only had myself to blame, since I already knew, from decades of live performances, what worked in my play and what didn't.

After closing the show, I still had the theater under lease, so—if only to give myself some sense of closure—I restaged the show with all of my original music and lyrics, returning both the play and my performance to full strength. Later, I invited an audience to see the show the way I wished it had been presented during its short and fatal Off-Broadway run. Those who had seen both versions vastly preferred my staging. Luckily, this is the version that was captured on DVD, one that audiences still watch and enjoy to this day. Who can say how Ben Brantley might have reacted had he seen my staging? He might have loved it or he might have disliked it just as much as the version he reviewed.

Either way, no one can rewrite history, no matter how much we wish it so. But it still makes me sad that those who saw the Off-Broadway production of my play did not see it at its best or at the fullness of its power.

But at the time, I was not merely saddened; I was devastated. *The Wilde Spirit* represented a full 20 years of my life, and an unrelenting push to get the show to the level of professional success that I felt it deserved. Most of this pushing was a lonely and solitary effort. I had put every last ounce of my emotional, financial, physical, and spiritual strength behind the show. For the play's last best chance, I had failed.

Now in my mid-40s, I had watched my guiding star Barbra Streisand growing older while making less and less films over time, even as I had seen my own chances at stardom diminishing, slipping away from me year by year, day by day, minute by minute. As I saw it, my Off-Broadway production was my last best chance to make my dreams come true, to become the star that I had always dreamed of becoming. And I had failed.

Taking into account the Los Angeles productions in the 70s, the critically acclaimed Off-Off Broadway production in 1982, the record-breaking three-year run in Provincetown in the 1990s, the 1995 Key West production, the countless presentations as a professional Guest Artist at some of the nation's top regional theaters and colleges and universities, and the ill-fated Off-Broadway production in 1996, over 40,000 people saw me perform in my play. The overall success of my one-man play would, in the end, be one of the great achievements of my life, yet the show's Off-Broadway failure cut into my heart the deepest.

Of course, I knew by then from years spent in therapy, that both my play's success and failure had come as a direct result of, and as a reaction to, whatever amount of shame still remained unhealed within me. As I saw it, my inner child had punished me again, not just for the deep betrayal I committed against him while fighting my *Holy War* at BYU, but also of again taking someone else's side—in this case, the director's side—over him, violating much of the trust that I had worked so hard to establish with him over the last two decades. In vindictive fashion, my inner child had withheld from me the one great success that I had worked most to obtain. It was almost as though I could hear him speaking to me, saying: "Now will you love me? Or should I make you pay even more? Until you stay on my side for good, I will never let you succeed at anything!"

After the play closed, I gave up any thought of ever writing, acting, or in any way ever working again in show business. I was too heartbroken to even contemplate it. So I took a job in classified advertising at *The New York Times*. But two questions remained: Could I learn to love myself in spite of failure? Could I love myself, knowing that I would never be a star?

After expending every last bit of energy that I possessed in bringing *The Wilde Spirit* to Off-Broadway, I should not have been surprised when I was hospitalized twice in 1998, and kept in Intensive Care for several weeks each time. My symptoms were so severe that doctors suspected that I had a heart problem. Subsequently, I underwent a cardiac catheterization.

As it turned out, my heart was broken, but not in the ways that they suspected. Since I did not have health insurance during my first two hospitalizations, I was left with $75,000 in medical bills, and I was eventually forced into bankruptcy.

The shame that I felt over my financial demise was excruciating, and no doubt contributed to another medical setback in 1999, when I was hospitalized again for two weeks, and again in October 2000, when I passed out at work and was carried out of *The New York Times* building on a stretcher. I assumed that, like before, I would be back at my desk at the *Times* in a few weeks at most, but this time I did not recover. Instead, I got worse, I was never able to return to my job at the *Times*, and I found myself permanently disabled. Meanwhile, a diagnosis of my mysterious illness proved illusive.

Eventually doctors determined through nearly constant and

highly specialized medical testing done only at the Mayo Clinic, that I either had a *Pheochromocytoma* or a *Ganglioneuroma.* Either way, I had a life-threatening, one-in-a-million condition.

In either case, such tumors are usually very tiny. Ninety percent of the time, they are located in the adrenal glands and can be easily located and removed surgically, and the patient can return to a normal life within a few weeks. But in my case, as with others unlucky enough to be in the ten percent category, the tumor was hiding elsewhere outside the adrenal glands.

When my tumor activated—regardless of whether it was a *Pheochromocytoma* or a *Ganglioneuroma*—it secreted an enzyme that forced my body to produce adrenalin in dangerous excess, creating life threatening panic attacks, surges of blood pressure— causing it to go extremely high and then to drop precipitously— and it usually brought on intense and prolonged vertigo, and many other horrifying symptoms.

Of all these symptoms, the frequent panic attacks were the worst. Each and every time I experienced a panic attack, I felt certain that I would be dead very soon if I didn't make it to the hospital as quickly as possible. Actually, I could have died during any of these panic attacks, since the symptoms they brought on mirrored and usually surpassed those of actual cardiac arrest.

I underwent dozens of full-body scans and other invasive tests, but my doctors could never locate the tumor within my body. This was not an unexpected outcome as this was the case with most patients in the ten percent category, like myself, whose tumor could not be found in the adrenal glands. For one thing, full body scans that had any chance of localizing a tumor such as mine, usually required a large injection of drugs just to make the tumor "light up." There was one problem with this: Patients like myself risked death each time they submitted to such scans. Indeed, after undergoing an MIBG scan at Saint Anthony's Hospital in Manhattan in November 2000, I ended up in Intensive Care for two weeks, recovering from the test. And the tumor still didn't light up!

Even the specialists at the National Institute of Health—where I was seen in 2001—found conclusive chemical evidence of a *Pheochromocytoma* or a *Ganglioneuroma*, but could not localize my tumor despite all of their scans. Referring me back to my New York doctors, they told me that unless my tumor could be localized and removed, I would likely be dead within two years.

It was shocking to me how the smallest of things could utterly change my life, and perhaps even end it. In my case, the confirmed presence of a rare tumor in my body brought my life and career to a screeching halt. It was a lesson in humility. I, who had believed since early childhood that I could make all of my dreams come true if I simply worked hard enough, had to face a brutal reality: I was defenseless against the tiniest of tumors, that my fate was no longer in my hands, that my life was but the tiniest spark of light in a vast, unending universe.

When I returned to New York City, I felt utterly hopeless. If the medical specialists at both the NIH and the Mayo Clinic—who knew more about my disease than anyone—could not help me, what hope did I have? Needing a walker simply to navigate my apartment without falling over, I made my way to my bedroom window and looked out upon the whole of Manhattan from 43rd Street, north to infinity. I unlocked the six-foot square window and swung it open. I was experiencing vertigo, and I had to cling to the walker simply to remain on my feet. Looking out the window and down to the pavement below, made me feel even dizzier, but I somehow managed to climb a chair, to stand at the gaping hole to eternity, only a step away from making a huge splat on the pavement 42 floors below.

At the very moment that I decided to jump, the now familiar voice of an unseen presence spoke to me, even as I felt the strong but invisible arms of my angel holding me from behind, actually steadying me on the chair, while preventing me from jumping out of the window. "Kerry, keep the faith," the voice said, comforting me, offering me love and solace and hope. "All is not lost."

In that moment, like the one I had experienced earlier at BYU when I nearly took my life, I had a choice to make. I chose life, and carefully climbed down from the chair, leaning both on the support of my invisible angel and on my walker for help. Then I closed and relocked the window, and took a step back.

"Kerry," the voice added lovingly, "you are never alone. I am with you always."

Knowing that I could no longer depend upon traditional medicine, I began seeing a psychic healer by the name of Suzy Meszoly, who was referred to me by my dear friend Danny, whom I had met in ACOA. In my case, Suzy proved to be nothing short of a miracle worker. Because it was difficult for me to simply get out of a chair without passing out, much less make the journey to her office, Suzy came to visit me in my apartment several times a week for the next several months, giving me hands-on healing treatments that included deep meditation among many other techniques. As Suzy explained it, she was merely helping me access my body's own inner ability to heal myself, largely thru Reiki, but also through other psychic and spiritual modalities I still don't fully understand.

As I lay on the gurney during one of these first healing sessions, I had a profound spiritual experience. Following Suzy's instructions as she gently guided me into a deeply meditative state, and as she continued her usual hands-on healing process, I suddenly saw in my mind's eye a personage of light entering the room, as though floating in the air, before coming to rest and standing next to Suzy. "Was this an appearance by my angel, the same spiritual guide that had spoken to me at so many pivotal moments in my life?" I wondered. But as the light surrounding the personage faded slightly, I could see in my mind's eye that it was, in fact, my mother's spirit that had just entered the room.

Smelling my mother's perfume in the room, I wanted to open my eyes and reach out to touch her. But something within me, an innate and wise source, warned me against it, that it might end the healing purpose of her visitation.

Still meditating and laying on the gurney—again in my mind's

312

eye—I saw my mother's spirit reach out to Suzy, taking Suzy's hand in hers, and guiding Suzy's fingers to a specific spot at the back of my upper neck. Then I saw energy—a dramatic white light—move through Mom's hands into Suzy's fingers. At precisely the same moment, I felt a powerful and warming energy flow into the back of my neck perhaps in the area of the pituitary gland, making a path into and under my brain, until I saw it confront the tumor, hidden and tiny though it was, while blasting it again and again with the white loving energy.

As the white light, like that of a laser beam, continued to attack the dark tumor within me, it reminded me of scenes out of *Star Wars*, when Jedi Masters confront the Dark Side of the Force. This spiritual surgery continued for a long time, until eventually Mom released her grip on Suzy's hands. She gave Suzy a hug, enveloping her in the light of her healing energy. Then, Mom caressed me and gave me a kiss on the cheek, as I felt her spiritual aura pervade my entire body. It was a mother and child reunion at its very best. Then, Mom's spirit departed the room as quickly and surprisingly as she had arrived, much the way Glinda the Good Witch made her quick entrances and exits in *The Wizard of Oz*.

Afterward, Suzy instructed me to stay in my meditative state, as she continued the rest of her healing ritual, laying her hands the parts of my body that spirit directed her to, before she finally said, "Okay, Kerry, take your time ... and come back to the room and to the bed. And when you are fully alert and ready, you can open your eyes, and slowly sit up."

When I finally sat up with my eyes wide and alert, I looked at Suzy to see if she had experienced or seen the things that I had.

"Your Mom is very beautiful," she reported. "Her energy is so strong. Did you see the energy move from her fingers into mine?"

"Yes! Yes, I did!" I replied, grateful for Suzy's confirmation of all that I had experienced during the session.

"Awesome!" Suzy exclaimed happily. "Your mom was just incredible! I feel so honored that I got to meet her."

I began weeping, and Suzy joined me in my tears of gratitude, holding me close and hugging me in another healing embrace.

After that, Mom appeared several more times at my healing sessions with Suzy. Each time, Mother's spirit guided Suzy to the back of my neck and into what both Suzy and I felt was my pituitary gland. We were both so certain of this, that I had my medical specialists scan my pituitary in a serious of tests in the hospital. But they still could not localize the tumor!

Because of those healing sessions with my mother's spirit and Suzy, the symptoms of my medical condition gradually improved. But my healing process was far more difficult than I make it sound. In truth, it was a grueling, up-and-down journey. In fact, between 1998 and 2003, I was hospitalized 13 times.

With my life reduced to hospitalizations, doctor's visits, horrific medical tests and full-body scans that endangered my life more than my illness, and a staggering number of medical bills, it was only through the healing work with Suzy that I found improvement and relief from my medical symptoms.

Incidentally, because Suzy knew that my illness had left me penniless, she never charged me a dime for her services.

******

When we next met at my place, Harlan held me tightly in his arms on the sofa, but his thoughts seemed a million miles away.

"Harlan, what are you thinking about?" I asked quietly.

"Leigh and the baby," he said, swallowing hard.

"Anything in particular?" I pressed.

"When I put my head on her stomach," he said wistfully, "I can hear the baby's heartbeat."

"Just think! If it's a boy, you can teach him how to play football and baseball, and all of those other manly things."

His expression soured. "Yeah? Maybe I can even teach him how to be a faggot like his dad!" he said, spilling out his inner shame. That day, I finally faced the truth: I couldn't give Harlan what he had to give himself.

By that time, Leigh was five months pregnant and excited for the baby to arrive. We all were in our own way. She spent her days knitting booties, decorating the small extra room in their apartment as a nursery, and collecting the baby things she would need.

And I started buying Leigh and Harlan things that they would need later, like baby bottles and diapers and other such items, if only to assuage my guilt.

It was after my weekly electroshock therapy session on Monday, April 7, 1975, when I finally asked Dr. Parker, "How many shock treatments does this make now?"

"I don't know, Kerry. I've never stopped to count."

"Well, I have! I've had two-hour electroshock sessions once a week since January 14, 1974. That's 65 sessions, or 130 hours of shock therapy! And do you know what I have to show for 130 hours of shock treatments? My hands shake so badly now that I can't even hold a pen steady! But I'm still gay, as I always was, as I always will be, as God intended me to be!" I stood up, took a deep breath, and stated my case emphatically. "Dr. Parker, this will be my last electroshock session. I graduate from BYU in 11 days. I'm done."

When I walked out of his office that day, I entered a new phase of self-acceptance.

The next afternoon, as Harlan and I held each other on the sofa in my living room underneath the chocolate factory, I explained my new feelings to him. "I won't apologize for loving you any longer, Harlan." I paused for emphasis. "I'll whitewash it on the mountains. I'll spit it in God's face if I have to!"

"Don't say that, Kerry," he retorted. "It's blasphemous."

"What isn't blasphemous around here?" I responded loudly, thinking if I said the words loud enough, I could reach inside Harlan's soul and force him to understand. "You and I have to get the hell out of here and find our own Promised Land."

"What am I going to do, Babe? Abandon Leigh and the baby?" he asked. It seemed more a question for himself than for me.

I felt a knot in my throat. "I should give you up," I replied.

He looked deeply into my eyes. "I can't hurt Leigh, but the

problem is … I could never let you go. I won't let you go, no matter what, so you can just forget that idea."

"Harlan, you've got to choose," I observed carefully and quite sadly. "I'll give you up before I see you torn apart."

After final exams came and went, I left my apartment on Monday, April 14, 1975 before the sun rose that morning, getting in Oscar for the ten-hour drive to Sacramento. On my way to pick up Stacey, I stopped to see Harlan.

He had left Leigh still sleeping in their bedroom in the back of the apartment when he greeted me on his porch.

"I wish you weren't going," he said. "I feel boxed-in, like there are no options left."

"We'll have time to talk after graduation," I replied. "I'll be back on the night of the 17th. After we graduate on Friday, the 18th, and my parents head back to Idaho on Sunday the 20th, we can talk it all through."

"You're right," he said, taking me in his arms and giving me a long and tender kiss on the lips.

"I love you, Harlan," I whispered, holding him in my arms.

"I love you, too, Babe," he replied. "Never forget that."

I smiled at him and he returned the smile.

"Oh," he added matter-of-factly after ending our embrace, "I wrote a poem for you, and I did some sketches on it!" He handed me the paper torn from his favorite sketchpad. "Don't read it now. Read it later on, after your audition."

"Thanks, Harlan," I said, climbing into Oscar's front seat.

As I pulled away, I added through the open window, "I'll call you tonight when we get to Sacramento!"

"You'd better!" Harlan replied, smiling even more broadly. "I'll worry about you until I hear from you!"

I called Harlan as I had promised, as soon as we arrived that evening in Sacramento at Stacey's parent's place. Our phone conversation was brief. I ended it by promising to call him after my audition on the morning of the 16th, and we said goodnight.

I spent the morning of April 15th rehearsing in Sacramento.

Then, in the afternoon, we drove to San Francisco to see *Funny Lady*, Streisand's film sequel to *Funny Girl* that had just opened. Since Stacey and I were both Streisand fans, we held each other's hand throughout the showing, and shared our enthusiasm over Barbra's performance afterward. We stayed with her sister that night at her home just outside the city. Since Stacey and I had to get up early the next morning to be in San Francisco for my 9am audition, we went to bed early that night.

Once on the main stage at the American Conservatory Theatre the next morning, I overcame my nerves and gave what I felt was a good audition. All seemed to go well, and the casting director said that I would hear from them soon. I now realize that I didn't do quite as well at my audition as I had hoped. Again, my inner child was out to sabotage me at every turn. Oblivious to this reality at the time, I went backstage feeling quite happy about my prospects.

Stacey greeted me with a hug, saying, "You did great, Kerry! You can't miss getting accepted."

"Thanks, Stacey!" I replied. "I have to call Harlan now."

******

In 2000, my longtime therapist Jim Enders retired. It was a difficult adjustment going without my weekly sessions with Jim. My 12-year relationship with Jim Enders had proven to be the most trusting, healthy and loving relationship that I had yet experienced. Jim had taught me what unconditional love looked and felt like. Over the course of my therapy relationship with Jim, I had learned how to love myself and to love others far better. More than that, I knew there was still a subconscious memory of something traumatic that had happened in my past, that I had yet to uncover. How could I uncover the truth now, without Jim?

Still battling cancer, I left New York in 2002, using my disability settlement to buy a cabin in a peaceful spot on the Bushkill Creek in the Pocono Mountains of Northeast Pennsylvania, where I continued my healing from the inside out.

317

Having gained a tremendous amount of weight after I became seriously ill, I now topped out at a whopping 345 pounds. But once I settled into the cabin, I began losing weight gradually, and over the next several years, I slowly began to feel better.

Eventually I was able to move about my cabin without a walker. My doctors were delighted by my progress, but they could not accept that my healing had taken place spiritually, that I had used my cabin as a bear might use a cave, healing not only my physical afflictions, but also the deepest wounds in my heart.

In late 2002, the IRS called on Rex at his Sacramento office one day, demanding the employee's payroll taxes not paid for the last seven years. Shocked, Rex explained that they had to go home to confront his business manager and lover, Craig. But when they arrived, they quickly discovered that Craig had disappeared, taking everything of value out of the house. Apparently, Craig had shoved most of the payroll taxes up his nose, as Rex soon learned, since Craig had hidden a cocaine habit. A warrant was issued for Craig's arrest, but they never caught him. They did make one discovery, though: Craig wasn't even the guy's real name!

To settle with the IRS, Rex was forced to liquidate his business, and sell his home and all of his assets. Pushed into bankruptcy and penniless, Rex was heartbroken. He had loved Craig and trusted him completely, but Craig robbed Rex of everything he had, even of his will to live. In despair, Rex visited a gay sex club, where he invited countless men to penetrate him anally without a condom.

In 2003, Rex called me to let me know that he had not merely contracted the HIV virus, but also full-blown AIDS, as well as a flesh-eating virus that had nearly chewed off his right foot. The cocktail of drugs, so effective with most AIDS patients, was not effective in his case, and he spent most of his next two years in hospital. Then in the summer of 2005, Rex's health improved. My health had improved as well, and I visited my family in Idaho that summer. Taking my niece Tara and her two children with me to California, we visited Disneyland, Yosemite National Park, and went on to visit Rex in Sacramento.

Tara explained the visit to her children in a simple way: "Uncle Kerry and Uncle Rex broke up years ago, but they remained friends just like Mommy and Daddy did after we divorced."

When we arrived at Rex's home in Sacramento, Patrick and Lea ran across the lawn to embrace Rex who was standing on his porch, saying, "Uncle Rex, we love you!" Their loving embrace of Rex as an Uncle, made Tara Lee and both of us grown men weep.

It was so good to see Rexy again. And I am so grateful that I made the effort, since shortly after our visit, Rex became gravely ill and was hospitalized not long after our visit to Sacramento.

Then, in October 2005, as Rex lay dying in a hospital, he called me at my cabin in the Poconos.

"Kerry," Rexy said, "You were the love of my life, but I was too big a fool to realize it at the time. Mom was right; leaving you was the biggest mistake I ever made in my whole life. Before I die, I want you to know how sorry I am for how I treated you."

Hearing him say those words made me sad, particularly when I thought of what might have been.

Rex died the next day. He was only 49.

A few months later, his mom—my California mom—died of a broken heart.

As the years passed at my Poconos cabin, as my ongoing battle with cancer continued, and as I gradually became healthier, my soul's deep need and desire to explore sexual role-play again grew increasingly apparent. My inner child was letting me know that he needed me to experience these things again, if only to reenact some forgotten sexual trauma from decades ago, for what purpose I was not yet consciously aware. Once I opened the door to this type of sexual exploration again, I opened the door for healing.

In the spring of 2012, at the age of 58, 40 years after my rape at the age of 18, the memories of that violent and brutal experience finally began to emerge from my subconscious mind.

The memories came back in tiny pieces in the beginning, first as a trickle, then as a stream, and finally as a torrential flood. One by one, I fit each piece of memory into a larger picture, like retrieving pieces of a jigsaw puzzle, until I could finally see and remember the whole ordeal of my rape as it had actually happened.

Only then could I look back on the journey I had taken throughout my life, particularly my sexual journey, and see that much if not most of it was driven subconsciously by the brutal rape I had survived as a young man. Only then could I fully comprehend what had driven me to the sexual experiences at BYU that had led me to such public humiliation. Only then I could I fully understand why I was drawn over and over again to a compulsive need for sexual BDSM, in a need to reenact and replay the trauma that had once played itself out in a seedy hotel room in downtown Salt Lake City in March 1972. Only then could I fully appreciate why the thought of being anally penetrated had terrified me for most of my life, and why I had avoided it at all cost.

All of this inner healing manifested in physical healing. After battling cancer for 15 years, my symptoms nearly disappeared. When this miracle occurred, some of my Pocono doctors put forward an exasperating medical theory that I had never really had a tumor at all. Their theory irritated me no end, as I had just spent the last 15 years of my life doing battle with it. In reality, these doctors could not accept the fact that I had healed my illness by alternative and spiritual means. At times, it made me wish that that they had met me when I was leaning on a walker, simply to keep from falling down.

But I knew the truth then, as I know it now: In order for my body to heal from cancer, I first had to heal the shame I had internalized over my rape, a secret I had kept hidden within my subconscious mind for 40 years.

******

I couldn't wait to tell Harlan about my successful San Francisco audition. With Stacey at my side, I found a pay phone in a hallway behind ACT's stage. But when I called, it was not Harlan who answered, but Leigh. She sounded so emotional that I could barely make out her words.

"Kerry," she said in a strange and distant voice, one I almost didn't recognize as hers, "I've been waiting for your call."

She stopped talking. The dead air on the phone was strange.

Finally she spoke again, stammering as she struggled to get the words out of her mouth. "I ... I ... would have called ... earlier this morning ... but I didn't want to ruin your audition."

She paused and began sobbing.

"Leigh, what's wrong?" I asked, as panic flooded over me.

"Harlan's ... dead," Leigh managed to sputter.

Both my mind and body went numb. I thought I had heard her incorrectly. I must have heard her incorrectly.

"He died late last night," she added, through her sobs.

"What?" I managed to utter, as I felt my knees beginning to buckle under me.

"He killed himself, Kerry," she said, having difficulty speaking.

The breath gushed out of me as though a truck had just slammed into me.

"Harlan disappeared after lunch yesterday and he never came back," she explained, before the horrifying sequence of events spilled out of her.

On the day prior, April 15, 1975, the day I had spent rehearsing in Sacramento, Harlan had driven to Salt Lake City and purchased a gun at a gun shop downtown. Later, after checking into a second-floor room at the Travel Lodge downtown, he had put a bullet in his head at 11:38pm.

According to witnesses, he had made his way from his room out onto the balcony, where he had called out for help before falling over the railing onto the pavement below.

He was rushed to the LDS hospital, but Harlan had been pronounced dead on arrival at 11:52pm.

Leigh had only arrived back in Provo an hour before my call.

"His brother Warren has arranged for a small family service to be held tomorrow morning in Layton," Leigh added.

"Tomorrow!" I exclaimed, now deep in shock. "I can't get back to Utah by tomorrow morning!"

"I know," she replied, "but Warren and Katharine want it over and done with already. If they could do it today, they would. The mortuary doesn't need time to get his body ready. It can't be an open casket." She began sobbing again. "They can't reconstruct his head. He blew most of it away."

I felt dizzy. I let the phone dangle in mid-air.

"What's the matter?" Stacey asked, suddenly frantic.

"It's Harlan. He killed himself," I said. And then I fainted.

When I unpacked my suitcase in Provo the following night, I found the poem that Harlan had written for me. Reading it again, I realized for the first time that it was a suicide note, the only one he had left anyone.

It was very early on the morning of Friday, April 18, 1975—the day of my college graduation—that my parents and grandparents arrived. They saw right away that I was in a fragile state. When I told them that Harlan had committed suicide only three days earlier, they seemed to understand. But I told them nothing of my true relationship with Harlan. That would have to wait for several more years, until after my mother's death.

BYU Commencement Exercises were held that morning in the huge Marriott Center and then in the afternoon in a separate ceremony in the De Jong Concert Hall, where all of the Fine Arts majors received their degrees. Feeling that the Mormons had killed Harlan, I was so angry when I crossed the Concert Hall stage to receive my bachelor's degree from Dr. Charles Metten, that I fantasized slapping him in the face while thousands watched.

Accepting Harlan's suicide was perhaps the hardest and most difficult thing I've ever had to do in my life. First, came the blaming phase in which I aimed my blame and the full extent of my rage at anyone and everyone I felt might be responsible for Harlan's suicide, first blaming the Mormon Church and BYU.

Not surprisingly, since I was in a state of shock, I stayed in Provo after graduation and remained there until the Christmas break. But for the first few spring and summer months after Harlan's suicide, I avoided the BYU campus like Hell itself.

When Dom and Maria decided to marry in the Provo Temple in May, I was invited to attend the wedding. I couldn't attend the Temple ceremony, of course, without receiving a Temple Recommend and no Branch President would give me one as long as I told the truth.

Like Harlan and Leigh, if Dom had told the truth about his recent sins, he could not have received a Temple recommend either. Dom, not unlike Harlan, had lied to his Branch President as he had lied to himself and to me, swearing that he had put his gay feelings behind him. As Harlan had done before him, Dom asked me to act as his Best Man at his wedding reception to be held in a local ward reception hall. I was happy to do so. But Dom began secretly having sex again with men at the rest areas only a few weeks after taking his marriage vows in the Temple.

Still blaming the Mormon Church for Harlan's suicide, I met with President Wilkinson to request excommunication from the church. Shocked, he nonetheless promised to look into the matter.

After Wilkinson received official word from Church Headquarters in Salt Lake City, regarding my request for excommunication, I met with him in his office on campus to discuss the matter. When he informed me that the LDS Church had denied my request, I became angry. "The church sucks! First they threaten me with excommunication, then they refuse to let me go!"

"There's still a place for you in the church," he replied.

"Thank you, President Wilkinson, but I don't think so."

I stared directly into his eyes, and added, "Regardless of what Church Headquarters says, I no longer consider myself LDS."

"Brother Kerry," he replied earnestly, "I hope and pray that one day you will reconsider your decision."

My reply was quiet but firm: "President, you have helped me through the worst kind of coming-out process that any gay man should ever have to go through, and for that I will always be grateful to you. But why would I want to remain part of a religion that wants me dead? Or if not dead, then hidden away, and shoved under the rug like so much debris?"

President Wilkinson took a long time to respond. "Brother Ashton, those like myself who have been called to positions of church leadership want only what's best for all concerned. In this, as in all things, we love the sinner but hate the sin."

"Let he who is without sin cast the first stone," I said softly.

That was the last time I saw President Cyrus W. Wilkinson.

******

In early January 2014, I made plans for a visit to South Florida to see my friend Liz Martin—a friend from my New York days. About a week prior to the trip, I received an email in response to a dating profile I had placed online, from a fellow by the name of Victor Ramirez, who happened to live in South Florida.

I became particularly intrigued with Victor when my niece Tara Lee—a gifted psychic—called shortly after I ended my first phone call with him, to inquire, "Who's Victor?"

After scraping myself off the floor, I replied, "Tara, how do you know about Victor? He's just someone I met online. In fact, I just got through talking with him on the phone just this minute."

"Well, how was it? The call, I mean?" Tara inquired.

"He seems authentic and very nice. I really liked him," I said.

At that point in my life, I prized authenticity over any other quality of character.

"Well, he's the one, Uncle Kerry. He's the man you've been hoping to meet for all of these years."

"As it happens," I explained. "I'm going to South Florida next week to visit Liz. And guess where Victor lives?"

She answered with the clarity of her own knowledge and conviction. "He lives in South Florida, not that far from Liz." She paused. "You have to meet him. It's your destiny."

When Victor and I met during my visit to Florida the following week, I heard the voice of my unseen angel speaking to me once again. This time the voice said, "Kerry, this is the man you will spend the rest of your life with. He is the great love of your life."

I have not heard the voice of my angel since then, but I have little doubt that I will hear his voice again, if only when he welcomes me home one day.

After spending a few days with Victor, I visited Liz at her home in Coconut Grove as planned. Since I had begun to experience a few medical symptoms again—mostly some intense vertigo—I sought out Liz's help. Ever since my health had improved, whenever I experienced any of the old symptoms, it scared the hell out of me. My first thought was that my tumor was back and active again. The second thought was always more fearful: Might the tumor become permanently active again, as it had years earlier?

A gifted massage therapist, a psychic healer, and a practitioner of *BodyTalk*—a way of balancing the physical, emotional and mental levels of the body and mind as a whole system—Liz gave me a treatment that night, as she did whenever she saw me. Much like my many healing sessions with Suzy, Liz lay me down on a gurney and then guided me into a state of deep meditation, even as her healing hands moved across and sometimes above my body, until she felt spiritually guided to the back of my upper neck.

I saw in my mind's eye the healing light from Liz's fingers, moving like a laser into my neck and brain and then underneath it, until the light confronted what remained of my tumor, with each blast of light causing secretions of black foggy clouds to emerge from the tumor. "Do you see that black icky stuff?" Liz asked.

"Yes," I replied, deep in a trance-like state.

"Visualize a window outside your body," Liz suggested, "and send the black gunk out through the window. You have no need of it any longer. Send it back to the Universe."

I did as Liz suggested, until at last I felt lighter.

After Liz ended the healing session, I felt immediately better. The latest symptoms dissipated again, quite miraculously.

As we sat and had tea afterward, Liz asked me what I had actually experienced during the session. "I saw the light and energy move from your fingers into the back of my head," I explained, "where it started blasting the tumor. It was very similar to the way I experienced all of those healing sessions with Suzy. And then I watched the black misty clouds move out through the window just as you told me to." And then I told her about Victor.

I had originally planned to spend only a week in Florida visiting Liz, but after meeting Victor I extended my trip until Valentine's Day, spending most of my time with him.

I was 60 and Victor was 47 when we met and fell in love, but he was worth the wait of a lifetime. Handsome, masculine, and bearded, Victor didn't come out of the closet until his mid-40s. As a Deacon in the Baptist Church, Victor was religious and had a difficult time accepting his gay identity. As a police officer, Victor rose quickly through the ranks, eventually becoming a Chief of Police in Miami-Dade County. Retiring at 45, he is still the highest-ranking openly gay officer to serve in his department. A self-made man of integrity and ability and authenticity, I am extremely proud of him.

After Victor and I fell in love, we both sold each of our homes and moved into a new home together in South Florida where we have lived happily and monogamously ever since. And I am so happy that we can now share a life together that is loving, stable and peaceful. This was where my yellow brick road led me. Like Dorothy Gale of Kansas, I learned that I didn't need to go in search of home beyond my own backyard, that I carried my Promised Land within me wherever I went.

******

When I visited my parents in Pocatello during the summer after Harlan's suicide, I told them that I had decided to leave the church. They were, of course, shocked and dismayed at my announcement, and reacted by adding my name to the Mormon Temple prayer list.

326

After I returned to Provo, I stopped blaming the Mormon Church and BYU for Harlan's suicide, and began blaming myself. Believing I had killed him just as surely as if I had pulled the trigger, I had the same nightmare every night, seeing Harlan's face in moonlight as I fired the gun, scattering his brains all over me.

Then I blamed Harlan. One afternoon I found myself in Provo Canyon, screaming out loud at the top of my voice while facing Bridal Veil Falls. "How could you do it, Harlan?" I screamed over and over again, until the leaves on the maple trees seemed to shake in response. But I found no solace in my screams. Later, I visited Harlan's grave at his family's cemetery plot in Layton. I placed the beautiful bouquet of flowers on his grave, but I found no solace there, either. Eventually I had a dream about Harlan that was not a nightmare, but rather a vision of comfort. In my dream, I saw Harlan standing in white light in my bedroom, smiling at me. "Please don't grieve any longer, Kerry," he said. "It was wrong of me to do what I did, and I take full responsibility for it. It wasn't your fault. Just know that I am at peace now, and that I will always love you." And then his spirit disappeared. Despite Harlan's visitation, I remained inconsolable.

It was difficult at times spending time with Leigh in the same apartment where Harlan and I had kissed and held each other so many times. Even so, Leigh and I spent many evenings that summer in her living room, quietly sharing our grief together.

On Pioneer Day, July 24, 1976, Leigh gave birth to a precious, blonde-haired baby boy, naming him Harlan Bradley LeClair.

Not long after the baby's birth, I heard back from ACT in San Francisco. They had liked my audition, but not enough to hire me.

Only grief can explain why I registered at BYU in the fall as a graduate student. I soon realized my mistake and dropped all courses except one, choosing to direct Maxim Gorky's *The Lower Depths* to fulfill the requirements of my only graduate course—a class in Directing taught by my nemesis Dr. Harold I. Hansen. The course required that graduate students direct and present a play as close to the author's original intent as possible. Since Gorky was writing about slum-dwelling folks surviving difficult lives, he used a lot of strong language in his play, including many a "son-of-a-bitch" and other curse words never permitted on campus. Naturally, I was expected to censor Gorky's text, but I refused to cut a single word. When Dr. Metten, now the Chairman of the Theatre Department, attempted to get backstage to stop my production in mid-performance, he encountered a stage door that I had already padlocked, anticipating such a reaction.

At the public discussion afterward, when I fielded questions and comments from the audience, Dr. Metten among several others felt that I should be burned at the stake, preferably on the campus green, and definitely that evening. There were a few who thought mine was the bravest production ever staged on campus, and somehow found the courage to say so.

In the end, Dr. Harold I. Hansen gave me a D- for my effort. I still consider it the finest accolade I ever received at BYU.

As I prepared to leave Utah, I looked at Harlan's paintings again and wept for the first time since his death. When tears finally came, they didn't stop. Out of my mind with grief and wanting to put an end to the pain, I burned all of his paintings and sketches, all of the notes and letters that he had written to me over the years, and even his suicide note, removing any evidence that Harlan Alphonse LeClair had ever existed, much the way I removed any memory of being violently raped, but I failed. It was a desperate act that I now deeply regret.

Saying goodbye to Leigh and little Harlan Bradley was difficult, but saying goodbye to Mormon Zion and Happy Valley was not, as I slowly moved through the remaining stages of grief.

Returning to Pocatello, I moved back in with my parents, but lived there only two months before making my new home in L.A. in February 1976. And it was in L.A., when I eventually accepted the reality of Harlan's suicide. But I never got over the senseless tragedy of it. Some losses cannot and should not be forgotten.

******

As Victor and I celebrated our first Christmas together in 2014 in our new home in South Florida and opened our Christmas card from Tara, we were astonished to find a written page torn from her diary, containing her notes from a psychic reading that she had given me a full decade earlier—most of the details of which both Tara and I had long since forgotten.

Apparently, it was only after rereading her old diary entries that she had decided to send her original notes to Victor and I as a very special Christmas gift.

Only after reading her notes made in 2004, did I remember all of the predictions Tara had made back then. Not only had Tara accurately foreseen Victor coming into my life a decade later, she had given me accurate details about his age (that he would be 13 years younger than myself), that he lived near a beach, but most astonishing of all, that his name was Victor. She had even written Victor's name in black-and-white at the bottom of the page, and circled it for emphasis. Of course, by the Christmas of 2014, I didn't need any additional convincing that Victor was my intended soul mate or that he was the love of my life, and that we were always intended to be together as a couple. But Tara's psychic predictions were remarkable, nonetheless.

During the summer of 2016, Victor and I attended a family reunion at my sister's home in Idaho Falls. I was happy that he and the members of my LDS family finally got to meet. Secretly, I was glad that my brother Dennis couldn't attend, as I still didn't feel safe being around him.

Since it was in the midst of the 2016 presidential campaign, I assiduously avoided any discussion of politics with anyone in my family. The last thing I needed was to have a political argument with any of the far-right members of my Mormon family. Though, when I became engrossed in a conversation with Jason—my niece Joy's husband—and our talk turned to the recent Pulse nightclub shooting in Orlando that summer, Jason said, "Islamic Jihadists want gay people dead."

Jason is one of the most moderate members of our LDS family, but nonetheless I responded provocatively: "As do many Mormons and many on the far right!"

"That's not true, Uncle Kerry," Jason replied defensively, unaware that his words had ripped a scab off an old wound, one I thought I had healed decades earlier.

In spite of myself, I found myself replying, "The Mormons tried to kill me! And they did kill my lover Harlan! So don't tell me Mormons don't want gay people dead!"

Surprised by my sudden outburst, I offered Jason and my beautiful niece Joy my immediate and sincere apology.

Later, to their credit, my sister Denise and brother Craig each made a point of telling both Victor and I, that they were happy for us, and that they were glad that we had found each other. Having said that, and despite the strong bond that I have always shared with my sister and with my niece Tara, a wall still stands between most of my Mormon family and me. It is a wall that I still hope that we can bridge someday. Sadly, the same wall that has divided my LDS family for decades now divides our nation.

In November 2016, America chose an incompetent and racist bully, a pathological liar, and a self-confessed pussy-grabber as the next President of the United States. But this idiotic and dangerous new president had a huge amount of help in getting elected, first from the Kremlin, then from the former FBI Director's unwise decision to make public statements about his opponent only days prior to the election, and lastly from our outdated Electoral College. Only with help like that, could such a buffoon and demagogue be elected president in the first place.

Since that fateful election two years ago, it has become harder to know what to believe in or in whom to believe. The current occupant in the White House lies about anything and everything, attacking the very institutions that uphold our democracy and the rule of law—solely to protect himself—even as his lies are presented as facts in the far-right media, while 40% of Americans believe every lie he utters. Indeed, a new Civil War is upon us, with each side claiming its own facts. But perhaps, given the nature of our current national politics, I should refer to it as our country's first *Uncivil War.*

I still hope and want to believe that Americans can find a way to reunite as one country and one people, but that seems unlikely at present. Indeed, the only goal of the current White House seems to be to *"Make America Hate Again."* Even our Vice President supports the same type of conversion therapy that I once endured at BYU, resulting in the fact that both of my hands still shake uncontrollably, as they always will. But I, and millions like me, will never return to the shadows. We will fight for our democracy and our civil rights if need be; we will fight hate with love, choosing enlightenment over ignorance and hope over fear.

Even prior to the presidential election of 2016, I realized that I still had important and unfinished spiritual work to do. As anyone knows who has followed a spiritual path, such journeys eventually demand forgiveness; otherwise, we can never fully let go of the past and move forward. Somehow I needed to find a way to forgive all those in my Mormon past whom I felt had wronged me. But could I fully forgive the Brethren at BYU for their well meaning but misguided decisions that affected so much of my later life? Could I forgive my oldest brother Dennis for the destruction he created in my childhood? Could I forgive my rapist? Could I forgive Harlan for taking his own life? Could I forgive Rex for deliberately exposing himself to the HIV virus and subsequently to AIDS? Could I finally and fully forgive myself?

For most of us, forgiveness doesn't come as a first step but as a last step in the healing process; it usually comes after giving up denial, accepting reality, and assigning responsibility. And that was certainly true in my case. Spending the two years since the 2016 election trying to understand what had gone wrong in our national politics, while working to forgive myself and to forgive others, proved to be a spiritual minefield.

Then, in late January 2018, a cyst appeared on my upper back and grew alarmingly huge within only a few days. When I went to see my dermatologist, he discovered a melanoma less than three inches from the cyst. In turn, he referred me to an oncologist who decided that the cyst would need to be removed first.

The surgery to remove the cyst, performed on February 15, left me with a hole in my upper back nearly four inches deep and two inches wide. It took months of home nursing visits and wearing a *Wound Vac,* before the huge, gaping wound finally closed over.

During the months of recovery that followed, as I prepared for the next surgery to remove the melanoma, I became discouraged due to the resistance I had encountered from dozens of agents an publishers in many attempts to publish this memoir. Though a few had shown interest, all had eventually said no. After talking on the phone with my niece Tara—who was now a highly gifted psychic and successful spiritual advisor based in Idaho Falls—she consulted with her spiritual guides and wrote me back a letter in response, saying:

> *"During the Holy War you fought at BYU, there was a part of you that accepted their judgments as correct. When you tried to become the person they thought you should be, your authentic self, your inner child, felt as though you had stabbed him in the back. This created the subconscious need to punish yourself, to withhold or block the success you deserve. This energy is also connected to the wound and the cancer on your back. Again, you have stabbed yourself in the back because you are still angry with yourself on some unconscious level. The key to healing the cancer and the back wounds and to publishing your memoir, is to forgive yourself and anyone else you feel may have wronged you."*

Clearly, I needed to have another talk with my inner child.

Having channeled my mother's spirit, Tara also included Mom's direct message to me in the same letter:

"I'm honored to be your mother and I am so proud of who you have become. You have battled and fought for every aspect of who you are: The actor, the writer, the director, the son, the brother, and the gay man. Now it is time to let go of the battle, and to live happily. I honor you. I see you. And my heart overflows with love and respect for you. Heal and carry on, and know that I am always with you."

On June 12, 2018, I entered the hospital for a same-day surgery to remove the melanoma. But after my surgeon removed the melanoma along with sentinel lymph nodes in both my neck and armpit, while I was still under general anesthesia, my long silent tumor—hidden within me for over two decades—suddenly reactivated, secreting enzymes for the first time in several years, causing my blood pressure to surge and then drop to zero.

My heart stopped, my kidneys stopped functioning, and my lungs filled with fluid. Though I essentially died on the operating table, the surgical staff brought me quickly back to life.

I remained in Intensive Care for a week thereafter, medically *intubated*, with a tube stuck down my throat and into my lungs, which kept me breathing. Throughout all of this, I remained heavily sedated, having only a few brief moments of consciousness, while Victor remained steadfastly by my side, holding my hand even when I wasn't conscious. Whenever I awoke, he was there, reassuring me each time that everything would be all right, especially when I discovered that I couldn't speak with the tube down my throat, and found it horribly difficult to breathe.

Each time I came to, I would take the writing pad and write out my same fearful question: "What happened?" Each time, he would explain it all to me, thinking I finally understood and accepted the situation, before I nodded off again. And each time, when I awoke the next time, he had to patiently explain it all to me all over again.

Only after the medical team determined that I could finally

breathe on my own, was the tube finally removed from my throat.

That same morning, a swarm of doctors gathered around my bed. Down to a one, they believed that my medical emergency earlier that week was caused, not by the tumor that was diagnosed years earlier, but by cardiac arrest, and they insisted that I undergo a cardiac catheterization immediately.

The catheterization was completed later that morning, with the medical team going in through my groin and up through a main artery to my heart, proving what I already knew: My heart was healthy; it was the tumor still hiding in my body—the same tumor that had created so many medical problems for me over the past two decades—that had caused my latest brush with death.

On the day I was released from the hospital, Victor confessed that while I was unconscious and when he was not by my bedside, he had taken up residence in a private room in the ICU, what he called his "war room," where he had prayed for me constantly.

I emerged from the hospital with clarity. For one thing, I knew that it was only due to the power of Victor's prayers, and the fact that I still had important work to accomplish here, that I was given another chance to live. More, I was reminded me yet again that each moment of one's life is a precious gift that no one should ever take for granted. I felt born again in a spiritual sense, but certainly not in a way that a religion could hope to understand.

In writing one's memoir, and choosing to go public with the most sexually intimate details of one's life—as I do within these pages—it's scary. It's like opening up one's private diary to everyone on the planet. Was I absolutely certain that I wanted to share my most hidden and well-kept secrets with the world? How would the members of my Mormon family react once my book was published? Would the conservative members of my family shun me once they read the graphic details of my sexual experiences, particularly the most vile and violent details of my rape? Would sharing these true experiences from my life with the world, even matter? Like so many in the #MeToo movement who have had the courage to come forward, to tell the truth of their sexual assault and to speak their truth to power—the most recent and powerful example being Dr. Christine Blasey Ford—would I even be believed? All rape and sexual assault victims struggle with similar questions when they contemplate coming forward and telling the ugly truth of what happened to them. Like them, I had to contend with the same inner conflicts and questions.

In the end, I decided that not only did I have the right to speak out, I had a sacred obligation to do so, and let the chips fall where they may. First and foremost, I owed it to my inner child to tell how he was betrayed and abandoned throughout much of my life. And I owed it to all rape victims and to all those in the #MeToo movement, especially the male victims of sexual assault, who might take comfort and find healing from my true story of overcoming shame, such that they might in turn find the courage to heal their own shame, and come out of hiding. So when I decided my book would reach the public somehow, even if I had to publish it myself, it was a solemn decision.

But I still needed to forgive all those whom I felt had hurt me in my past, and to find a way to finally forgive myself. Ultimately, my search for forgiveness led me back to Stephen Sondheim's song, "No One is Alone," from his Broadway musical—lyrics that had guided me for decades:

> "People make mistakes, holding to their own,
> Thinking they're alone.
> Honor their mistakes, fight for their mistakes,
> Everybody makes, one another's terrible mistakes."

Completing this memoir led me to a new place where I could at last honor all of our mistakes.

At Tara's suggestion, I wrote my inner child what she calls an *Aloha Letter*. In the letter, I asked for my inner child's forgiveness and offered him mine. I explained that the memoir was my way of sharing his story with the world, and honoring him for all that he had survived, and that I was taking his side. I asked him to support my efforts in publishing the book. Most of all, I promised him that from that day forward, I would earn his trust every single day.

Victor joined me for the burning ceremony, standing with me on our patio, when I put the letter in an empty firepot and set it ablaze. In burning the letter, I was saying *aloha* and goodbye to all that had gone before, while saying *aloha* and hello to all of the love and miracles that the Universe had yet to bless me with.

While watching the letter burn to ashes, I reminded myself what Victor had advised me of the night before: "Forgiveness is every day." Self-forgiveness would always be part of an ongoing and daily process. But the commitments I made to my inner child in the letter were—and would remain—sacrosanct.

"My inner child is on my side now," I explained to Victor, as I wiped away the tears forming in my eyes. "Because I am now on his side, and I am going to remain on his side for the rest of my days." Victor just smiled in his gentle and understanding way.

Perhaps now that my memoir is published and my relationship with Victor is publicly and proudly acknowledged, LDS Church Headquarters may want to honor the request I made decades ago and remove me from their membership roles. But it is of little consequence to me now whether they do or they don't.

I spent much of my life as a victim, but I am no one's victim now. For 40 years, I kept everyone, including myself, from knowing anything about my rape, but I have no secrets now. For decades I fought for recognition as an actor and author, but I was always told, "You need a name!" Now, whether professionally successful or not, I've got a name. It is the name of a man with integrity, who is finally both honest and authentic, and I am proud of my name. Though stricken with a rare and dreadful cancer, I have won every battle that I have waged with it over the last 20 years. Though I lost my first Mormon love to suicide, and another to AIDS, and though I have experienced many heartbreaking losses along my life's journey, I believe it all happened *for* me, not *to* me, making me stronger. Through it all, love has triumphed over hate, and I believe that it always will.

As for Bridget and her husband Grant, they subsequently raised all of their four children as LDS. Their children are all grown now, some with children of their own. Besides being a housewife in Salt Lake City, Bridget has written and published several books and thousands of freelance articles. When I make the trip west to visit family, I always try to see Bridget and Grant if at all possible.

I never saw Jack Young again after he left BYU, but I heard that he later married in the Temple and had several children.

I haven't heard from Leigh since she sent me a photo of Harlan Bradley when he was seven-years-old. At that time, he still had his mother's blue eyes and blond hair and his father's handsome features. Harlan Bradley LeClair is now twice as old as I was when I met his father.

Not a day has passed since Harlan's suicide that I haven't thought of him.

I spent years looking for him in dark alleys and smoke-filled bars, but found only shadows there.

Later I tried to forget him, but he haunted me wherever I went.

But I believe I will see Harlan again, when God Himself joins Victor and I in a marriage meant for time and all eternity.

Photograph of Kerry and Victor, taken in Paris, France in May 2016, shortly after Victor's 50th birthday.

ACKNOWLEDGMENTS

There are several people who aided me in the process of writing and bringing my memoir to publication, who I would like to thank. Among my fellow writers, I must acknowledge Raymond Luczak, Damian McNicholl, Andy Ambraziejus and Stephen Roos, as well as Mitch Douglas, my literary agent from the 1980s who first encouraged me to write my story as fiction. All of these gentlemen provided me with literary guidance, editorial suggestions, or emotional support along the way, but I particularly thank Raymond who, without being asked, did a complete edit on one of the early versions of the manuscript.

I also need to thank three psychic healers, who utilized Reiki and other spiritual methods either to help me to recover from my rare cancer or to guide me through the process of rewriting this book. I cannot sufficiently thank Suzy Meszoly—the Psychic Healer who literally saved my life when the medical profession could not, and never required any financial compensation from me at the time. You can contact Suzy at SuzyMeszoly-Healer.com. I also acknowledge my dear friend Liz Martin who not only helped me maintain my health, but also provided me with psychic insight into what scenes to include in the book. For more information about Liz, go to LizMartinMassageAndHealing.com. My niece Tara Lee also aided me with a suggested rewrite and guided me toward more spiritual growth, healing and forgiveness. To find out more about Tara, go to facebook.com/tara.simmons.31.

Lastly, I want to thank all of you who have purchased and read my book. If you have any comments to share with me, you can email me c/o my publisher at LynnWolfEnterprises@gmail.com or you can follow me at Facebook.com/KerryAshton.Author and at Twitter.com/KerryAshtonNow. Also, please consider writing a small review of the book at www.amazon.com/author/kerryashton or at www.goodreads.com/book/show/42506111-saint-unshamed. Even a couple of sentences can make a huge difference in spreading the word. Again, many thanks for reading the book!

CPSIA information can be obtained
at www.ICGtesting.com
Printed in the USA
LVHW021239121218
599888LV00003B/3/P